THE PRACTICE
OF PUNISHMENT

THE PRACTICE OF PUNISHMENT

Towards a theory of restorative justice

Wesley Cragg

Routledge
Taylor & Francis Group

LONDON AND NEW YORK

First published 1992
by Routledge

2 Park Square, Milton Park, Abingdon, Oxon OX14 4RN
711 Third Avenue, New York, NY 10017, USA

Routledge is an imprint of the Taylor & Francis Group, an informa business

First issued in paperback 2016

Transferred to Digital Printing 2006

Typeset in 10 on 12 point Garamond by
Falcon Typographic Art Ltd, Edinburgh

British Library Cataloguing in Publication Data
A catalogue record for this
book is available from the
British Library.

Library of Congress Cataloging in Publication Data
Cragg, Wesley.
The practice of punishment: towards a theory of restorative
justice/Wesley Cragg.
p. cm. — (Readings in applied ethics)
Includes bibliographical references and index.
1. Punishment. 2. Corrections—Philosophy.
I. Title. II. Series.
K5103.C73   1992
345′077—dc20
[342.577]   91–22364

ISBN 978-0-415-04149-2 (hbk)
ISBN 978-1-138-99520-8 (pbk)

To the cause of penal reform
and
those who work for it

CONTENTS

CONTENTS

PREFACE

The motivation for writing this book comes from twenty-five years' experience as a volunteer with the John Howard Society, a complex Canadian organization working locally, provincially, and nationally with people in conflict with the law. Over the course of those years, I have assisted offenders both inside and outside of prison, played an advocacy role, and studied proposals for penal reform in the company of other volunteers and with professional staff. All of this has given me first-hand knowledge of the radical changes that have been sweeping through sentencing and corrections for more than two decades, and that have resulted in widespread loss of confidence in the efficacy of punishment, or at least harsh punishment, as a deterrent, and in the value of rehabilitation. Principles that have dominated sentencing theory and practice for much of this century are now very much in doubt.

These events have stimulated new thinking about the purpose of punishment. In spite of this fact, however, there remains a serious vacuum at the level of sentencing theory and practice. From a practical point of view, this has meant that it has become very difficult to formulate consistent, fair, and humane criteria for evaluating legislative, judicial, and correctional developments.

My purpose in writing this book is to fill that vacuum. I begin by examining the traditional philosophical accounts of punishment with a view to discovering why they have failed to provide an adequate basis for designing a coherent and humane approach to sentencing and corrections. I then turn to a discussion of the function of law and the nature of legal obligation with the aim of discovering the basic principles that ought to guide law enforcement. The function of law, I argue, is to reduce justified recourse to violence in the resolution of disputes. Understanding the implications of this for coercing compliance with the law allows the construction of a theory of punishment built on principles common to policing, adjudication, sentencing, and corrections, an account, furthermore, that is able to capture the strengths of the traditional theories of punishment while avoiding their defects.

I have been aided in my efforts by many people whose contribution I wish to acknowledge. First are many John Howard friends, both volunteers and professionals, who have assisted and encouraged me in many ways. In particular, Graham Stewart, now the Executive Director of the John Howard Society of Ontario, deserves special thanks. His wealth of experience and analytical insight have been invaluable.

Many others have also offered assistance. Conrad Brunk's counsel, and his knowledge of the peace and conflict studies literature, assisted me to bring my thoughts on those subjects into focus. Anthony Duff read portions of the manuscript and offered helpful advice. Anthony Duff, David Garland, and Martin Wright provided invaluable assistance in identifying important developments in penology and penal reform in Britain. Leslie Wilkins' hospitality provided the occasion for a week-end of conversation from which I learned a good deal.

Early drafts of various sections of the book were read in a number of settings: special Nordic Conferences of the International Society for Philosophy of Law and Social Philosophy (IVR) in Iceland, Finland and Canada, the University of Western Ontario Department of Philosophy, Laurentian University colloquia; and meetings of the Canadian Section of the IVR. I am grateful for many helpful comments received in those various settings. Laurentian University colleagues, particularly Henri Pallard, Brian Donohue, Gary Clarke, Michel Giroux, and Ashley Thomson, have been generous with their time and assistance.

Finally, I am grateful for the assistance of my wife, Mary, Daintry Clarke, and Pat Seguin, all of whom have contributed to the final stages in the writing and editing process.

There remains a word to say on the use of gender-specific pronouns. Clear conventions on this subject have yet to emerge. I have been reluctant to follow the advice of some people simply to avoid the use of third person singular pronouns altogether. The weight of punishment falls on specific individuals. To talk only in the plural obscures this fact. I have resolved the problem by switching gender from chapter to chapter: odd numbered chapters use the masculine form, even numbered chapters the feminine form of relevant pronouns.

AN INTRODUCTION

Punishments and rewards are pervasive features of social life. We meet both almost everywhere. As parents, we must come to terms with both and seek to assess their proper role in the education and discipline of our children. As employers and employees, we must wrestle with their role in ordering productive relationships. Contract negotiations are unavoidably about both. What is a just wage for this job in contrast to that one? Are pay scales equitable? Under what conditions should an employer have the right to discipline an employee? What kinds of disciplinary responses are justified under what conditions and for what reasons? And so on. In our social lives, we find ourselves wondering whether someone's snub was a tit for tat, or what the neighbours up the street did to deserve the anger directed their way.

Punishment and reward give rise to perplexing questions. Is corporal punishment morally acceptable in the home, or in school? Should we use rewards to encourage our children, for example, to respect others, or to do their homework, or to shovel the neighbour's sidewalk? Where is the line properly drawn between punishment and abuse or intimidation?

The answers to these questions are not easily found. They become even more difficult and controversial when the focus is on state punishment. The power of the state to punish is enormous. The state is able to execute, incarcerate for long periods of time, extract heavy fines, and require restitution and compensation.

Though the notions of punishment and reward are not easily separated,[1] the focus for this book will be the practice of punishment, particularly punishment as it is inflicted by the state. However, the discussion will not centre exclusively on state punishment. Rather, my intention is to explore the relationship of state punishment

1

to the informal common sense understandings of the purpose of punishment that are a part of everyday life. I shall argue that reforming penal institutions and correctional practices can only succeed where widely held informal understandings and formal patterns of punishment are brought into harmony with each other. The demand for state punishment comes from people whose understanding is shaped by common sense notions which are then used to evaluate the state's response to what they regard as harmful or offensive behaviour.[2] Rejecting these understandings as simplistic, or 'barbarian', or as irrelevant to the development of social policy which, it might be argued, ought to be shaped by modern scientific accounts of human behaviour is mistaken in my view and renders the task of reform difficult or, what is worse, impossible.

Launching into a systematic discussion of punishment requires some preliminary justification, however. There is a sense, of course, in which the discussion of punishment is virtually unavoidable in our complex society. Punishment is an accepted feature of our everyday lives. It is a pervasive feature of family life, education, employment, games, the law and so on. Few people think that we could do without it. Hence, there is an obvious sense in which the fact of punishment is not controversial. Why then does the practice warrant a sustained evaluation?

Two responses to this question are possible, one radical in nature, the other more practical and closer to everyday concerns. The radical response would suggest that the practice of punishment in modern societies such as our own is so deeply flawed and the principle that human beings have a right to inflict pain and suffering on wrongdoers is so suspect that punishment should in principle be abolished and replaced with a humane alternative.

The sense of moral outrage implicit in this response is not altogether unjustified, as we shall see. However, to approach an evaluation of punishment in this spirit is in effect to reject a basic feature of criminal law as it has evolved over hundreds of years. What is more, most of those who reflect critically on our culture can see the unavoidability of punishment as we practise it in spite of concerns with specific aspects of its administration. To suggest therefore that state punishment is by its very nature radically suspect is likely to be rejected as thoroughly impractical or utopian. There seems a wide consensus that punishment, for all its warts, is needed for the protection of society and its members.

My question is therefore directed to the great majority in our society who, as just described, are not prepared to reject punishment out of hand. Rephrased it now reads: are there reasons of a pragmatic and down-to-earth variety for thinking that punishment as it is practised in our contemporary western European and North American societies is in need of careful scrutiny?

There are many reasons for thinking that the appropriate answer to this question is 'yes'. To begin with, we are at a point in our history where sharp disagreements have emerged on what punishments are morally appropriate or acceptable for criminal activity. The persistence of capital punishment as a public issue is perhaps the best example of this fact. There is also widely shared uneasiness with the treatment of offenders by our courts and correctional institutions. What are not widely shared are the grounds for this concern.

There are, on the one hand, many people who think our courts have become offender oriented, handing out unjustifiably lenient sentences for serious offences. Correctional institutions are not infrequently described as resorts. Parole boards have in recent years been subjected to fierce criticism for their decisions. Meanwhile, confidence in the capacity of our system to rehabilitate or deter has been declining. This has led some to conclude that offenders should be ostracized from normal society and forced to live under austere conditions with limited access to treatment, education, recreation, and social activities of a sort the rest of us enjoy and take for granted. It is not uncommon, for example, to hear commentators suggest that those who have committed serious crimes like murder or violent assault should be regarded as having forfeited the right to be treated with dignity and should be either permanently isolated from normal society in some way or executed.

In contrast to these attitudes are the views of many others, spearheaded often by organizations committed to penal reform, that our approach to punishment has become excessively punitive and counter-productive.

Do these attitudes reflect more than just the normal range of opinions found on most topics in our society? There are good reasons to think that they do. There is today much less agreement on the administration of punishment than there has been for many decades. Research has revealed surprisingly wide disparities in sentencing among judges. Evaluation of rehabilitation-oriented pro-grammes in correctional institutions has resulted in widely shared discouragement about their efficacy. The 'nothing works' syndrome is now common among correctional officials, and academics. The goals of reform and rehabilitation whose values have dominated the field of corrections virtually since the turn of the century have been sharply criticized and widely abandoned. And while deterrence is still a mainstay of sentencing rhetoric, the value of most sentences as either general or specific deterrents is very much in doubt. In short, the justifications of punishment that have dominated sentencing and corrections through most of this century have lost their capacity to persuade. What has taken their place is 'justice-oriented' sentencing, whose goal is to assign punishments fairly by reference to what is deserved. In short, we seem to be returning to just retribution as the goal of punishment.

This 'reformation' in punishment theory has begun to have a dramatic effect on how the task of sentencing offenders is carried out. While the goal of rehabilitation dominated sentencing, judges required wide discretion to fulfil their responsibilities. This in turn resulted in wide disparities in sentences handed down for apparently similar offences. Many people have now concluded that wide judicial discretion is itself a serious source of injustice.[3] As a consequence many jurisdictions have implemented policies designed to reduce disparities in sentencing by reducing and in some cases virtually eliminating judicial discretion in deciding sentences.

Changing attitudes toward the role and purpose of punishment have impacted on the practice of punishment in two other significant ways. The focus on just sentences has directed attention to questions of fairness as well as questions of offender rights. However, it has also opened the door to increasingly harsh sentencing practices. There are two reasons for this. First, considerations of fairness that require that like cases be treated alike have increased the pressure for determinate sentences. This in turn has undermined rehabilitation-oriented practices like remission of time for good behaviour and early release mechanisms like parole which have the effect of reducing the time offenders spend in prison in ways that are not directly related to the seriousness of the crime committed.[4]

Second, desert-oriented theories of punishment provide guidance to sentencing authorities once the types of punishment for various offences have been established. On the other hand, their advocates have not reached common views on acceptable ranges of punishment. Some advocates of the desert model of punishment support capital punishment, for example. Others are opposed.[5]

4

Some have argued for very limited use of imprisonment and very short sentences, while others advocate harsh sentencing policies, for example life imprisonment for serious crimes.[6] In a public climate of fear and uncertainty, this aspect of a just deserts approach to punishment seems to have opened the door to increasing severity in sentencing policy, as evidenced by prison overcrowding and vastly expanding capital budgets for prison construction, among other things.

Another weakness of desert-oriented punishment is that it provides little guidance on how those sentenced to imprisonment should spend their time while imprisoned. This fact combined with discouragement about the effectiveness of rehabilitation and a lack of public sympathy for those who break the law has resulted in a serious vacuum in correctional policy. Increasingly our prisons resemble warehouses whose primary function is incapacitation for the duration of an offender's sentence.

One concrete sign of public unease with how offenders are dealt with by our criminal justice systems is the rush on the part of governments in recent years to appoint inquiries and commissions whose mandate is to review sentencing and correctional practices. Equally disconcerting is the unease with which the authors of resulting reports have greeted their own recommendations. Willard Gaylin and David Rothman, writing in the 'Introduction' of *Doing Justice*, one of the most influential early defences of the justice model of punishment, describe their solution as 'one of despair not hope'. The desert model they advocate is described as 'intellectual and moralistic', emphasizing 'justice not mercy' and turning back on 'generosity and charity, compassion and love' (von Hirsch 1976: xxxix). The Canadian Sentencing Commission, having undertaken a task similar to that of the American Committee eleven years earlier, endorses a similar model of sentencing but is equally pessimistic in that endorsement. Punishment cannot be justified, they imply. Yet contemporary society insists, apparently without sound reason, that punishment be inflicted for criminal acts. The best that we can do is to limit the damage that punishment inevitably inflicts (Archambault 1987: 145).

Finally, at the level of pure theory, we find a similar range of difficulties arising. Pure retributivist theories are notoriously difficult to defend and widely thought to be indistinguishable from the thoroughly disreputable goal of revenge.[7]

The chief rivals of retributivist accounts of punishment are

5

forward-looking and utilitarian in nature. These theories have been widely criticized both on empirical grounds – actual rehabilitative regimes have not generated results required to justify their continuance – and for their inability to provide sentencing criteria that respect fundamental moral principles, particularly widely shared notions of justice.

What is more, though each theory seems to require the other if punishment is to be justified, they also seem to be incompatible.

All of this suggests, then, that there is ample reason for thinking that punishment as it is practised in western liberal democracies in the late twentieth century needs careful and sustained scrutiny.

How to proceed?

The account offered thus far suggests that we are unlikely to make progress by moving case by case through current sentencing and correctional practices and current criminal law. Our current system is too badly fragmented and the current malaise too pervasive. Approaching our task by plunging into abstract theorizing is equally unpromising. This is because the work of recent theorists has resulted in justifications that either embrace the status quo uncritically or are inapplicable in anything but utopian settings.[8]

Consequently, I propose to begin from an assessment of what I shall suggest are deeply held beliefs about punishment and its function in our modern societies. They are four in number.

1 *Something like punishment as we understand it is an unavoidable element of modern social life.*

The strength of this belief is evidenced by the abrupt and derisive public rejection that invariably greets proposals for the abolition of punishment. The strength of the belief is also indicated by the fact that it is accepted as a ground level reality both by formal commissions like the Canadian Sentencing Commission and by most theorists writing on the subject.[9]

2 *The practice of punishment, reflecting as it does the evolution of our criminal justice system and the kinds of penalties it typically imposes for criminal acts, from imprisonment to fines, is in principle defensible and understandable.*

This belief reflects the common view that the way our society approaches the enforcement of law, though perhaps capable of improvement and even substantial improvement, is none the less intelligible and defensible.

6

3 *Punishment as it is practised in North American and western European societies is in need of significant reforms.*

This belief is perhaps less widely shared than the others. Yet it reflects the realities of the evolution of our penal system. At various times in the last century, our societies have been persuaded that serious penal reform was required. Movements for penal reform have given rise to significant changes in what we view as legitimate punishments and how those punishments are administered. The most recent evidence of this fact is the gradual rejection of capital punishment as legitimate punishment by most western liberal democracies since the last war. Yet many of the reforms introduced with public support in the past are now suspect. And there are significant efforts to reintroduce harsher sentencing practices.

4 *Any account of punishment to be useful must provide us with criteria for evaluating whether current practices are in need of reform, and whether concrete proposals for reform constitute genuine improvements.*

Many discussions of punishment fail this test, as we shall see in what follows.

I propose to start with practical concerns and practical problems. Most of us have in fact thought a good deal about punishment in one form or another throughout our lives: as children faced with parental disapproval and discipline, as parents confronted with the need to establish and maintain family discipline, as employees and employers, as friends and neighbours, and just as citizens required to obey the law. Most of us have therefore given thought to who should be punished under what conditions and for what reasons. It is also true that the moral dimensions of punishment have been and continue to be widely explored, though not always as systematically as philosophers would like. Finally, it is relatively obvious to those familiar with everyday accounts of punishment and with the philosophical literature on the subject that philosophical discussions on this subject tend to echo common sense views on the subject. For all of these reasons, to begin a study of punishment with practical concerns and practical insights seems, at first glance at any rate, a sound strategy.

I shall not ignore theory, however. Rather, what I am proposing is something more akin to a dialogue between theory and practice. Philosophy of punishment is practical philosophy.

It is important therefore that it engage experience in practical ways.

A guide to the argument

The purpose of the first three chapters is to evaluate traditional approaches to the justification of punishment: retributivism, utilitarian theories and two relatively recent attempts to capture the virtues of each of these theories in a single hybrid account. One of the purposes of the discussion will be to show how these traditional theories arise naturally from practical concerns to which harmful and offensive behaviour give rise. However, on careful examination, none of them is able to provide an account of punishment that is free of serious practical and moral objections. Neither can the theories be combined in a way which captures only their virtues while avoiding their objectionable qualities.

We are left then with a dilemma. Although punishment is widely thought to be an unavoidable feature of the criminal law, the practice of punishment seems to be very difficult to justify taken by itself.[10] This suggests that, to understand the necessity for punishment, we need to turn to an examination of the need for law and the role of punishment as a part of legal systems.

Legal systems arise, I shall suggest, in response to a universal human need for cooperation as well as human vulnerability to violence, or to the use of force as a means for achieving human objectives. Law provides a potentially useful way of resolving disputes in a manner that encourages cooperation and reduces recourse to the use of force in the settling of disputes. Legal systems seek to accomplish these goals by giving designated officials the authority to make, change, interpret, and enforce laws. The use of this authority is morally justified, I shall argue, when it reduces recourse to the morally justified use of force in dispute settlement.

Legal systems can fulfil these basic functions only if those who fall under the law's authority are confident that for the most part others with whom they interact can be trusted to live within the law. The proper function of enforcement, then, is threefold: to demonstrate that for the most part people are law abiding and that those responsible for enforcement are committed to fulfilling their responsibilities conscientiously; to persuade people to obey the law when they might otherwise fail to do so; and to provide assistance to those who need help in obeying the law.

I shall argue that each of these functions does in fact play a central role in both policing and adjudication in modern western societies. Furthermore, once we understand enforcement to have these three functions, not only are the complexities of both policing and adjudication more easily understood, but the relationship of each to sentencing and the development of correction policies becomes evident. This in turn provides an interesting perspective from which to both understand and evaluate much of the general contemporary unease with sentencing as well as the persistent and persuasive demands for significant reforms that have dominated public policy debates in recent years.

We now have a setting in which to understand the role of sentencing and corrections. The function of a sentence, this account suggests, is the resolution of disputes to which criminal offences give rise in ways designed to sustain confidence in the capacity of the law to fulfil its legitimate functions on the part of victims of crime and the public at large. To do this effectively, the sentencing process must demonstrate commitment on the part of authorities to law enforcement, while seeking to persuade and enable offenders to live within the law.

The function of enforcement is therefore essentially restorative. And the goal of sentencing is restorative justice. As we shall see, what results is a theory of punishment that captures the essential features of the traditional accounts, accepts the inevitability of punishment as a feature of criminal justice, but goes beyond the traditional accounts by suggesting that, while punishment is unavoidable, imposing hard treatment is not the purpose of sentencing but rather its result. The purpose of sentencing is and ought to be restorative justice.

9

1

PUNISHMENT AS RETRIBUTION

There is a straight-forward sense in which punishment could be said to be a natural feature of human existence. History, literature, and religion confirm its central role in human relationships from the dawn of society. It is perhaps the sense that punishment is an inevitable or unavoidable feature of social life that leads many people to dismiss as impractical, or silly, or hopelessly utopian all suggestions that punishment is something we could and should do without.

At the same time, there is another side to the picture. Even while admitting its socially fundamental character, many acknowledge that punishment has many troubling features. We may agree that punishment is an essential tool for parents, teachers, employers and employees, the courts and so on. Yet we are often concerned with how that tool is employed by those in positions of authority. Knowledge of the history of punishment does little to allay that concern. Looking at the past from the perspective of today's values, it is hard not to be appalled at what has been justified in the name of punishment.

It is no doubt these troubling features that have led some people to experiment with the task of describing a world in which punishment was allotted no place. Neither is the project as other-worldly as some might at first suggest. After all, for most of human history, corporal punishment has been seen as essential to the education of children. Yet this assumption has been frequently and persuasively criticized over the course of the last half-century to the point where corporal punishment has been virtually eliminated from our educational systems. Equally, the once unbridled right of parents to use corporal punishment is now being progressively curtailed.

Perhaps more important than these developments is the fact that punishment seems to conflict with values like forgiveness, mercy, compassion, and benevolence, all of which reflect non-punitive ways of solving problems of human conflict. Punishment sets out to cause suffering. Its approach is essentially negative and coercive. In contrast, the values in tension with it are positive, forward-looking and build on cooperation.

None of this would convince most of us to set aside punishment as unnecessary or outdated. However, these considerations do suggest that the practice of punishment is not unproblematic. Neither are appropriate forms of punishment easily described, structured, or justified. As a result, we are left in a position of considerable moral tension. If punishment is an inevitable feature of social life, under what conditions is inflicting punishment justified?

The common view

One way of answering this question is to try to construct a common sense picture of punishment based on everyday experiences. This should not be a difficult task in the first instance if it is as common as I have suggested. And it may help us to understand the features of punishment as we commonly experience it. We can then ask whether, given its basic properties, punishment as we normally encounter it is unavoidable in some form.

One fundamental feature of human relationships is that they are rule governed. Since the function of a rule is to prohibit what otherwise might be done, rule enforcement seems unavoidable. If those who broke the rules were treated no differently from those who followed them, we would normally conclude that the rule had ceased to apply. It does not follow that in every case where there is no enforcement there is no rule. In times of emergency, there may be no time for enforcement. Alternatively, ignoring a breach of the rules may be politically expedient, and so on. All that having been said, however, if no one ever reacted when a rule was broken, that would in normal circumstances be grounds for concluding that there was no rule.

Normally, we can also determine the strength of a community's commitment to a rule by determining how it is enforced. The greater the effort put into enforcement and the more stringent the penalty, the more important the rule to its enforcers. The same is true of the sanction attached to breaches of a rule. Most of us would think it unfair to treat those breaking fundamental rules no differently from those breaking insignificant ones.

Finally, what a person intended in breaking a rule is normally very important. Someone who takes what is not his inadvertently is easily excused; someone who knowingly takes what is not his is not. The second person's behaviour is much more disturbing. It suggests a lack of concern for others, a willingness to put his own interests first in ways that challenge basic values.

Punishment has a place in this picture. As a consequence, the practice of punishment is for most people unproblematic. Punishment, when it is imposed, does not normally generate rebellion or outrage. Most communities share a sense of what is appropriate in most circumstances and what is not. A teacher is justified in ejecting unruly students from the class. An employee is entitled to compensation and an apology for unjust dismissal. Parents should normally not attempt to discipline other people's children and so on.

However, there are significant areas where consensus is much harder to obtain. Mostly, disagreement occurs where proposed punishments are severe and potentially harmful to those on whom they are inflicted. For example, there are today sharp disagreements about the justifiability of capital punishment and the appropriate uses of imprisonment. There can be strong disagreements over what rules should be enforced. Is abortion or euthanasia immoral? If so, should it be prohibited? Should polluters be prosecuted under the criminal law?

Punishment is problematic, it might be suggested, because it inflicts suffering. Most of us believe that a basic rule of civilized society is that we should never impose unnecessary suffering on others. Where punishment appears to do this, its moral status in thrown into doubt.

It would seem to follow that, since punishment imposes suffering, it is justified only if it can be shown to be necessary. The discussion suggests that punishment is necessary because it is unavoidable. But is this true? The answer, surely, is 'no'. It would be nice if it were otherwise. For we would be in a position to bring some of the more difficult aspects of our discussion of punishment to a halt. However, nothing that we have said shows that punishment *is* unavoidable. Rules do not exist, we have argued, if they are never enforced. Enforcement in its most basic form requires that those who break the rules be treated differently from those who respect them. However, there are options beyond just punishment. We might create a system in which those who broke basic rules were simply ignored while those who obeyed the rules were systematically rewarded. Alternatively, we might create a system where those who broke the rules were put in institutions and treated as, for example, we treat those who are sick.

Both options have been canvassed by commentators.[1] However, their value for our purposes at the moment lies in the challenge they put to the common sense account. Why, we want to know, is punishment so widely thought to be unavoidable? The answer lies in a more thorough look at the role of rules and the need for their enforcement in everyday life.

Rules are a fundamental feature of human society. There are many reasons for this. Most of us accept that we must live and work in communities if we are to meet effectively even our most basic needs for food, shelter and clothing. We also know that this makes us vulnerable in particular ways. We cooperate to produce the material goods we need. However, what we produce is easily taken from us. Unless there are rules that govern how goods and services are exchanged, what we produce will be of little value to us. Why labour to build a house or grow crops if they can be taken away on a whim?

Our lives are vulnerable in a similar way. Working with others requires that we 'disarm' ourselves for the purpose of engaging in common tasks. In the absence of shared rules protecting human life, for example, fear of violent assault would render cooperation virtually impossible.

Those who break the rules benefit without contributing. They gain personal advantage by doing what the rules forbid. The benefit they gain, furthermore, is of no value to them unless the rules they break continue to be respected for the most part by others. There is no point in stealing a bicycle if no one respects private property. For what has been stolen will not remain in the possession of the thief for any length of time.

Those who break the rules on which cooperation is based generate anger and resentment, but only if they do so intentionally. A person who mistakenly walks off with a bicycle which he believes to be his own may have harmed its owner. But he will not cause offence (unless what he did was the result of carelessness) if he returns the property when the mistake is discovered. People who steal cause anger and resentment because they have put their own interests ahead of the interests of their victims in particularly selfish ways.

Inevitably, failure to respect basic rules raises the issue of fairness.

The offence creates an imbalance where someone who has a right to something has lost it and someone who has no right to it has gained it. The result is a winner and a loser where neither merits what he has.

A basic moral outlook that is widely shared is that a world where those who live moral lives end up worse off than those who do not is an unjust one. Preventing this state of affairs is one reason for insisting that basic rules be respected. One obvious way of making this point is to correct the injustice that has occurred by restoring the balance that has been disturbed. The person who has been harmed does not deserve the harm he has experienced. The person who has done the harm does not deserve the benefit he has gained thereby. The purpose of punishment is to restore both the victim and the offender to their appropriate positions relative to each other.[2] It does this by returning to the offender a harm equivalent to the one he imposed on his victim and offering the victim the satisfaction of knowing that the rules he respects have social support, that he has been harmed and that the offender has been brought to justice.

This account of punishment has many virtues. It accords with experience. The harm caused by those who break basic rules arouses resentment and anger. Punishment calms this anger by giving offenders their just deserts. It accords closely with dictionary definitions of punishment.[3] Finally it is compatible with the most common definitions of punishment contributed by theorists.[4]

Four questions

The account of punishment as it has developed to this point offers answers to three questions. Whom are we justified in punishing? Why are we justified in punishing them? And what kind of punishment are we justified in inflicting? We are justified in punishing those who have broken fundamental rules by inflicting on them a penalty that reflects in an adequate way the harm caused in breaking those rules. We are justified in taking this action because, by breaking the rules in question, they have taken unfair advantage of their victims and the community generally by depriving their victims of benefits conferred by those rules and reaping benefits they did not deserve.

However, our account leaves unanswered a fourth question. Who is justified in imposing the punishment that offenders deserve?

Perhaps the best answer to our last question is that, in practice, responsibility for punishment rests with those who have a special responsibility for the particular area of life to which the rules apply: parents for their children, teachers for students, employers for employees, and so on. If we follow the analogy, this would suggest that the state has responsibility for enforcing the law since this is the area of life for which it has special responsibility.

The analogy, however, does not really explain why we need formal as opposed to informal methods of punishing those who break our laws. Neither does it explain why state punishment should override or take precedence over other ways of accomplishing the same end. Perhaps the reason is essentially pragmatic. Or perhaps, as I shall suggest below, the explanation lies in the power that the right to punish confers and the need therefore to control its use, to curb excesses, and to ensure that punishment is inflicted only for appropriate reasons.

Be that as it may, it is significant that the popular view of punishment implies very little about how the right to punish is conferred, particularly on state authorities, especially when conferring on the state the authority to punish effectively removes it from those most directly affected by offences, namely their victims.

Punishment and retribution

We need now to step back from our account to set out its essential characteristics and to consider some basic concerns to which it gives rise. First, it is backward-looking. It justifies punishment only as a response to a past event. Second, this account links punishment to moral wrongdoing. It justifies punishment as a response to an injustice. Finally, this account emphasizes notions of merit and desert. An offence by its very nature inflicts unmerited harm on a victim, or inflicts harm in an unmerited way. By acting in this way, the offender gains an advantage which he does not merit. Punishment sets this imbalance straight. It removes the undeserved benefit by imposing a penalty that in some sense balances the harm inflicted by the offence.

This account is, of course, a retributivist one. It takes the view that punishment is justifiable if it is merited or deserved. It is deserved when it is a response to injustice or wrongdoing.

15

Retributivism: practical and philosophical concerns

The most common and pressing concern with retributivism is its link with vengeance. Vengeance is simply retaliation for a harm done. As such, it seems, as many have taken it to be, another word for retribution. It is hard to deny that this association exists in the public mind. Punishment is how we get even with those who have hurt us. It balances accounts and teaches perpetrators what it feels like to be treated in a certain way. Perhaps even more significant is the extent to which this link is taken for granted in academic discussions. For example, the *Dictionary of Philosophy* asserts that one of the main elements of the retributive theory of punishment is the view that 'the purpose of punishment is revenge' (Angeles 1981: 230). Social scientists are equally prone to the same association. Thus, it is no coincidence that Ezzat Fattah, who produced much of the key research that lay behind the movement to abolish capital punishment in Canada in the 1970s, describes the deterrence arguments in favour of capital punishment as 'more civilized than arguments based on revenge and retribution' (Cragg 1987: 141).

It would be hard to deny that the desire for revenge comes naturally where people to whom one is emotionally attached are victimized. It would be equally hard to deny that giving vent to the desire for revenge can be extremely destructive. Indeed, vengeance, associated as it is with anger, bitterness, hatred, and resentment, seems to negate the human capacity for love, compassion, forgiveness, and mercy. It is not surprising, therefore, that many have been led to reject retributive accounts of punishment because in their view retribution and revenge were one and the same thing.

Is this association justified? Unquestionably, the two have something in common. Both are responses to wrongs inflicted on innocent victims. Both aim to correct the wrong. Vengeance, however, takes as its focus the personal hurt caused by the wrong and is a response to that hurt and the anger it generates. Consequently, those seeking revenge frequently misjudge the harm or wrong to which they are responding. They over-react, with the result that the punishment that is inflicted is often excessive.

Revenge also has a haphazard quality. It leads to punishments that vary with the degree of anger provoked. Wrongs that provoke no anger get no response even when they are similar in all respects save the identity of the victim.[5]

Just retribution, on the other hand, requires that punishment

16

should be in proportion to the seriousness of the offence. Punishment should not vary with the identity of the victim and it should be inflicted only for genuine wrongs.

Contrasting just retribution and vengeance may also help to explain why modern societies have delegated responsibility for inflicting serious penalties to formal state institutions. Where the practice of punishment rests on informal mechanisms, it is subject to all the distortions associated with vengeance. The merit of formal institutions is that they can be structured so as to reduce the possibility of bias and distortion in assessing whether a genuine wrong has been committed, the nature of that wrong, and the response merited. Formal institutions with a trained and impartial judiciary would also be more likely to treat like cases alike, which is also central to just retribution.

Our discussion of revenge points to another virtue of retribution. The desire for revenge is in many ways a natural response to perceived wrongs. To ignore those emotions invites further conflict. When offenders are punished in accordance with their deserts, the desire for revenge is quieted. Feelings left over that demand further punishment can then be seen to be unjustified. Just punishment is therefore a way of redirecting natural but potentially very destructive emotions in morally acceptable and socially constructive ways.[6]

This first concern with retributivist accounts can be seen therefore to be unfounded. Nevertheless, there are other and, as it turns out, more serious problems. To begin with, retributivist accounts seem to incorporate criteria for assessing the appropriate response to any given act of wrongdoing. On examination, however, this turns out not to be the case.

The most obvious formula for this purpose is the *lex talionis*, the principle of an eye for an eye, a tooth for a tooth, a life for a life. The *lex talionis* is virtually as old as law itself. Careful examination of the Biblical record, however, shows that the principle was never applied literally, at least by the Hebrews.[7] This is not surprising since literal application is impossible in many cases and certain to be morally repugnant in others. What, for example, is the appropriate response for violent sexual assault, or defamation of character, or dishonesty, or kidnapping or terrorism? No easy answers appear.

The *lex talionis*, however, is closely related to another principle, namely that punishment should fit the crime. This principle requires that the weight or punitive quality of a penalty should vary with the moral seriousness of the offence committed. For example, stealing a bicycle should not receive the same response as armed robbery. A minor assault should be treated differently from assault with the intent to kill.

The proposal that the punishment should fit the crime brings into focus a principle of proportionality. It does provide guidance in determining an appropriate scale of sanctions. It requires that various offences be rank-ordered by reference to their relative seriousness. A similar rank ordering of sanctions would then allow offences and sanctions to be matched.

What this proposal does not help with is determining what is to count as appropriate sanctions. It cannot help us determine the acceptability of life imprisonment, or capital punishment, or maiming, or banishment and so on. These judgements have to be made independently of the principle of proportionality. Further, it is not at all clear that the retributive account of punishment can help us with them.

The inability of retributive accounts to generate a determinate scale of sanctions or to help us evaluate the appropriateness of proposed or existing sanctions like capital punishment points to a gap which the account itself cannot fill.

Secondly, the values central to retributivist attitudes would seem to conflict with other values that have traditionally played important roles in human relationships. Formalized retributive justice requires that the punishment fit the crime and that like cases be treated alike. It has, as a consequence, an unrelenting, remorseless character that leaves no room to adapt penalties to what we might call the human dimension. The traditional image of retributive justice is of a goddess who is blindfolded and thus unable to see the individual who has come before her for judgement. The verdict is guided only by the weighing of guilt and the requirements of justice in measuring the appropriate penalty.

Normally, people are prepared to modify their attitudes in the light of special considerations. A friend fails to meet a commitment. But we know he has been under serious financial pressure and forgive the oversight. An employee of someone with whom we have contracted for house repairs steals money and is detected. When he is confronted with his act, he confesses but asks not to be reported. This is the first job he has been able to find and he has a family to support. He will certainly lose his job if the theft is reported. And so we agree out of a sense of compassion for his situation to overlook his theft on the promise that he has learned his lesson.

Many other examples could be set out. However, each has the same quality, namely a willingness to overlook or 'bend' justice to fit the human dimensions of those who have committed an offence. There is no place in formal systems of retributive justice for these qualities. Mercy, compassion, forgiveness can apply only where we are prepared not to treat like cases alike, since the qualities to which they respond are not directly related to the issues of guilt or innocence or to the seriousness of the offence. When they find expression, they override notions of desert.[8]

Because retributive justice is incompatible with values like compassion it has an inhuman aura. It is true that some see a place for the prerogative of mercy within retributive systems. However, the place they assign it is almost always outside the judicial system in the hands perhaps of a sovereign. Further, its exercise is normally thought to be restricted to very special cases like terminal illness or crimes committed under highly unique circumstances. Thus, although a retributive account of justice can sometimes find room for virtues like mercy, it is virtually always at the expense of justice and not in concert with it. Hence, the effect is to emphasize the fundamental incompatibility of retributive justice with other values.

Retributive justice stresses impartiality. This is one of its strengths, since it ensures that individuals receive equal treatment at the hands of the court regardless of their station in life. The effect, however, is to depersonalize the process. Justice on this account is concerned with wrongs and not with persons, except in so far as they are the perpetrators of wrongs. However, the inability to focus on the individuals involved blinds justice to the crime's victim as well as to the personal characteristics of the offender. This too is a virtue. It distances justice from those intense emotions that can distort an objective assessment of guilt and the nature of the offence. This means, however, that the victim loses his central role in the drama whose focus is the wrong committed and not the person wronged.

This points to a further problem. Retributive justice is depersonalized. It is also decontextualized. To merit punishment, one must break a rule and thus commit a wrong. Typically that will involve theft or assault and so on. Punishment is in response to the wrong committed. Thus, to punish someone who has committed no wrong is clearly unjust. Again, this is the central strength of the account. However, the effect of focusing on the crime and not the criminal is to abstract from the social context in which the crime occurs. This means that the powerful are treated no differently from the poor. It also means that those who are socially disadvantaged are treated no differently from those who are not. The theft of food on the part of a mother on welfare is therefore not materially different from the theft of a camera by a young adult from a well-to-do family. Two adults on trial for child abuse must be treated alike where their offences are the same although the one may be a man who has carried the frustrations of a stressful occupation home with him to be vented on his children, while the other is a man who was himself abused as a child and has never managed to establish mature relations with others.

That is to say, retributivism requires that we ignore factors that would otherwise seem significant. We know that someone who has been raised in a series of foster homes is more likely to come into conflict with the law than is his counterpart from a stable home environment. People on welfare are more likely to end up in court than people with stable incomes. Children who have been abused by their parents are more likely to abuse their own children, and so on.

We might sum up this series of concerns with retributive justice in the following way. Most of us believe that justice requires that people be treated in accordance with their just deserts. A world in which those who merit rewards do not receive them while those who have failed to respect the rights of others benefit from their wrongdoing is a paradigm of injustice. Retributive justice responds to these values. However, the justice it imposes leaves no room for other values to which we are equally committed, values whose focus is human needs rather than human deserts. It is this element of exclusivity or 'moral imperialism'[9] that renders it seriously suspect.

Philosophical objections

I have already suggested that the principle of desert accords with our deepest intuitions. At the same time, that same principle generates serious philosophical puzzles and concerns. To begin with, even if we grant that punishment should be in accordance with desert, it does not follow that punishment is justified. Retributive punishment occurs when someone deliberately inflicts hard treatment on an offender for his offence in accordance with his desert. Previous discussion has suggested reasons for thinking that such a principle is more likely to be fairly or justly applied if the authority to punish is delegated to formal judicial institutions. These considerations assume that if punishment is deserved it should be deliberately inflicted. There is, however, nothing in the principle of desert itself which justifies that assumption. Neither is it supported by our moral intuitions.

It is a commonplace of moral life that people do not get what they deserve in many instances. Conscientious business people have their business fail as the result of the operation of economic forces over which they have no control. People find themselves caught by rising interest rates and lose their homes though they had taken every conceivable precaution in setting up their finances. Scholarships are not necessarily won by the most deserving. Indeed, there is no principle that ensures that success goes only to those who merit it and failure only to those who do not deserve to succeed.

Neither is desert the only or the most important principle ordering human relations. Many of our social practices and institutions are structured to respond to need and not desert. People with self-inflicted illnesses do not in the normal course of events receive a lower priority in our hospitals than those whose medical problems are in no way self-inflicted. Universal health insurance, workers' compensation plans, adult re-education and retraining programmes do not allocate spaces on grounds of desert. Child custody and divorce proceedings largely ignore questions of blame. And so on.

Perhaps more important, there seems to be no overriding social obligation to correct those misfortunes that lead to undeserved results, whether positive or negative. This does not mean that our modern societies are ungenerous or uninterested in justice, though they may be in some respects. Undeserved misfortune does arouse sympathy. Undeserved success can be the occasion of regret. However, there is no moral imperative that requires that all such imbalances be corrected.

It is true that actions that break basic rules require a response. This might be said to be a necessary condition for the existence of a rule. However, this in no way implies that the response be a punitive one or that it should be measured by notions of desert. Equally possible is the idea that intervention might be guided by a desire to achieve some good, for example quieting the desire for revenge, or securing respect for the law. What is more, it is widely accepted that structured punitive response to some even quite significant moral wrongs is not warranted even when they cause deep hurt. Breaking promises not directly related to economic matters is one example of this.

In short, the principle of retribution does not explain why punishment should be inflicted on those who break fundamental rules. At best it implies that, if a punitive response to moral wrongdoing is warranted, punishment should reflect desert.

There is a second significant problem with the notion of just retribution. Retributive accounts link punishment directly with moral wrongdoing. One immediate problem with this is that not all illegal activity is immoral in and of itself. Traffic laws and zoning by-laws provide good examples of this.

To this objection there is a relatively easy response. Once a law is established, people come to rely on its being respected. Those who do not respect the law take advantage of those who do in a variety of ways. They pose unfair competition or create risks or inconvenience that result directly from their refusal to respect the laws in place. Hence, it is not unreasonable to assume that there is a general moral obligation to obey the law even where the law itself has no explicitly moral content.[10]

This argument meets one objection to linking moral and legal guilt as required by retributivism. However, it points in the process to related difficulties that are not so easily resolved.

To begin with, while on the retributivist account the function of the law is to punish moral wrongdoing, in fact the law does not punish all moral wrongdoing. Neither does it pick and choose in a way that reflects the moral seriousness of the wrongdoing involved. Some moral wrongs the law simply refuses to become involved in. For example, increasingly over the second half of this century, the law has decided that the issue of child custody should be resolved independently of considerations relating to the sexual conduct of one or other of the parents.

Further, there are some kinds of moral wrongdoing that the law simply ignores. Deceit in commercial and consumer relations, for example, is punishable. Dishonesty in personal relationships often is not. There is no obvious moral justification for these distinctions. Presumably the reasons lie elsewhere. This being the case, it is hard to avoid the suspicion that the reason for enforcement where it occurs is grounded not on morality but on some non-moral goal or purpose. If this is so, retributive accounts of punishment may serve to disguise in illegitimate ways the real nature of law and punishment.[11]

This leads to a second serious difficulty. Retributivism seems to rest on an assumption of widespread moral agreement about right and wrong. Yet contemporary western societies are morally diverse and reflect substantial disagreements about the nature of morality and about what kinds of actions are immoral and what are not. Examples where this disagreement shows itself are not hard to find. Our obligations toward the environment are one. Abortion, euthanasia, gun control, the treatment of animals, corporal punishment in the discipline of children, compulsory education, are just a few others. When the law punishes people in these areas, it implies, on the retributivist account, that those being punished are guilty of moral wrongdoing, when, in fact, those being punished may see their behaviour as morally permissible or even morally required. Equally, when the law fails to punish in these areas it fails to act against people whose behaviour is regarded by some as deeply immoral.

This dilemma is deepened if we are prepared to acknowledge that the law sometimes reflects values that are in conflict with morality. It is not hard to find examples of this in the past: slavery, enforcement of religious conformity, discrimination on a variety of grounds, and so on. Unless we assume that contemporary systems of law exhibit a kind of moral superiority or infallibility not shared by their precursors, we have to assume that immoral values are reflected in contemporary legal systems as well. This must inevitably generate serious problems for a view that assumes that the function of the law is to punish moral wrongdoing, when it seems that, at least sometimes, the law is doing just the opposite.

All of these problems point to a final difficulty that captures the central dilemma. The plurality of often incompatible moral beliefs has led many to the view that there are no absolute or universal moral values or principles. Moral values are now widely seen as relative either to cultures or to individuals. This view, which lies behind a good deal of contemporary liberal political theory, appears to offer an explanation for moral diversity. It also seems to imply that assessments of moral desert and attributions of moral blame are bound to vary in irreconcilable ways. Since the law cannot give equal place to incompatible moral values, a legal system which assigns punishment in accordance with moral blame must unavoidably favour one view of morality over other competing views. If this is so, aiming at retribution in punishment would seem to require a kind of favouritism.

Although none of these arguments is conclusive taken by itself, they point to two things. First, in a morally pluralistic society, to justify punishment as a response to moral wrongdoing creates severe problems. Second, to show that the notion of just retribution is sound would require that it find a place within a much broader moral theory designed to prove the existence of universal moral values on which a legal system could and should be grounded. It would also have to show that the resulting moral and political theory could provide an adequate account of central liberal political values such as individual liberty.

Moral guilt and the problem of determinism

An essential element of retributivist accounts of punishment is the view that punishment for wrongdoing is justified only where the person responsible acted voluntarily. Punishing people for actions over which they had no control is morally unacceptable. It is for this reason that retributive systems differentiate between the behaviour of adults and children, those who are sane and those who are not, those acting under compulsion, mental or physical, and those whose actions spring from voluntary decisions. The concept which captures that requirement in common law jurisdictions is *mens rea*.

This raises two difficulties for retributive accounts of punishment. To assess guilt is to assess the degree of responsibility properly attributed to someone who has broken the law. Inevitably, discovering what someone's state of mind was and whether he could have acted otherwise is complex and difficult. Whether a person's act was voluntary does not seem to admit of black and white answers. Judgement is often clouded by severe illness, great stress, emotional upset, intoxication, mental retardation, and so on. What is more, it seems quite clear that in our everyday moral interactions we take these kinds of considerations into account. We find it easier to excuse or forgive a friend who has let us down in a hurtful way if we are convinced that the context in which he found himself made it extremely difficult for him to meet his commitments. These judgements, however, almost always depend on our knowledge of the individual in question, his character and past patterns of behaviour, and our knowledge of the prevailing situation.

One would expect similar conditions to prevail where people are charged with criminal offences. Yet a court is not in a good position to make the necessary judgements. Ascertaining the mental state of an accused is extraordinarily difficult and uncertain. Yet often severe punishments hang on the outcome.

The difficulty of assessing with any certainty the degree of responsibility properly attributed for a particular action is paralleled by a theoretical problem. To a large degree, the science of human behaviour is dominated by the view that all human behaviour is determined. This is normally understood to mean that what people do is, in principle at least, capable of being predicted in advance, given an adequate knowledge of genetic and environmental determinants. If this is true, nothing that human beings do is voluntary in the required sense. It follows that punishment is never justified.

Assessing the theoretical merits of determinism is a task too large to pursue here. Hence the spectre of determinism cannot be sufficient taken by itself to justify a rejection of retributive accounts of punishment. Nevertheless, it is worth pointing out that in practice determinism is also suggested by our knowledge of the social conditions conducive to criminal behaviour. It is hard to accept, for example, that the fact that the murder rate is so much higher in the United States than in Canada is to be accounted for by lower standards of morality. We know that crime rates rise as economic conditions deteriorate. We know that a child brought up in an abusive home is much more likely to become an abusive parent than those with non-abusive parents. We know that most sexual offenders experienced sexual abuse at some point in their lives.

This suggests strong social determinants in criminal behaviour. Poverty, little incentive at home to pursue an education, broken homes, alcoholic parents are all important factors over which the individuals concerned have no control. All of this suggests that the concept of responsibility has no place, or a substantially reduced place, in our response to criminal behaviour.

Although assessing the merits of determinism is beyond the scope of our discussions, I take it that the general plausibility of determinism should lead at any rate to real caution in the application of retributivist accounts of punishment. Whether a plausible alternative account of punishment can be constructed, one which does not link punishment with a concept of moral guilt resting on a doctrine of freedom of the will, remains to be seen.

Retributive justice: a test case

The focus of discussion in this chapter has been twofold. We have seen first that, in a number of fundamental respects, retributivism has had a deeply formative impact on the way we think about punishment. At the same time, we have seen that that approach to punishment has significant flaws. The argument, however, has proceeded in an abstract way. This no doubt is inevitable in an account of this sort. However, it does lose track of the fact that our conceptions of justice have developed in response to social, political and religious realities in concrete historical settings. Thus retributive notions of justice were not first abstractly conceived and then implemented. Rather, they developed as responses to real needs.

Although the concept of retribution can be found in one form or another within the thinking of most societies, our own conceptions have been most deeply influenced by Old Testament ideas. The Old Testament is in turn in part a record of the attempt of the Hebrew people at a particular stage of their history to build a system of law that would enforce in a just way the rules that they saw as vital to their survival. Reviewing that historical development will help to illustrate and give a concrete form to our evaluation of the notion of just retribution.

The Hebraic notion of just retribution is first developed in the five books of the law called the Pentateuch. The popular understanding of these books focuses on the Ten Commandments and the *lex talionis*. This picture is both distorted and incomplete. The *lex talionis*, that is, the idea that people should be punished for moral wrongdoing in a manner which directly replicates the wrongdoing, does not find literal application at any point in the Old Testament account. Neither does the rationale of the Hebraic approach to justice mirror or rely on ideas grounded in a *lex talionis*.

The key to understanding Old Testament notions of punishment lies in the notion of covenant. The formative experience that generated the need for a formal legal system was what the Hebrew people themselves understood to be an encounter between their leader Moses and their God. That encounter, which issued in a covenant, had two elements. The first was a promise given by Moses on behalf of the people that they would as a people undertake to order their daily lives around a set of fundamental moral rules in a way they believed was in accordance with God's will. Since their conception of God was that of a deity who had ordered his creation in accord with principles of justice, the notion of justice was at the centre of the moral law formulated in the context of the covenant.

The second element was what they understood to be God's promise that, if they respected the moral law, all would go well for them. This idea of well-being included some explicit and very concrete elements. However, in its broad form, it conveyed the very general idea that if the moral law was obeyed the Hebrew people both as a people and as individuals would flourish.[12]

The covenant also implied harsh punitive attitudes. However, those attitudes had a very specific grounding. If the moral law was not obeyed, both the individuals responsible and the community as a whole would suffer just punishment merited by a failure to respect their obligations under the covenant.[13] The result was a picture guaranteed by an all-powerful, all-knowing, and just deity where those entering into the covenant were assured that those who ordered their lives around the moral law would flourish and those who ignored that law would receive their just deserts.

The covenant placed a collective responsibility on the Hebrew nation to ensure that the moral law was obeyed. The strategy they adopted, not unreasonably, was to build a legal system whose task was to interpret and enforce the basic moral law, that is to say, the Ten Commandments. The law they developed reflected its purpose. Punishment for breaches of the law varied with the seriousness of the offence. Since punishment was for moral wrongdoing, care was taken to ensure that only those actually responsible for their actions were convicted. Special care was taken to ensure that those who were innocent were not convicted of offences they had not committed. In short, to punish unjustly was itself as serious a breach of the covenant as disregarding any of the basic laws.

The system was not perfect. However, so long as the system was implemented in good faith, it met their obligations under the covenant. Furthermore, the Hebrews believed that those who did not come to justice at the hands of the community would not escape it at God's hands, just as those who respected the law could know that eventually they would receive their just rewards.[14] In this sense, justice was both assured and inescapable.

We are better able to evaluate the Hebraic approach to punishment if we examine it in light of the moral criticism it generated. The most searching criticisms were generated by a group of social critics who came to be called prophets. Of these, Amos, though a minor prophet, is exemplary. Amos lived at a point in Hebrew history at which the nation of Israel had achieved its greatest power and prosperity. Since this would count as a kind of flourishing, the people, or at least the ruling elite, saw their success as an indication that they were fulfilling the terms of the covenant. Amos disagreed. He pointed out that the covenant promised prosperity for all in return for obedience. However, what he found was abject poverty, the manipulation of power with a view to ensuring ever greater accumulations of personal wealth, and a callous disregard for the well-being of those who lacked wealth and power. For Amos, serious poverty and victimization in a society were all the evidence needed to demonstrate an unjust legal system.

A second type of moral criticism even more profound than that generated by the prophets is found in the New Testament. The story is told of Jesus, who lived under the Old Testament law, coming upon a woman about to be stoned for adultery. Jesus is asked for his view of the law. He responds with the words: 'Let him who is without sin cast the first stone.'[15] Stoning was in fact the appropriate punishment for adultery.

What this criticism did was highlight one implication of just retribution. A system that punishes only some but not all wrongdoing is itself unjust. In fact it implies that the justification for punishment is not desert but something else. If it were desert alone, all wrongdoing would evoke the required response. The story also suggests that, where wrongdoing is the focus of punishment, no one can be spared because everyone is guilty in some form of failing to live up to the high standards set by the moral law.

Conclusions

This New Testament criticism of the notion of just retribution is in many respects the most compelling. It suggests that retributive fairness cannot be achieved in a human system of justice. The operation of the law is too uneven, too open to manipulation by those in positions of power to achieve just retribution in punishment. The notion might well have a place in an ideal setting where the full disclosure of the facts could be assured and in which everyone was treated equally, that is to say, a system in which those who deserved to prosper did and those who deserved punishment all received it. The Hebrews believed themselves to be a part of just such a system of all-encompassing justice. But that belief rested on a faith that, where human institutions failed, divine justice would not and could not. This promise of absolute justice was central to their understanding. Human systems do not operate within a similar context of divine guarantees. Therefore, the pursuit of justice in retribution is bound to fail.[16]

It would seem, therefore, that either punishment is not justified, or, if it is, its justification lies elsewhere.

2

THE POINT OF PUNISHMENT: FORWARD-LOOKING ACCOUNTS

From retributivism to utilitarianism

As we have seen, retributive or backward-looking justifications of punishment reflect values that are in many ways fundamental to how we view the world. Life shared with others is something most of us value. Yet it carries with it significant burdens. For example, living together requires respect for basic values. It seems seriously unfair when those who respect those values end up worse off than those who do not.

How these basic values lead to a retributivist account of punishment is explored in the previous chapter. What is important for our present purposes is the realization that backward-looking or retributivist justifications of punishment seem to entail that we are justified in inflicting hard treatment on offenders, and perhaps actually have an obligation to do so even when we are quite certain that neither the community nor the offender will benefit as a result. Thus Immanuel Kant, whose discussions of the topic have been very influential, was led to conclude that

> [e]ven if civil society resolved to dissolve itself with the consent of all its members, the last murderer lying in prison ought to be executed before the resolution was carried out. This ought to be done in order that everyone may realize the desert of his deeds . . .
>
> (Ezorsky 1972: 105)

As many commentators have pointed out, it is this aspect of retributivism that seems to tie it most closely with the idea of revenge.

When we set out to punish someone, our goal is to inflict suffering or pain. Taken by themselves, pain and suffering seem to be as close

30

to things that are intrinsically undesirable or evil as anything in our experience. Hence, inflicting either on someone without justification is normally condemned as wrong or immoral. Sometimes, of course, they are unavoidable. Under these conditions they are accepted as necessary evils, for example, in the pursuit of renewed health. To impose punishment on the grounds simply that it is deserved and for no other reason would *not* seem to fall into this category.

There is a second consideration. The kind of punishment we normally think justified is closely tied to the enforcement of rules. Punishment takes its value from the rules to which it is attached. Most of us would agree, for example, that to punish someone for refusing to obey a command or law that was thoroughly immoral would itself be thoroughly immoral. Equally, it would seem that if punishment is justified, it is because it is needed if rules seen as necessary or valuable are to be respected.

The ideas just described are virtually as old as the *lex talionis*. Few have put it better than Plato who has Protagoras point out in the dialogue of the same name:

> In punishing wrongdoers, no one concentrates on the fact that a man has done wrong in the past, or punishes him on that account, unless taking blind vengeance like a beast. No, punishment is not inflicted by a rational man for the sake of the crime that has been committed (after all one cannot undo what is past), but for the sake of the future, to prevent either the same man or, by some spectacle of his punishment, someone else from doing wrong again.
>
> (Plato *Protagorus*: 324)

Where nothing is to be gained by punishment, it should not be imposed even, this view suggests, when it is deserved.

The values highlighted by our deep unease with particular aspects of retributivism are essentially forward-looking. They require that if punishment is to be justified, it must be shown to advance human welfare in a significant way.

Forward-looking welfare-oriented justifications of punishment have significant virtues. They have a humanitarian focus. They require that punishment be evaluated by reference to the welfare of offenders, victims, and the public at large. They appear to direct us past irrational and vindictive behaviour toward responses whose merit is open to the test of experience. Finally, they would seem to place on those responsible for sentencing offenders an obligation to search out the least harmful, most effective way of achieving the good toward which the punishment is directed.

Forward-looking accounts of punishment have other virtues as well. Rival retributivist accounts link punishment and immorality. Punishment is justified, they suggest, only if it is deserved. To deserve or merit punishment one must do what is wrong. This feature of retributivism is mirrored in the requirement that only those who can be shown to be morally responsible for their actions should be found guilty and subsequently held to account. It is also mirrored in the requirement that the severity of the punishment must fit the moral gravity of the crime. To punish a morally insignificant act with a heavy penalty, for example incarceration, would be morally offensive and therefore unacceptable.

As many commentators have pointed out, this view ties legal guilt to the notion of moral wickedness.[1] It implies that crimes are 'sins with legal definitions'.[2] And with that link come many problems. Contemporary western liberal democracies are now morally very diverse. On many questions on which consensus perhaps at one time reigned, substantial differences now appear. The moral acceptability of capital punishment is just one example. Those same democracies have also become secularized. Christianity no longer claims the active adherence of even a substantial minority of their populations. Immigration has introduced a plurality of religious traditions where previously only one dominated.

Equally difficult is the assessment of responsibility. Using moral criteria, the degree of guilt for one's actions depends on the extent to which one could have avoided doing what one did. As Hart puts it: 'can human judges discover and make comparisons between the motives, temptations, opportunities and wickedness of different individuals?' (Hart 1968: 162).

Forward-looking accounts of punishment offer a way out of these difficulties. They suggest that the seriousness of criminal acts be gauged by the seriousness of their impact on society. The notion of harmfulness provides the needed tool. Harm seems to be something that can be objectively identified. It is free of direct moral overtones. Whether something is harmful can be determined as a rule quite independently of subjective moral considerations, or so it would appear. The standard of harm can also be used to evaluate various ways of responding to offenders, placing an onus on those involved to find the least painful punishment capable of producing the greatest benefit.

Finally, the standard used to determine the harm caused by an offence can also be used to measure the harm inflicted against the benefit to be gained. Any punishment likely to cause more harm than the offence it was trying to prevent could then be seen to be unjustified.

Distinguishing law and morality, as forward-looking theories propose, has additional benefits. First, it allows the justification of punishment to be linked directly with criteria for deciding what should and what should not be prohibited by law. Offences warrant serious punishment if they cause serious harm. Less harmful actions warrant less punitive intervention. It follows that punishment should not be inflicted for actions that are not harmful or where the harm caused by punishment outweighs anticipated benefits.[3]

Second, it allows us to distinguish between legal and moral obligation. This is of value for a number of reasons. Many laws have no moral content. Traffic laws are a good example. Laws in a modern society are sometimes created before moral attitudes have had an opportunity to settle. Environmental laws and laws regulating medical research are possible examples. In some areas there is no moral consensus. Abortion, euthanasia and medical ethics in new areas of research provide examples of this phenomenon. Finally, there is no guarantee that law and morality will mesh. Modern codes of law frequently prohibit activities that are not seen as immoral by the people subject to them. In these cases, what the law requires and what morality requires are quite different. It would seem, therefore, that the notion of harm is a more objective guide than morality to the creation of law.

Third, forward-looking theories do not carry with them the idea that punishment implies wickedness. Rather punishment implies only that an offender has broken a law. By separating punishment from the notion of wickedness, we are also better able to distinguish the proper aims of morality from those of law. The criminal law, on this account of the matter, should aim to protect those who fall under its jurisdiction from harm. The goal of morality is to guide people toward the achievement of a morally commendable life. This second goal cannot be achieved through coercion. The moral quality of someone's life is a matter of intentions and attitudes and one's reasons for doing what one does. This is a realm of personal life that the law ought not to penetrate. Distinguishing between legal guilt and moral guilt helps to make that clear.

Finally, distinguishing between moral and legal guilt opens the door to the introduction of a scientific understanding of criminal behaviour and its control. It shifts the focus of attention from the moral quality of offending behaviour to its empirical characteristics. The goal of the law, on this view, is social control. The purpose of punishment is not moral reform, except in so far as moral reform can be shown to be the most expeditious way of controlling the offending behaviour. Rather, the purpose of punishment is to reduce the likelihood that harmful behaviour will recur. Approaching the matter this way allows the law access to the social sciences. Forward-looking theories allow proposals for legal reform and sentencing and correctional strategies to be tested empirically.

Illustrating the theory: three examples

Ted, though still a teenager, is old enough to be considered an adult in the eyes of the law. One night, while drinking at the student pub, he is angered by an idle comment of a passerby. He replies emotionally and in the exchange that ensues his adversary is knocked to the ground. Ted is apprehended by the authorities and finds himself in court.

Under our current system of law, certain facts would be essential to proceedings. What was Ted's age? Was he old enough to be held legally responsible in adult court for his actions? What happened? Was Ted acting in self-defence? Did he intend to knock down his antagonist? Was Ted acting in a negligent or reckless way? What damage was caused? And so on.

Assume, however, that the system that Ted has encountered is governed by purely forward-looking principles. The goal of the system is to prevent forbidden acts. All of the facts already mentioned remain relevant. But they will not determine proceedings, as they would under our current system. They are relevant only to the extent that they provide clues as to how best to respond to the threat that Ted poses. Since the system is forward-looking, its focus will be the person and not his offence, the future and not the past.

This approach has an air of benevolence about it. After all, if Ted has problems, should they not be dealt with before someone else is hurt? And is it not in Ted's interest that his problems be sorted out before he seriously damages his own future?

The central question before the authorities, therefore, is what response would best ensure that the kind of altercation in which Ted became involved will not recur? Hence what actually happened, and the degree of Ted's responsibility for the events that transpired, may or may not be important. Let us assume, for example, that Ted has a history of hard drinking and losing his temper when he is drinking hard. The judge orders Ted to be committed to a detoxification centre until such a time as the authorities are assured that his drinking problem has been cured. The sentence is imposed although Ted, in this particular instance, is innocent of moral wrongdoing, since, though angry, he knocked down his antagonist accidentally while trying to move away from his seat to avoid trouble.

The same events occur the next evening. The culprit this time is Peter, a juvenile attracted to the pub by older friends introducing him to the bar scene for the first time. Peter has a good school record, no history of hard drinking, and has never been in trouble before. Peter too is drawn into an altercation by an offensive comment. He takes the bait, and swings at his adversary who is knocked down and injured. The judge decides that Peter needs to be taught a lesson and puts him on probation.

Jake enters the same establishment on the third evening. He is a regular and is not known to cause trouble. But on this occasion he is infuriated by an offensive comment, loses his temper, and deliberately assaults his antagonist using all the force he can muster, knocking him to the ground and injuring him. Jake is not a heavy drinker, has never been in a fight before, and comes from a very good family. He admits his mistake to the court and promises not to repeat the offence. There is every reason to believe that he will keep his word and hence no reason to penalize him for his behaviour, even though he has caused serious injury. The judge gives him an unconditional discharge.

Evaluating forward-looking theories: three worries

These three examples illustrate well three basic elements of forward-looking theories of punishment. Punishment should fit the offender and not the offence. Punishment should not be inflicted where it will generate no benefits. And punishment should not be inflicted if it will cause more harm than good. However, the examples raise real worries.

The first worry has to do with the principle of responsibility. Is it fair or just to treat differently people who have committed what is in essence the same offence? Is it just or fair to allow the courts to assign what seem to be onerous penalties for what might be relatively minor infractions and light penalties for serious infractions? And, perhaps most significantly, is it fair or just to hold people criminally liable for actions for which they would not normally be held morally responsible? This third question is a crucial one. Ted, in our example, did not intend to strike the person he injured. He was trying to get out of the way. The harm done was an accident. Peter is immature. Should this not be taken into account in assigning penalties? In short, what place is there for the principle of responsibility in a forward-looking theory of punishment?

One of the basic components of modern criminal justice systems is the idea of responsibility or *mens rea*, which requires that criminal trials proceed in two distinct steps. The court's first task is to determine the guilt or innocence of the accused. If an accused is found guilty, it remains to determine an appropriate penalty for the offence that has been committed. Our system implies that to punish someone for an act for which he was not responsible is unjust. What this has meant in practice is that, 'subject to certain important qualifications, liability to punishment is excluded if the law was broken unintentionally, under duress or by a person judged to be below the age of responsibility or to be suffering from certain types of mental disease' (Hart 1968: 174). To put it otherwise, people should not be blamed for what they could not help doing.

On the surface, forward-looking theories seem to imply that this traditional notion of responsibility should be eliminated. This is strongly suggested by our three examples. By traditional standards, Ted receives the most severe sentence even though he attempted to avoid a fight. Jake, who set out to hurt his opponent, receives an unconditional discharge. And Peter, who is still a juvenile, is sentenced to probation even though it is a first offence. To use legal terminology, a forward-looking approach to punishment would seem to imply that the principle of *mens rea* should be replaced with a requirement that people be held strictly liable for their actions. It should be obvious that, were this to happen, criminal law would undergo significant changes.

The fact that the principle of responsibility seems to have no place in a forward-looking theory of punishment highlights a second worry. Forward-looking theories of punishment focus on the offender and not the offence. That being the case, why should the provisions of the criminal law extend only to those who have committed offences? If the purpose of the law's intervention is to prevent harm from occurring in the future, why should the authorities wait until an offence has been committed before intervening?

The example of Ted is a good one here. If it is known that Ted has a drinking problem and that he becomes violent when he has been drinking, why should the law wait until he has hurt someone before it acts? Punishment, on a forward-looking account of the matter, is justified only as a way of preventing greater harm than would likely occur if there was no punishment. If this justifies sentencing Ted to treatment for his drinking problem so that he no longer poses a threat to others after he has already hurt someone, why should it not also justify imposing treatment on him before he hurts someone? On the surface, there seems no reason for a forward-looking account to make this distinction. This in turn would seem to imply that perhaps the notion of crime itself is outmoded and should be replaced by more direct and scientific responses to human behaviour, allowing us to respond to problems as they arise and to resolve them before serious harm is done.

What would justify such a radical restructuring of the criminal law? The appeal of forward-looking theories of punishment is their focus on human welfare. Punishment should never be inflicted unless its benefits outweigh the harm it causes. What this formulation leaves unclear, however, is whose benefit counts and what is to count as a benefit. Must Ted's treatment benefit Ted? Or is it enough that it benefit those who might otherwise be harmed by Ted? If the purpose of treatment is to protect those Ted might otherwise harm, then forward-looking theories seem to justify subordinating the interests of those being treated to the interests of others.

These considerations give rise to a third worry. If law and morality are indeed distinct, there is no reason to assume that enforcing the law will advance human welfare. A particular legal system may work to the benefit of most people most of the time, or it may not. Particular laws may contribute to the general good or they may not. Whether any of this is true or not is irrelevant to whether a law is a law. It would seem to follow that forward-looking accounts cannot avoid evaluating the law or laws for whose breach punishment is being considered. If that is the case, what reason is there to think that the judgements that forward-looking accounts of punishment require are easier to make or more straight-forward than those required by backward-looking accounts that rest their justification of punishment on the notion of moral guilt?

Responsibility and deterrence

The obvious way to begin to deal with these worries is to show that there is a place in a forward-looking account of punishment for the principle of responsibility. Two proposals have been particularly influential.

Some commentators have suggested that the notion of responsibility can have a useful place in a forward-looking theory of punishment because it marks a distinction between actions that can be deterred through punishment and actions that cannot. Patrick Nowell-Smith captures this idea in the following way:

> Why are men who steal as a result of a decision said to be worthy of punishment while those who steal from some other cause are not? The reason is we believe that the fear of punishment will affect the future behaviour of the thief but not that of the kleptomaniac.
>
> (Nowell-Smith 1948: 60)[4]

The virtue of this explanation is that it reinterprets a practice deeply embedded in our criminal justice systems in a manner that shows it to be consistent with a forward-looking approach to punishment. The explanation, however, is not convincing.

To begin with, deterrence is not the only forward-looking justification of punishment. Reform and incapacitation are alternative justifications and neither is open to drawing the line where Nowell-Smith thinks it should be drawn. Kleptomaniacs, to use his example, can be treated and they can be incapacitated. In this regard, they are no different from those who steal voluntarily.

More importantly, it is not true that only behaviour that would be recognized in a court of law as voluntary can be influenced though the application of punishments and rewards. This is most immediately obvious when we consider that we use punishment to train animals. Yet we would never consider animals appropriate candidates for criminal sanctions. Equally, we know that severely retarded and even autistic children will respond to punishment and reward regimes. Aversive therapy which uses punishment as a conditioning device is now a well-known though controversial technique that has been used to condition people whose behaviour is seemingly out of their control.[5] Finally, Nowell-Smith's argument seems to imply that recidivists should not be punished since punishment does not seem to affect their behaviour. Yet this is certainly not consistent with the principle of responsibility as it is reflected in the sentencing practices of modern criminal justice systems.

It follows that the relation between responsibility and deterability is not strong enough to justify retaining the doctrine of responsibility in the absence of other reasons.

Responsibility and freedom

A second type of argument designed to show that the notion of responsibility in determining guilt in a criminal trial has a place within forward-looking non-retributivist accounts of punishment emphasizes the connection between punishing only voluntary acts and protecting people's freedom. By holding people responsible for only those things they do voluntarily, the law increases their ability to avoid coming into conflict with the law. This very influential view has been eloquently defended by H.L.A. Hart, with whom it is closely associated. What should we lose, he asks, if the doctrine of responsibility were eliminated? He answers:

> Among other things we should lose the ability which the present system in some degree guarantees to us, to predict and plan the future course of our lives within the coercive framework of the law. For the system which makes liability to the law's sanctions dependent upon a voluntary act not only maximizes the power of the individual to determine by his choice his future fate; it also maximizes his power to identify in advance the space which will be left open to him free from the law's interference. Whereas a system from which responsibility was eliminated so that he was liable for what he did by mistake or accident would leave each individual not only less able to exclude the future interference by the law with his life, but also less able to foresee the times of the law's interference.
>
> (Hart 1968: 181–2)

Is Hart correct in thinking that individuals enmeshed in such a system would lose their ability to predict and plan their lives within the coercive framework of the law? And if so, why would this be the result?

Let us examine this question in two stages. First, do strict liability laws restrict the capacity of individuals governed by them to 'plan and predict' their lives? Second, do they render people less able to 'foresee the times of the law's interference'?

Testing this view should not be too difficult. Many of our laws already have this character. In fact, a substantial proportion of sentences handed down in modern systems of law are for offences of this type. It should be possible, therefore, to work out whether strict liability offences reduce the freedom of those falling under their authority.

When we review the evidence, it is clear that strict liability laws do not necessarily have this effect. On the contrary, strict liability seems to enhance people's ability to plan and predict within the coercive framework of the law. For example, why has strict liability become such a pervasive feature of our legal system? The answer becomes clear when we consider a few examples like traffic offences. Under Canadian law, anyone who drives while under the influence of alcohol, that is to say, with a blood alcohol level higher than 80 milligrams of alcohol in 100 milliliters of blood, is guilty of an indictable offence (Section 236 (1)). Drivers suspected of driving while under the influence of alcohol can be required to submit to a breathalyser test and subsequently to a blood test (Section 234.1 and 235). Random testing is also permitted. No excuses (or virtually no excuses) are allowed. And refusing to give a sample for testing is itself a criminal offence. Consequently, conviction is virtually certain for those who test above the limit. That is to say, the law imposes strict liability in this case.

What has this to do with predictability? If you drink and drive and are apprehended, you will almost certainly be convicted. It is widely thought that fewer people drink and drive than was the case before the law was enacted. But how is this possible if strict liability reduces people's ability to predict how to avoid coming into conflict with the law? It would seem to follow from the evidence that, where traffic laws are concerned, eliminating responsibility in determining guilt does not have this result. Because the law imposes strict liability, drivers have a clearer picture of the consequences of drinking and driving than would be the case if *mens rea* had to be established prior to a conviction. Eliminating responsibility therefore makes it easier for drivers to predict what will happen if they drink and drive and provides them with an incentive for not doing so.

We can see the same kind of logic working where environmental protection laws are being debated. Many advocates for stronger legal protection of the environment insist that anti-pollution regulations be formulated as strict liability offences. The reason is that convictions will be more easily obtained and polluters more effectively deterred. Such laws would not result in more effective deterrence if they made it more difficult for potential polluters to plan and predict the future course of their business lives within the coercive framework of the law.

In short, the chief argument for moving to strict liability in our system is that it enhances the deterrent impact of the law by making the application of the law easier to predict and harder to evade.

But would this continue to be the case if *all* our criminal laws imposed strict liability? It seems that it would not. There are many reasons for this. For our immediate purposes the most important reason is that giving strict liability a more central role in our criminal law than it now has would require significant changes in the sentencing process.[6]

Let us imagine, for example, that assault was a strict liability offence. A person would be liable for conviction simply by coming into physical contact with another person. The law forbidding assault would now throw a very wide net. Everything from accidental hitting to traffic accidents, to fights, to intentional wounding would be encompassed.

It seems obvious that this new law prohibiting assault could not have a simple sanction attached to it. Rather, a broad range of sanctions, if any were specified at all, would have to be made available to the sentencing judge, allowing wide discretion in determining the appropriate penalty. The consequences of committing a strict liability offence of assault could only be made definite by specifying different kinds of assault and assigning to each a different penalty by reference to the intention lying behind it. But this new set of laws, though perhaps drafted somewhat differently from our own, would in fact be very similar to what we now have.

What this argument shows is that to move toward a more comprehensive regime of strict liability would require moving toward a more systematic use of indeterminate sentences. This inevitably would make it very difficult to predict and plan one's life within the coercive framework of the law.[7] If the law does not lay out in advance the consequences of breaking the law, individuals cannot evaluate the risks associated with particular activities. For example, if being involved in a traffic accident was one species of a strict liability offence of assault, and if the penalties attached to that offence were indefinite and allowed sentences ranging from an absolute discharge to life in prison, deciding whether to drive would become at the very least substantially more complex than is now the case.

But would this be a bad thing? Under modern conditions, many of the important decisions about how individuals should be treated are left in the hands of professionals, or assigned to legal and quasi legal bodies with substantial powers. Family courts have powers of this sort to deal with young people and decide questions of child custody. Government boards dealing with such things as compensation for injured workers are now common. The medical profession has substantial powers to control patients with or without their consent, and so on. Why should avoiding that outcome be so important when dealing with the criminal law?

To answer that question, we need to look more closely at the implications of forward-looking or utilitarian theories of punishment for sentencing.

Punishment and the treatment of offenders

For a retributivist, the purpose of a sentence is to correct a past wrong. Forward-looking theories are attractive in part because they accept that in a very straight-forward sense we cannot change the past. The best we can do is to seek to prevent similar wrongs from being committed in the future. This implies that the goal of sentencing should be to prevent future offences and to do so in the most beneficial and least harmful way possible.[8] This suggests approaching punishment from the perspective of reform or deterrence. To evaluate the implications of this approach to sentencing we need, then, to look at both reform- and deterrence-oriented sentencing with a view to understanding the implications of each for punishment and the treatment of offenders.

Reform as moral education

Offenders are people who have ignored their obligations. They are wrongdoers. Bringing them to see themselves in this light is one of the oldest and historically the most influential justifications of punishment in the literature. Its rationale is explored as early as the Book of Job in the Old Testament, and its continuing influence is reflected in the vocabulary of corrections. Those we have accused of offences are offered the opportunity to acknowledge their guilt by pleading guilty. We send offenders to penitentiaries that were introduced, as the word suggests, as places of moral and spiritual reflection and penance. The term corrections, or correctional institution, though somewhat more neutral than that of penitentiary, nevertheless connotes error and the need for improvement.

To see punishment as a tool of reform is consistent with informal practices. We often justify punishment in dealing with children, students, employees and even friends as a way of 'bringing someone to their senses'. When parents punish their children their goal often is to bring them to see the error of their ways. Punishment is inflicted in school settings with a view to trying to convince those involved that they should cooperate with the educational enterprise for their own benefit and that of others.

Finally, it is widely thought that what many offenders lack is a basic concern for others. What this implies is that what is needed is the inculcation of appropriate moral values. But this raises real problems.

Inculcating moral values requires that those being educated are brought to believe that the values being advanced are morally sound. Moral reform can play a role only if obeying the law is a moral obligation. Approaching the law this way, however, is not consistent with the view that morality and law are distinct. If law need have no necessary moral content to be law and to generate legal obligations, then compliance cannot be advanced as a moral obligation. To put the matter another way, if the aims of law and morality are distinct, and if the goal of enforcement is to 'announce that some actions are not to be done and to secure that fewer of them are done' not because they are immoral but because they are forbidden, then the relation between law and morality will be purely contingent. Acting as the law requires may be morally commendable and it may not. If the purpose of a trial is to determine legal but not moral culpability, then the purpose of punishment cannot be moral improvement. Moral improvement is not a legitimate objective in sentencing offenders if the purpose of a sentence is to ensure conformity with the law quite independently of its moral character.

Reform as rehabilitation

In light of these criticisms, it is not surprising that modern reform theories have shifted from the idea that the goal of reform is to improve moral character to the view that the goal of reform is to rehabilitate offenders. On this modern view, criminal activity is a symptom of personal inadequacies. The purpose of rehabilitation is to diminish offenders' criminal propensities through psychiatric therapy, counselling, vocational training, educational up-grading, substance abuse programmes, and any other scientifically grounded techniques for reducing recidivism.

What does this imply for sentencing and sentence administration? The answer would appear to be indeterminate sentences. As Lady Barbara Wootton explains:

> If the primary object of a sentence is to discourage further offences at the cost of minimal interference with liberty, then the moment at which this discouragement is effective enough to justify the offender's release can hardly be forecast in advance: it must depend upon his progress. Logically, there-fore, the conception of criminal procedure as preventive rather than punitive involves acceptance of indeterminate sentences.

It also implies that:

> custodial sentences should be indeterminate in respect of the type of institution to which an offender should be committed, and indeed that the rigid division of institutions into the medical and the penal should be obliterated.
>
> (Wootton 1963: 112)

It follows on this view that relinquishing control over offenders is not justified unless they have been rehabilitated. Further, since the purpose of a sentence is to discourage offences, there is no convincing reason for distinguishing between offenders and non-offenders in providing treatment. In neither case are they being punished because they have done something wrong. Indeed, as Lady Wootton again makes clear, such persons are not being punished at all. They are being reformed, treated, cured, or rehabilitated.

Reform and rehabilitation: dilemmas and contradictions

Purely forward-looking rehabilitation-oriented accounts of sentencing have a humanitarian quality. Their focus is the welfare of offenders and non-offenders alike. They do not seek to change what cannot be changed. Rather their concern is ensuring that the wrongs of the past are not repeated in the future. It is also clear that their impact on criminal justice policy has been progressive.

44

Emphasis on rehabilitation rather than punishment has encouraged the introduction of new programmes into prisons and encouraged the search for alternatives to incarceration.

In spite of all this, however, it is clear that rehabilitation-oriented sentencing is exposed to each of the three criticisms raised earlier. Where the justification for 'punishment' is rehabilitation, there is in principle no reason to distinguish between those who could have avoided breaking the law and those who could not. Certainly, why someone failed to obey the law might have a bearing on the appropriate treatment. But it might not. Neither is there any reason in principle to differentiate between offenders and non-offenders in devising methods of social control.

For radical reformers, these observations would not count as objections since the effect of shifting to a medical or rehabilitation model of sentencing is to eliminate any justification for imposing punishment. Nevertheless, the approach under consideration is subject to two related and very fundamental objections.

First, to approach sentencing this way would remove the right of individuals to choose not to obey the law. It would also undermine their freedom to shape their lives in accordance with values or ideas that the state viewed as incompatible with the overriding public interest in ensuring continuing compliance with the law, including the right to criticize the law where it was thought this might lead to disobedience. It would therefore seriously undermine the capacity of people generally and not just offenders to plan their lives in accordance with values of their own choosing. It would also lessen their capacity to predict both the conditions under which the law could be expected to intervene and take control of their lives and what to do to avoid that intervention or to bring it to an end when it occurred.[9]

Second, the process of rehabilitation disguises a fundamental conflict. It appears to focus on the welfare of those to be rehabilitated. Yet its goal is to discourage further offences on the part of those being rehabilitated. If the commitment to the public welfare is honestly represented, rehabilitation represents the coercive subordination of the interests of some, those identified as potential offenders, to the public interest as defined by the law.

This conflict is disguised by the assumption that the behaviour of offenders is disordered or deviant. Offenders cannot be rehabilitated unless those assigned that task know what is to count as normal or acceptable behaviour. That standard is set by the law. However, if

45

there is no necessary connection between law and morality, then there are no grounds for assuming that the standard is a good one. It may be or it may not. From a non-legal perspective, the standards of behaviour created by the law may be objectionable or even reprehensible.

Those assigned the task of rehabilitation cannot make these distinctions. The standard against which an offender's behaviour must be judged is that set by the law. The acceptability of that standard cannot be questioned. The object of the exercise is to ensure that the person being rehabilitated complies with the law. However, the process cannot be presented to those toward whom it is directed in these terms. Subjecting someone to a process of rehabilitation implies a concern for her welfare. It cannot be seen or accepted as rehabilitation otherwise. Punishment cannot be justified as an exercise in rehabilitation unless its purpose is to enhance the welfare of those required to undergo it.

It follows that to justify punishment as rehabilitation, when in fact its goal is simply to reduce offences, is hypocritical. If law and morality are distinct, the standards set by the law may be commendable or they may not. Inducing people to obey the law coercively may count therefore as rehabilitation or it may not. It can count as rehabilitation only if the standards the law sets are commendable standards from something other than a purely legal perspective. Forward-looking accounts of punishment cannot guarantee that this will be the case.

It is for these reasons that reform-oriented sentencing must have a manipulative character in any account of punishment that builds on the assumption that law has no necessary or minimum moral content.[10]

The deterrence option

The idea that the function of punishment is to warn and deter people from actions identified as criminal by the law is an attractive forward-looking justification of punishment, in part because it would appear to avoid the problems of reform-oriented alternatives. It appears to be consistent with recognizing a fundamental distinction between law and morality. Unlike rehabilitation, deterrence can be justified in relatively neutral terms. Its function can be set out in morally neutral terms as simply social control. It assumes only that virtually everyone has an interest in avoiding pain and suffering and implies nothing about the quality of the behaviour it is put in place to discourage.

Justifying punishment as a deterrent has other virtues as well. The idea of influencing behaviour, our own and others', through the use of rewards and punishments is one with which virtually everyone is familiar. We all know that punishment is often thought of in those terms. Most accept that society is justified in preventing actions considered harmful to others. Punishing offenders is one way of accomplishing this goal. Further, our experience suggests that seeking to deter unwanted behaviour in this way is or can be effective. It is one of the ways in which we train children. It is also one of the ways in which adults are disciplined.

Using punishment as a deterrent has other advantages. Common sense recommends it as a way of discouraging undesirable behaviour. Reverting to a deterrence justification is not an effective way of rescuing the principle of responsibility directly as a matter of principle. But it does seem to imply that punishment imposed should be relative to the harm done. That is to say, deterrence-oriented punishment builds on the forward-looking principle that pain or suffering should not be inflicted unless the good achieved that way is greater than the harm imposed, thus respecting the principle that the severity of a punishment should not exceed the gravity of the crime committed.

Theories that justify punishment by its capacity to act as a deterrent are nevertheless subject to serious criticism. To begin with, the requirement that minor harms should not be punished with a severity that creates greater misery than the offence unchecked[11] cannot ensure that punishments inflicted match the gravity of offences committed. Take, for example, traffic offences. Most people would not regard moderate speeding as a serious offence. But, if the authorities thought the accident rate could be reduced by slowing up drivers, then imposing severe penalties on speeders would presumably be justified. On this account of the matter, a judge would be justified in imposing a heavy penalty on someone charged with speeding even though her particular offence was not a serious one, taken on its own merits. Equally, if a judge thought on reasonable grounds that even a single serious accident could be prevented by making an example of someone who had been speeding, the sentence would presumably be justified as a deterrent.

The same reasoning would apply even where no great physical

harm was involved either directly or indirectly. Parking offences provide a good illustration. If parking habits could be changed and illegal parking reduced or eliminated by imposing a few severe penalties for parking offences, the cumulative benefits might well justify doing so even though the benefits involved were largely matters of convenience.

We can now see that deterrence theories are open to a second and even more fundamental objection. If the severity of a penalty need not be related to the gravity of an offence, does this not imply that there might sometimes be justification for punishing someone who had committed no offence at all? Punishing innocent people could deter as effectively as punishing only the guilty, particularly if those who were to be deterred were convinced of the victim's guilt. We also know that people can be deterred by threatening harm to others close to them. Parents, for example, often drive more carefully when their own children are in the car. Might it not then be the case that threatening to punish occupants of a car other than the driver and occasionally doing so would be a more effective way of preventing traffic violations than punishing just the driver?[12] Might a government not then be justified in threatening vicarious punishment where it could be shown that to do so would be a particularly effective way of deterring criminal activity?

Deterrence and the problem of unjust punishment

It is an inherent feature of all purely forward-looking accounts of punishment that they regard the relation between an offence committed and the punishment we are justified in imposing as a contingent one. The actions that bring someone to the attention of sentencing authorities may be relevant to the sentence that ought to be imposed; but they may not. This means that all forward-looking approaches to punishment open the door in theory to unjust punishment. But do they do so in practice? Some very complex arguments have been developed to show that deterrence theories do not have this implication. The general lines of arguments designed to show why are quite easily sketched.[13]

Those committed to defending a deterrence view of punishment often begin by pointing to the highly improbable character of the examples frequently used by their critics. A city has been terrorized by a child killer. The *only* way to calm its fears is by concocting a case against an innocent, socially isolated victim who can be punished

48

with minimal consequences except to herself and whose suffering is likely to be heavily outweighed by the social benefits of obtaining a conviction and imposing a severe penalty. A mob is bent on revenge. An innocent person must be sacrificed if the mob is to be placated. To fail to offer up a victim would ensure widespread violence.

Usually the examples used against deterrence theories postulate crises that can be effectively resolved only by victimization. As a consequence, the solutions proposed also as a rule require secrecy. And this, it is argued, is their fatal weakness. In anything but the most unusual and therefore clearly distinguishable circumstances, the harm that would be done if the authorities were found out would be so great that the risk could not be justified. What this shows is that to punish innocent victims in either an occasional or a systematic way would as a practical matter so undermine a legal system that the benefits realized would never outweigh the harm that would be caused. For example, if it became known that innocent people were being punished, people would simply stop believing the authorities when they laid charges. Equally, to victimize or threaten to victimize family members of offenders with a view to deterring criminal behaviour would arouse so much opposition and fear that it could not serve as an effective and efficient deterrent.

Other defences are also available. One might argue that the kind of situation that would justify clearly unjust practices is in the normal course of events so unlikely to arise that it can safely be ignored. Alternatively, it might be argued that situations requiring this kind of response are so unusual and so abnormal that ignoring principles of justice in these cases would pose no threat to normal legal practices.[14]

Are these counter-arguments convincing? It would seem that they are not. What they fail to acknowledge is that, where punishment is concerned, principle and practice meet often in unusual ways. In practice, utilitarian calculations are made by fallible individuals who can never do more than simply estimate the benefits and harms that might result from their actions. If the rationale justifying the imposition of a punishment is deterrence, and a decision has to be made about the most efficient way of achieving that goal, there is no guarantee that sacrificing the interests of a single person might not present itself as the most effective solution in even the most ordinary situations. Experience confirms this observation. Individuals, for example police officers and court officials, do on occasion override principles of justice to obtain or avoid convictions when they are convinced it is in the public interest to do so. Were this not so, charters of rights protecting individuals from decisions putting the public interest ahead of individual rights would not be likely to have the importance contemporary societies assign to them.

How might these objections be avoided? Is there a way of insisting that punishment should be inflicted only where it could be shown to be useful or beneficial, yet provide a defence against any abuses to which the principle might in practice be put? It has been suggested that building a rule into the legal system that prohibited the punishment of those who had not in fact committed a crime would be justified in practice as a way of reducing harm by preventing abuses.

This move could not be effective, however, unless the reason for it was disguised and presented in non-utilitarian terms. Assume for the moment that the reason for prohibiting punishment of those not in fact legally guilty of a crime was that such a rule was needed to protect the system against mistakes and unacceptable risk-taking. Presumably, the constraint would itself consist of a law prohibiting the punishment of innocent people. But what grounds would judges in a system that was in all other respects deterrence-oriented have for respecting the rule if they thought they could break it undetected? It could not be argued, as would be the case if principles of justice were respected for their own sake, that to break the rule would be immoral if breaking the rule was justified in a particular instance on utilitarian grounds. Neither could it be claimed that breaking the rule would undermine public confidence if in fact the breach remained secret. It seems that even if the rule was justified in general there would be no way of ensuring that the reasoning that justified the rule would not be used to justify breaking it under special conditions.

This concern cannot be dismissed as fantastic or unrealistic. There are simply too many cases where rules prohibiting particular kinds of behaviour, dishonesty for example, have been overridden by officials whose jobs required them to evaluate various courses of action by reference to their consequences. Situations involving national security are a good example, but there are many others.[15] There is no reason to doubt that similar pressures might be, indeed no doubt have been, experienced by the courts.

Finally, what this discussion reveals is the inherently manipulative character of deterrence-oriented sentencing, particularly where it is advanced in support of a theory which assumes there is no necessary connection between law and morality. Where the goal of punishment is simply to secure compliance with the law, the welfare of those whose behaviour is being controlled in this way is not a primary or even necessarily a secondary consideration.

For all of these reasons, purely deterrence-oriented sentencing cannot avoid undermining the capacity of those falling under the law's authority to predict and plan their lives within the coercive framework of the law. The sentences generated by deterrence-oriented sentencing will be determinate. However, the punishments announced by the law will not be, since there is no way that legislators can know what punishments will be effective deterrents in particular circumstances. The result can only be to reduce individual freedom in significant ways.

It would seem that there is no way in principle or in practice in which respect for individual freedom as well as respect for fundamental principles of justice can be accommodated within purely forward-looking theories of punishment.

The empirical character of forward-looking justifications of punishment

Forward-looking accounts see punishment as a tool whose use is justified because it can help to reduce the incidence of crime. For this reason, forward-looking theories can be tested empirically, at least in theory. For retributivism, establishing the appropriate punishment for a given offence is a matter of assessing what the culprit in question deserves. Forward-looking theories appear rational and scientific because they argue that punishment should not be inflicted except where some good will come of it. This suggests that once the good to be achieved is specified, it should be possible to determine what range of interventions is most likely to achieve that end. Whether the intervention is justified can then be assessed by its anticipated results.

The appearance of testability is misleading, however. Forward-looking views appear to imply that punishment is justifiable only if it is effective in bringing about the end it is designed to achieve. For this reason, only if it is thought to be the most efficient way of preventing crime in specific cases is inflicting punishment justified. For this reason too, forward-looking accounts imply that the same offence committed by two different people might warrant quite different responses.

It would seem to follow that if it could be shown that the

practice of punishment achieved its general aim badly or not at all, the practice should be either drastically curtailed or eliminated. Unfortunately, there is an important sense in which the evidence we need to evaluate the practice is always out of reach. Assume, for example, that the available evidence demonstrated quite clearly that up to the present punishment has not worked very effectively to reduce crime. Would this show that to continue the practice was unwarranted? The answer, it would seem, is 'no'. The evidence need not be regarded as conclusive. It is possible that the conditions under which punishment was administered in the past were not ideal. Techniques available might not have been properly applied or properly designed. Furthermore, it always remains open to punishment advocates to argue that the failure lay not in the practice itself but in our limited understanding of it and its effective use.

Our current situation has many of these features. Reform-oriented accounts of punishment have dominated the thinking of social scientists, professional policy advisers trained in criminology and related fields, and reform advocates for most of this century. Although the public has remained sceptical, forward-looking principles of punishment have come increasingly to dominate correctional policy and, to a varying degree, sentencing policy over the past century.

What does the evidence tell us, then, about the justifiability of rehabilitation- or deterrence-oriented punishment?

The twentieth century: a test case

As David Garland (1985) describes it, our modern system of corrections began to evolve around 1895 and was largely in place by 1914.[16] Over this period, classical notions of justice and responsibility began to be replaced by modern, scientifically ordered alternatives. Individual reform gradually became a central organizing principle of sentencing and penology. Arguments for the individualization of penalties came to be seen as persuasive. And alternatives to incarceration were designed and put into practice. Finally, the idea that a sentence should be seen not as a moral judgement but as a prescription for a return to an acceptable way of living began to dominate if not judicial practice at least academic commentary.[17]

It would be inaccurate to say that forward-looking accounts of punishment have dominated sentencing or corrections in the intervening period. It would not be inaccurate, however, to say that they became progressively more influential over the intervening years. The two decades following the second world war saw forward-looking penal theories introduced with varying enthusiasm and consistency in virtually the whole of the western world.

The resulting shift in sentencing and correctional practices manifested itself in three ways. First, sentencing principles came to focus increasingly on offenders as individuals and not on their crimes. Correctional administration was directed increasingly toward the goal of rehabilitation and treatment, and toward risk assessment. Second, the moral character of punishment was de-emphasized. This was essential if the goal of the sentencing process was to shift from determining responsibility and measuring desert to preventing recidivism. Finally, the range of discretion granted to both sentencing and correctional authorities was progressively broadened. This was reflected in a number of ways. The range of penalties for particular offences was substantially widened. Offenders became eligible for parole often after as little as one-third of incarceral sentences had been served. Wide discretion to release on parole was granted to correctional authorities or parole boards. Perhaps most indicative was the appearance of indeterminate sentencing. In a least some jurisdictions, for example California, indeterminate sentences became quite common.

Contemporary criticisms of the welfare model of punishment

Until very recently, the welfare model of punishment dominated, particularly the field of corrections.[18] However, the past two decades have seen a remarkable reversal of outlook. Few would dispute that individual offenders have benefited from programmes they encountered in serving their sentences. Yet, as a central sentencing goal, the rehabilitation ideal is now thoroughly suspect. The issue here is coercive rehabilitation. The evidence is that it is not effective for the most part.[19] Studies of predictive restraint have been equally damaging. Research has shown that there are no techniques currently available that can reliably indicate those and only those likely to commit violent acts or engage in other forms of criminal activity.[20]

These criticisms of coercive rehabilitation and predictive restraint have an obvious place in the discussion of the individualization of sentences. If coercive rehabilitation is not effective, then varying sentences based on the need for treatment cannot be justified. Equally, if there are no reliable techniques for predicting dangerousness or recidivism, then varying the length of sentences on public safety grounds is equally unacceptable.

But the argument goes well beyond this. It is now well documented that sentencing systems and judges whose goal was rehabilitation or incapacitation generated longer and harsher sentences on average than did retribution-oriented judges and the retribution-oriented systems they replaced. There are many reasons for this. The logic of welfare-oriented sentencing requires that those responsible for sentencing and for the administration of sentences be granted substantial discretion. The inability to predict dangerousness or recidivism combined with public pressure pushes authorities toward assuming the worst where there is doubt.[21] That judges and other correctional authorities did in fact emphasize public safety, imposing as a result more and stiffer sentences, is therefore hardly surprising.

Welfare-oriented sentencing also increased the harshness of sentences by diminishing and undermining the control that offenders had over their own lives. The discretion granted to those administering sentences made it difficult to predict when one would be released.[22] Since there are no reliable ways of establishing that someone has been rehabilitated, those under sentence could be given no reliable way of knowing what criteria those responsible for administering their sentence would use in deciding to 'terminate treatment'. The frustration and alienation this caused inmates is well documented.[23] As a result, punishment came to be seen by offenders as the exercise of arbitrary power.

Deterrence-oriented sentencing fares little better in the face of empirical evaluations of its effectiveness. There can be no doubt that sanctions attached to criminal laws act as deterrents in some general sense. However, there is no evidence that their impact is what deterrence theorists suggest ought to be the case. Specific deterrence is simply a variation of the welfare model. It constitutes a form of treatment whose goal is to alter the behaviour patterns of an individual offender. As a treatment technique, the results of punishment imposed for deterrent purposes are no more predictable or reliable than alternative treatments.

Gauging the deterrent effect of punishment on the general population is also notoriously difficult. What can be said with some confidence is that, while imposing sanctions does deter in some situations to some degree, there is no obvious generalizable correlation between the severity of punishment and its deterrent effect.[24]

Forward-looking models: an overview

Experience with reform, rehabilitation, and deterrence models of punishment cannot disprove their value for reasons already explored. Indeed, there is increasing evidence that support for forward-looking sentencing is beginning to return.[25] I propose to return to discuss that phenomenon in a later chapter. However, combined with our earlier assessment of the conceptual implications of forward-looking accounts of punishment, the empirical accounts now available of the impact of forward-looking sentencing and correctional administration are significant.

C.S. Lewis was one of the first to invite people to consider whether they would actually prefer the welfare-oriented approach, implying as it did indeterminate sentences, to 'old-fashioned' desert-oriented sentences. He suggested that when you replace justice with welfare you 'start being "kind" to people before you have considered their rights and then force upon them supposed kindnesses which they in fact (once) had a right to refuse, and finally kindnesses which no one but you will recognize as kindnesses and which the recipient will feel as abominable cruelties' (Lewis 1953: 230). Benevolence undisciplined by justice, he suggests, becomes a tyrant.

Recent influential criticisms have been offered by many people who once endorsed welfare-oriented sentencing. One critic, H.L.A. Hart, whose views we shall examine at some length in the next chapter, rejects a purely forward-looking approach to sentencing because it implies treating people as 'merely alterable, predictable, curable or manipulable things' (Hart 1968: 183). To approach criminal justice in this way, he suggests, would require a radical change in our understanding of human relationships.

Hart's observations are well grounded. How we respond to people is a function of what we perceive to be their intentions toward us. When we feel that others are interested in us only because of our value to them in the pursuit of their own goals, we feel resentment. We don't like to be used. When we are caught up in events over which we seem to have no control, a normal reaction is anger or frustration or discouragement. Often we will just refuse to respond to threats or bribes, even at great personal cost, when we feel they are illegitimate.

It is not surprising that offenders respond in similar ways. Little separates them from law-abiding citizens except their offence. While their offence may be significant to us, the reason is almost certainly because we believe they should share our way of looking at these things. In fact, for the most part they do. Hence, when they find themselves caught in a system that assumes it has the right to manipulate them for society's benefit, or a system that tries to cudgel them into appropriate ways of acting, they react with resentment, anger, frustration and despair, just as we would in their place.

The only thing surprising about this is that we should be surprised by it. Neither should we be surprised that our twentieth-century experiment with forward-looking accounts has not been a success. Our correctional systems today are better than they were one hundred years ago. No doubt this is in part a reflection of greater social wealth. However, improvements made in the last century also reflect shifts toward more humanitarian ways of dealing with people who come into conflict with our laws. The interest in rehabilitation has also played a role in improving access to medical treatment, education, training programmes, counselling, recreation, and so on.

All of this having been said, however, forward-looking accounts of punishment are not satisfactory. What a person actually did has an unavoidably central role in our dealings with that person, a role for which forward-looking accounts of punishment cannot give an adequate account. It is equally true that we cannot understand our relationship to the law independently of moral considerations. To attempt to determine how to deal with offenders independently of moral considerations is to dehumanize them. Morality plays a central role in our understanding of human relationships. The fact that someone has broken a law does not somehow dissolve the need to understand and respond to his actions from a moral perspective.

What then does this imply for an understanding of punishment? Purely forward-looking theories cannot adequately account for values central to the evolution of modern liberal democratic systems of criminal law. This has led some commentators to conclude that only retributive theories can provide a morally acceptable basis for responding to offenders.[26] Yet, as we have seen, backward-looking accounts are equally unsatisfactory.

Are there any other options? Some commentators, having arrived at the conclusion that neither a purely forward-looking nor a purely backward-looking account of punishment taken alone can provide an adequate justification of punishment, have suggested that the two approaches be combined into a mixed theory that avoids the defects of both while incorporating their several virtues. Of these, a proposal by H.L.A. Hart has been the most influential. However, recently, R.A. Duff has offered a second alternative. The purpose of the next chapter is to evaluate both these proposals.

3

TWO HYBRID THEORIES

In Chapters 1 and 2 we looked at accounts of punishment that were either exclusively backward-looking or exclusively forward-looking. Neither approach it seems can justify the practice of punishment. In each case, the central reason is similar. Each approach lacks what the other offers. Backward-looking accounts fail because they are unable to accommodate the widespread belief that unless inflicting pain can be shown to have beneficial consequences it is immoral. Forward-looking accounts are unable to acknowledge that punishment should, as a matter of moral principle, be inflicted only on those genuinely guilty of an offence and should vary in proportion to the seriousness of the offence committed.

An obvious solution to this dilemma is to combine the two accounts. This option, however, poses serious difficulties since the principles that dominate the two distinct approaches seem incompatible. How then is this fundamental incompatibility to be overcome? Those seeking to construct a hybrid theory must first decide whether forward-looking or backward-looking values should dominate the account being constructed. Once this is determined, the challenge is to demonstrate that there remains room in the account for the central values of the contrasting approach. Let us assume, for example, that our goal in punishing is backward-looking, that is, just retribution. It would follow on this view that punishment was justifiable only if it was deserved. The challenge then would be to show how this approach could be rendered consistent with the view that nevertheless punishment should be inflicted only where it was likely to have beneficial consequences.

It is not surprising that, as the inadequacies of each account taken by itself have become increasingly apparent, commentators have turned to a search for compromise solutions. The proposals that have emerged are too numerous to review here. For the most part, they have been shown to suffer from defects similar to those of the 'pure' theories they are designed to replace. However, two proposals merit special attention, the first because it has been very influential, the second because it serves as a particularly persuasive attempt to find a place for forward-looking values in what is essentially a retributive account.

PART I: H.L.A. HART'S COMPROMISE SOLUTION

Three questions distinguished

Perhaps the most influential attempt at a compromise solution to the problems of both forward-looking and backward-looking theories of punishment taken alone is that developed by H.L.A. Hart. His account is a response to what he perceived as a growing confusion caused at least in part by what he describes as a 'persistent drive towards an oversimplification of multiple issues which require separate consideration' (Hart 1968: 3). What is required, he suggests, is 'the realization that different principles (each of which may in a sense be called a "justification") are relevant at different points in any morally acceptable account of punishment' (Hart 1968: 3).

Hart proposes that we distinguish three questions. First, what justifies the general practice of punishment? Second, to whom may punishment be applied? And third, what amount of punishment should be inflicted? Approaching each question in a distinct step should allow us to see clearly, Hart argues, that endorsing retributive principles in the application of punishment in particular cases does not entail endorsing retribution as the general aim of punishment (Hart 1968: 9).

What answers, then, does Hart give to each of these questions? The answer to his first question, Hart seems to suggest, is that the practice of punishment is justified by the belief that penalties are required as a threat to maintain conformity to the law (Hart 1968: 25–7). Who then are we justified in punishing? Hart's answer is that we are justified in punishing only those who break the law voluntarily. To fail to limit punishment to those genuinely guilty of an offence would, he argues, be unfair and unjust and would undermine the capacity of people to live satisfactory lives within the coercive framework of the law. What is more, we should accept this constraint, Hart argues, even though it will inevitably hinder the pursuit of the general aim of punishment, namely to ensure conformity to the law.

It would seem to follow that, by distinguishing these two questions, we can endorse what Hart calls retribution in the distribution of punishment, while rejecting retribution as the general aim of punishment.

We have then Hart's answer to his first and second questions. But what answer does he propose for the third? That is, by reference to what values should sentencing authorities determine the amount of punishment that should be inflicted for particular offences? In particular, should retributive or utilitarian principles guide the sentencing process after guilt has been determined?

Unfortunately for those attempting to assess the strength of Hart's proposal, it is not at all clear that Hart provides an answer to this question. The focus of his discussion is on the first two questions. Little attention, however, is paid to question three. It is true that he does discuss particular sentencing practices like capital punishment. However, no clear general answer to the third question emerges from those discussions. What answers, then, are available?

How should offenders be punished: a first interpretation

One obvious possibility is that the amount of punishment that should be inflicted on offenders for their offences should be determined by what they deserve. That is to say, punishment should be inflicted in proportion to the moral gravity of the offence committed and that like cases should be treated alike.[1]

However, if this is what Hart had in mind, it is open to serious objections. If we accept that only those who deserve to be punished because they have broken the law voluntarily should be punished and furthermore they should be punished in accordance with their desert, what role in punishment is left for the principle of utility? If the answer to the second and third questions is a retributivist one, then what room is left for the view that the general aim of punishment should be forward-looking since in every case who is punished and how they are punished is to be determined by backward-looking criteria. That is to say, to approach the justification of punishment this way implies that punishment should be inflicted even when it is obvious that it will benefit no one. And this is one of the principal reasons for rejecting retributivist accounts of punishment in the first place.

How should offenders be punished: a second interpretation

A more plausible interpretation is that Hart thought that principles of utility *and* principles of justice should play a role in determining the amount of punishment to be inflicted on offenders for specific offences. However, this suggestion is a perplexing one. Utilitarianism comes equipped with its own criteria for determining what is an appropriate sentence in a particular situation. But so too does retributive justice.[2] A judge cannot impose a sentence that is both an appropriate retributive and utilitarian response to an offence where the two are in conflict. The central challenge for hybrid theories of the sort Hart is proposing is to show how this conflict should be resolved.[3]

There would seem to be only two ways out of this dilemma. The first is to take the view that insisting that punishment be assigned in particular cases in accordance with the requirements of justice is the most efficacious way of pursuing the utilitarian goal. There is some evidence that Hart was at least tempted by this option.[4] On the other hand, he also quite explicitly rejects this way around the problems of combining justice and utility in punishment at various points in his commentary and in ways that have direct application to this dilemma.[5] There are convincing reasons, Hart argues, for accepting that principles of justice are as likely to frustrate the pursuit of utility as they are to facilitate it.[6]

The second way out is to suggest that the role of the language of retribution is so important to the way we think about our social relationships that it should not be overridden or diluted excessively, even if and when it collides with the aim of social protection. This view gives to those values associated with backward-looking accounts of punishment a status that is independent of the general aim, which is a utilitarian one.

In practice it is certainly possible to direct sentencing authorities to use both forward-looking and backward-looking criteria when sentencing offenders. Indeed, there is a very real sense in which modern systems of law do exactly this. However, simply insisting that both types of values have a necessary place in punishment does nothing to explain their relative place. If they come into conflict, and they cannot avoid doing so, which set of values should prevail?

Solving this problem is in fact one of the basic problems in law enforcement. In effect, Hart's compromise solution on this interpretation amounts to little more than a direction that, when conflict occurs, common sense should mediate. Sometimes that will result in a weakening of the role of justice and fairness. Sometimes it will result in sacrificing social protection in the interests of justice or fairness. However, in either case the outcome will vary with the particular judge who is called upon to make the decision, a decision which, unless guided by a coherent set of sentencing principles, must inevitably have an arbitrary quality to it.

No doubt, common sense is what those responsible for making these decisions will normally rely on. We might expect the result to be a kind of uneasy equilibrium. Furthermore, this may turn out to be the best we can do.[7] However, if it is, it suggests that a basic practice in our social lives is beyond understanding and analysis in a fundamental way.[8]

How should offenders be punished: a third interpretation

There is a third obvious interpretation left. Punishment should be inflicted on those found guilty of breaking the law as required by the goal of general deterrence. The argument supporting this interpretation proceeds in four steps.

1 If the goal of punishment is deterrence, as Hart appears to believe (Hart 1968: 27), then, when we punish people for breaking the law we are using[9], manipulating[10] or sacrificing[11] them to some social good.
2 In using people by punishing them in pursuit of a social good we are overriding principles of justice (Hart 1968: 172) that 'pervade the whole of social life' (Hart 1968: 183).
3 It is their decision to break the law when they could voluntarily have avoided doing so that gives us a licence to punish offenders and thus use them as instruments in the pursuit of a social good.[12]
4 However, we should exercise our moral licence to punish people in this way only if we need to do so in pursuit of the main aims of punishment.[13]

This justification raises a serious problem. Why does the fact that someone has committed an offence give society a licence to use him in ways that are in conflict with principles of justice and fairness? Hart's response to this question is not at all clear. On the other hand, his account of why we should *not* treat people this way is impressive, and deserves careful discussion.

The case against ignoring principles of justice in sentencing

Hart offers three interlocking reasons for not ignoring principles of justice in determining the punishment that should be inflicted on offenders for their offences in particular cases. First, we do as a society value individual freedom. As we saw in the previous chapter, indeterminate sentences are the logical outcome of a sentencing system dominated by purely forward-looking principles. And indeterminate sentences put those subject to them under the control of designated authorities in a way that to all intents and purposes removes from them the right and the capacity to guide their lives in accordance with values of their own choosing.

Second, and of equal importance, is the impact a purely forward-looking sentencing regime would have on how we see ourselves and others. Under normal conditions, people do not see each other:

> as so many bodies moving in ways that are sometimes harmful and have to be prevented or altered. Instead, persons interpret each other's movements as manifestations of intentions and choices, and these subjective factors are often more important to their social relations than the movements by which they are manifested or their effects. If one person strikes another, the person struck does not think of the other as just a cause of pain to him; for it is of crucial importance to him whether the blow was deliberate or involuntary. If the blow was light but deliberate, it has a significance for the person struck quite different from an accidental much heavier blow.
>
> (Hart 1968: 182–3)

What does this imply for the law? Hart replies:

> If as our legal moralists maintain it is important for the law to reflect common judgments of morality, it is surely even more important that it should in general reflect in its judgments on human conduct distinctions which not only underlie morality, but pervade the whole of our social life. This it would fail to

do if it treated men merely as alterable, predictable, curable or manipulable things.

(Hart 1968: 183)

What this implies is that to allow purely forward-looking principles to dominate sentencing can only result in a system of corrections that treats those who come under its control 'merely as alterable, predictable, curable or manipulable things'. Second, there is substantial danger that punishing offenders for purely utilitarian reasons will turn them into hardened enemies of society, as Hart acknowledges (Hart 1968: 27).

Finally, Hart suggests that to depart in a significant way from the principle of proportionality, a backward-looking principle, and from the principle that like offences be treated alike, which would be necessary if sentencing were to be dominated by forward-looking considerations, would risk 'confusing common morality or flouting it and bringing the law into contempt' (Hart 1968: 25).

Taken together these arguments seem persuasive. How could punishment be justified if it required such a substantial flouting of fundamental social values? The difficulty is that taken together they seem to have direct application to Hart's own justification of punishment if we interpret it in this third way.

To conclude, on all three possible interpretations of the answer he might give to the question 'how much punishment should be inflicted on offenders for particular offences?', his hybrid account is exposed to just the criticisms that Hart himself levels against either purely forward-looking or purely backward-looking theories.

The general aim of punishment: a final criticism of Hart's forward-looking hybrid account

The hybrid account Hart offers is subject to a second type of criticism. Hart assumes that the purpose of punishment is social protection. But is he consistent in this view and does he show that a justification of the practice of punishment can in fact be built on this assumption?

Two observations are relevant here, one very brief, the other more substantial. First, Hart does not in fact offer a justification of punishment. This is particularly obvious when we consider the costs that previous argument suggests attach to sacrificing offenders to the public good. To actually justify punishment, Hart would have to show that it was on balance the least harmful and most efficacious way of accomplishing what he says is its goal, namely the need for general deterrence. What appears a simple requirement hides an extraordinarily complex calculation. Hart avoids the calculation by appealing to what he regards as widely shared beliefs.[14] This tactic, however, comes up against empirical research into the efficacy of punishment as a general deterrent undertaken over the past several decades, which suggests that public assumptions about the efficacy of punishment as a deterrent are not a reliable foundation on which to build a justification of that practice.

Let us set this 'quibble' aside, however, and turn to what must surely be the fundamental concern. Does Hart provide us with a general aim that could in principle justify the practice of punishment? The answer is that he provides us not with one general aim but with two. In some places he points to social protection as the general justifying aim of punishment. Elsewhere, however, his argument implies that the general aim of punishment is to maintain conformity to the law.

It is clear that it is the second general aim to which Hart is committed. There are two reasons for this. First, Hart makes it clear that the purpose of the law is 'to announce to society that (prohibited) actions are not to be done and to secure that fewer of them are done' (Hart 1968: 6). The function of punishment is to encourage compliance with the law.

When we put it this way, we can see that Hart's way of justifying punishment creates an illusion. The function of punishment is to deter people from breaking the law. Punishment is justified, on this account of the matter, if it fulfils its purpose. But this is a functional not a moral justification. It can work as a moral justification only if imposing a legal system can be shown to be justified as a moral good.

Hart is committed to the view that there is no necessary connection between law and morality.[15] This is one of the basic reasons for his rejection of retributivism both as a justification for retaining the requirement of responsibility in the criminal law and as a justification for punishment. If we accept Hart's view on the relation of law and morality, however, there is no reason to assume that enforcing the law in general or specific laws in particular will have socially valuable consequences. It follows that establishing that punishment helps to secure that the law is obeyed explains the rationale for punishment but does not justify it.

It is true, though he does not make reference to the fact in his discussion of punishment, that Hart is of the view that all legal systems come into existence in response to certain 'natural necessities', of which vulnerability to violence is one of the most basic. However, as Hart himself acknowledges, this will not carry him the needed distance. A legal system could meet the basic requirements described in his account of the minimum content of natural law. But this would still not entail that the system provided social protection in a form that justified enforcement through punishment.[16]

Separating law and morality generates a quandary for Hart's hybrid theory. If obeying a particular law is conducive to the general good, then punishing those who break that law will be justified, since punishment is necessary by hypothesis to ensuring that the law is obeyed. However, if the law is a bad one, punishing those who break it will not be justified. This of course implies that there is and can be no general moral obligation to obey the law. It also implies that there is and can be no general moral justification of the practice of punishment of the sort his own account assumes to be possible, even on the assumption that a particular legal system was on the whole a morally commendable one.

Alternatively, it might be argued that even bad laws should be enforced, because accepting that people have the moral right to pick and choose which laws to obey would inevitably undermine the authority of the law, with unfortunate social results. It would follow, on this argument, that punishing people even for breaking bad laws would be justified if requiring that people obeyed the law in general could be shown to enhance general welfare. As it turns out, this approach to the problem is a promising one. Indeed, it forms the basis for the approach I shall develop below. But Hart does not make this argument. Neither is it clear how he could make it without falling back into a form of rule utilitarianism, an approach to the justification of punishment which he quite explicitly rejects and which, as we have seen in the last chapter, has fundamental weaknesses.

A concluding assessment

It would seem then that Hart's attempt to combine retributive and utilitarian principles into a single hybrid theory does not succeed. However, it does provide some useful pointers. It provides persuasive arguments for rejecting purely forward-looking as well as purely backward-looking accounts of punishment. It suggests strongly that we should seek to understand the role of punishment from within an account of the nature and function of legal systems. And it points to the fact that an understanding of the relation of law and morality cannot be escaped simply by rejecting retributivist accounts.

PART II: TELEOLOGICAL RETRIBUTIVISM

Duff's alternative account

Hybrid accounts of punishment that assume that punishment ought to be forward-looking in its general aim but constrained by backward-looking considerations in its application are unlikely to result in coherent accounts for reasons already set out. However, they do have the virtue of identifying the value of looking at punishment in the context of other important aspects of the law. Teleological retributivism proceeds in the same way. However, teleological retributivism also asserts what forward-looking accounts try to avoid, namely, that law has an irreducibly moral character that must be understood if punishment is to be explained and justified.

Hybrid theories try to find a place for both forward-looking or utilitarian principles and backward-looking or retributive principles in their accounts of the practice of punishment. Their fundamental task is to show how these two apparently incompatible ways of assessing how sentences should be arrived at in particular cases can be combined in the sentencing process. Since most hybrid theories avoid this task, most are fundamentally defective.[17]

An exception to this is the account offered by R.A. Duff in *Trials and Punishments* (Duff 1986).[18] He argues that punishment is an expression of moral criticism, whose central characteristics it therefore shares. To criticize someone is to blame him for something for which he is alleged to be responsible.

Criticism in this context has a clear point, Duff argues. Its goal when directed at a wrongdoer is to bring him to acknowledge his misdeed(s) and to alter his behaviour. It therefore has an unavoidably forward-looking character. At the same time, it is also backward-looking in as much as moral criticism is a response to something that has already been done.

The criminal law, Duff argues, takes its place as a formal element in an ongoing process of dialogue whose goal is to persuade offenders that their behaviour is blameworthy and merits criticism. The form of the dialogue is conditioned by the fact that it occurs in a community of moral agents who are autonomous and rational. We respect another person as a rational and autonomous moral agent when we:

> treat him and respond to him as one who is able, and should be allowed, to conduct his own life and determine his own conduct in the light of his own understanding of the values and goals which command his allegiance. It involves a refusal to manipulate him, or to use him merely as an instrument for the attainment of social or individual goals; insofar as I may properly attempt to modify his conduct (or, more accurately, attempt to bring him to modify his own conduct), I should do so only by bringing him to understand and accept the relevant reasons which justify that attempt.
>
> (Duff 1986: 6)

The point of the dialogue, therefore, is to persuade a wrongdoer to change his ways through moral criticism.

Moral criticism is itself a way of blaming someone for what has occurred.[19] It communicates, if expressed, a judgement that the person being criticized acted wrongly. Duff argues that one of its central purposes is to induce suffering in the wrongdoer for his offence, what he calls 'the pain of recognized and accepted guilt' (Duff 1986: 59).

Duff argues that both the trial process and punishment should be understood as a formal process of moral criticism of offenders (Duff 1986: 41). Punishment is the formal expression of moral criticism for wrongdoing, specifically an illegal action, by a community. Its goal is to 'induce suffering in an alleged offender for an alleged offence' (Duff 1986: 41). Seen as an element in a moral argument, the goal of punishment is to bring a wrongdoer to recognize that what he has done is wrong. That is to say, the goal is to persuade the wrongdoer to accept the criticism to which he is being subjected, to recognize his behaviour as blameworthy and to change his ways. Punishment allows an offender to acknowledge wrongdoing and reinforces his commitment to change. Seen from this perspective, punishment constitutes a form of penance.

The view of punishment that emerges is both forward- and backward-looking. It is backward-looking in so far as it voices a moral criticism in response to an action. However, it does not argue that punishment should be inflicted for that reason alone. Rather, built into the idea of moral criticism is the forward-looking goal of reform. The result is a view of punishment that is both retributive and teleological in character.

Persuasion and the moral character of law

The view that claims that the obligation to obey the law rests simply on the power of the state authorities to impose their will by force is also compatible with the claim that the purpose of trials and punishments is persuasion. However, this alternate view implies that the basic element in the process of persuasion is prudence, where obedience rests in the last analysis on fear of punishment.

Where punishment is designed to give people a prudential reason to obey the law, it is intrinsically manipulative. This is because the fear on which compliance rests is only contingently related to the content of the law being enforced. That is to say, deterrence-oriented sentencing seeks to influence and change attitudes by manipulating in artificial ways the interests of those being punished. It does not seek to convince those toward whom it is directed that the law seeks the welfare of others, or is intrinsically worthy of obedience and requires compliance for that reason. Although all or some of this may be true, the persuasiveness of the threat bears no relation to the truth of this claim.

Deterrence-oriented punishment seeks to convince those toward whom it is directed that obeying the law is in their self-interest. But it does so by manipulating those interests. It manipulates by inserting a threat or a fear that bears no direct relationship to the goals or life plans of those whose attitudes it seeks to influence. Hence, it has a fundamentally arbitrary quality. The reasons for compliance that it offers operate quite independently of the content of the law being enforced or the moral or the legal authority of the enforcer.

Reform-oriented sentencing is equally manipulative though not necessarily punitive. It does not operate through threats. It seeks to change attitudes. However, where reform is purely forward-looking and does not respond to the moral character of the behaviour of the person targeted for reform, then the goal of reform is conformity with the law, whatever the law's content. It may be that the law merits respect for any number of reasons. But the reason that reform is being demanded is not the merit of the law. Rather reform is required because conformity with the law is demanded.

The model for achieving reform may be treatment, behaviour modification, counselling or even moral exhortation. In all cases, however, the measure of success will be whether the person being treated conforms, not his reasons for conforming. Any reason for complying will be as good as any other so long as it is effective.

Respecting a person's autonomy, on the other hand, requires that reform result from a conviction on the part of the person whose behaviour is in question that there are morally persuasive reasons for changing his ways, reasons that relate to his understanding of the kind of person he would like to be, or the kinds of values he ought to respect. That is to say, the goal of persuasion is to bring him to see that the hard treatment being imposed on him is merited.

Duff argues that moral persuasion can be an integral part of the legal process only if law has an 'essential and ineliminable moral dimension' (Duff 1986: 76). From this it follows that 'an essential and proper purpose of law [is] to serve the common good' (Duff 1986: 91). It also follows that any system of rules properly described as a legal system will contain 'certain notions of value and purpose, concerned with the common good and with the moral status of the citizen within the concept of law. These [will] provide an *ideal* model of what a system of law *ought* to be.' (Duff 1986: 91–2). Once this is recognized it will be clear that our legal obligation to obey the law rests on a moral obligation to care for the good of the community.

Teleological retributivism: its strengths

Teleological retributivism shares one of the central virtues of hybrid accounts of punishment. It locates the practice of punishment within functioning legal systems and attempts a justification that accepts that punishment has to be understood as just one aspect of a complex legal system. Teleological retributivism shares, therefore, the view common to hybrid accounts that punishment cannot be justified independently of other aspects of the legal process.

Teleological retributivism also shows how we might overcome one of the basic problems with hybrid accounts like that of Hart in which retributive considerations play only a restraining but not a justificatory role in an account of punishment. Hart's account, it will be recalled, assigns punishment the role of general deterrent whose central function is to support the basic aim of any legal system, namely to announce that certain actions are not to be performed and to reduce the likelihood that they will be performed. This approach locates the practice of punishment within the context of an operating system of law. Yet, as an account of punishment, it explains the role of punishment quite independently of the characteristics of particular legal systems in which it finds its place.

Accounts which have this character can explain the function of punishment. They can also offer a justification of punishment, but only on a case by case basis where it can be shown that the state is morally justified in prohibiting the behaviour which it has proscribed by law.[20] However, this leaves the practice of punishment unjustified. It also carries with it the apparent implication that there is and could be no general moral obligation to obey the law.

This conclusion clashes with common sense. It also clashes with the stated aim of Hart's hybrid theory, which is to justify the practice by reference to its general aim.

Teleological retributivism avoids this problem by ascribing a necessary moral content to law. Law by its very nature is concerned with the common good, reflecting its authors' views of what that common good requires by way of laws. Justifying the law involves identifying those values and demonstrating that they are sound. The trial process and punishment itself have this function. Both seek to persuade offenders that their conduct merits moral criticism and punishment. Punishment is justified on this view of the matter as a component in a process designed to win an offender's respect for the law and the vision of the public good for which it stands.

A second strength of teleological retributivism is its focus on moral autonomy. Here too we find a point of agreement with the first hybrid account examined. Central to Hart's account, as we have seen, is the view that purely forward-looking accounts of punishment are inconsistent with values that give a high priority to individual liberty. They also imply an understanding of human relationships that is quite inconsistent with those that currently prevail. This is because purely forward-looking theories imply that intervention designed to control and manipulate the behaviour of individuals is justified only by future and not by past considerations. Hart rejects purely forward-looking accounts of punishment on the grounds that respect for individual liberty and autonomy requires that if someone is to be used as an instrument in the pursuit of a social good, specifically general deterrence, that person must first be shown to have broken a law he could have chosen to respect.

Teleological retributivism points to a central weakness in that view. Hart argues that respect for individual liberty and autonomy requires that retributive criteria be used to determine whom the state is entitled to punish. This has the effect of ensuring that only morally autonomous individuals are found guilty and exposed to the burden of punishment. One purpose of a trial, therefore, is to establish that someone charged with a crime is morally responsible for his act. Having established this point, however, the state is now justified in treating those found guilty as mere instruments that the state is justified in manipulating in the pursuit of a public good.

Teleological retributivism points to the incoherence of this view. The fact that someone has broken the law he could have chosen to respect cannot justify treating him in a way that ignores his moral status. If moral autonomy is central to the question of guilt and therefore central to the justification of punishment in particular cases, then respect for the moral autonomy of offenders should have a central role in the imposition of punishment as well.

To view trials and punishments as integral elements in a process not of manipulation but of persuasion grounded on a view of the common good accomplishes that goal. Punishment can be imposed on this view in a manner that is consistent with the values central to the process of determining guilt, particularly with those values associated with respect for the freedom and autonomy of individuals.

In spite of its attractive features, however, teleological retributivism suffers from some irremediable weaknesses.

Moral persuasion and the nature of modern legal systems

One central difficulty with Duff's account of punishment is that it requires that moral persuasion play a role which it does not and seemingly cannot play in modern legal systems. The goal of persuasion, on Duff's account of the matter, is to convince an offender that the state is justified in prohibiting what he has been charged with doing. There is much about the trial process that lends itself to this interpretation, as we have already seen. In particular it fits the requirement that only those who are capable of understanding a charge brought against them and participating in their trial are fit to stand trial.

Unfortunately, there are other equally important aspects of the trial process that cannot be accommodated within Duff's account. Although the evidence brought before the court in a criminal trial may have the effect of bringing a culprit to see the moral quality of his act, in fact this is not its point. The point is to establish a matter of fact. Is the person on trial guilty of the offence for which he has been charged? What is more, discussion or argument about the moral quality of the prohibited conduct is expressly excluded. The court by law takes the law as given and prohibits discussion of its merits. The court is concerned only with whether it can be established beyond a reasonable doubt that the person on trial acted in a way that the law prohibits.

What is more, a criminal trial is not a debate between equals. The rules of the debate are set by the court. Furthermore, the interpretation of those rules lies with the court. The person charged may attempt to persuade the court of his view of how the law should be applied. Nevertheless, the power to decide and enforce the decisions arrived at lies with the court and with the authorities that look to the court for direction.

Duff acknowledges that the separation of powers in modern legal systems which 'is not found in non-legal moral contexts' creates problems for his account (Duff 1986: 138). He argues in response that this does not obviate the need for modern legal systems to justify their laws. It is just that the process of justification is more complex, with different aspects of it being assigned to different contexts. Specifically, the justification of laws is a function of the legislative process while the interpretation and application of the laws is the responsibility of the judiciary. The court is required to assume that the rules it is called on to apply are morally justified. Hence, the court refuses to allow those appearing before it to argue their merits.

What Duff says about the separation of powers is true. However, it cannot be brought into harmony with his under-riding claims. To begin with, in a democracy, the authority of a legislature does not rest on its capacity to justify its actions. Rather, the authority of the legislature rests on its claim to represent the views and wishes of the majority of the citizens of the state. There is no requirement that the governing party justify its legislative proposals with coherent moral argument. Further, there is no guarantee that laws created by democratic regimes will be morally defensible, a fact for which history provides ample evidence. Yet unjust laws are laws for all of that and require compliance on pain of punishment, as does any law.

Second, the complex of laws in actual democratic states does not in fact display the moral coherence required or assumed by Duff's notion of transparent persuasion. Modern democratic societies are morally pluralistic societies. Their lack of moral homogeneity is unavoidably reflected in their laws. Lack of thorough-going consistency is therefore virtually inevitable. Some people will be faced with legal burdens others are not required to carry. Everyone will be required to respect laws that significant numbers may believe to be unjustifiable.

What all of this illustrates is that teleological retributivism, as Duff describes it, could only justify punishment in an ideal political and legal system which reflected a coherent vision of the common good. This in turn implies that punishment as we actually encounter it in the real world cannot in practice be justified.

Duff's account must now face a real difficulty. First, he argues that punishment is an unavoidable feature of modern legal systems. Modern legal systems in turn play an essential role in modern society. It follows that offenders will have to be dealt with in accordance with law.

What does this imply? It would seem that what it implies is that sentencing in modern societies must fall back on utilitarian principles.[21] This in turn means that, when all is said and done, the hybrid theories of Duff and Hart lead to the same conclusion. Punishment as they describe it is an unavoidable feature of modern legal systems. Yet the accounts they offer imply that there is no coherent and morally defensible set of principles by which to guide its application.[22]

Moral persuasion and the notion of a common good: a second criticism

A central feature of teleological retributivism is the view that legal systems by their very nature encapsulate a vision of the common good. It does not follow, of course, that the vision reflected in any given legal system is coherent or sound. It does follow, on Duff's account of the matter, that those responsible for creating and implementing the law will justify their actions by reference to that vision.

Why then are communities justified in imposing a vision of the common good on all those falling within the law's jurisdiction? The answer Duff gives to this question is a communitarian one. 'Human communities', he argues, 'provide the necessary context within which we can make sense of any kinds of value, and within

74

which individuals can find their identity and their good' (Duff
1988: 789). The law can now be understood as a system of rules
designed to protect and enhance the common values around which
a community can form. The practices and institutions to which these
values and rules give rise then provide a context in which individuals
can shape their own values and create a coherent view of what in life
is worth doing. Communitarianism implies that, in the absence of
community structures, individuals cannot develop a sense of who
they are and the values they wish to guide their lives.

This approach to law and punishment has clear virtues. Not only
does it assume that punishment can be understood only within the
context of a working legal system, it goes further and argues that
both punishment and law have to be located within a system of social
and political values that can give shape to a community's institutions
and practices, including its legal institutions and practices. It follows
that punishment can be justified only if those values are sound.

This approach to an understanding of the practice of punishment
has important strengths, as I have attempted to argue. However, it
does highlight what seems a serious difficulty with the account of
punishment Duff defends.

For teleological retributivism, moral autonomy is a basic value.
As Duff puts it:

> to respect another person as a rational and autonomous moral
> agent is to treat him and respond to him as one who is able,
> and should be allowed, to conduct his own life and determine
> his own conduct in the light of his own understanding of the
> values and goals which command his allegiance.
>
> (Duff 1986: 6)

To respect someone as a morally autonomous individual, therefore,
requires that he be granted what has been described as 'value
sovereignty'.[23]

How can a society create a legal system which requires that all
members of that society respect the vision of the common good
reflected in that legal system while claiming to respect their value
sovereignty? Value sovereignty would seem to require that individuals be left free to choose the values which will guide their lives,
even where those values come into conflict with those generally held
by the people among whom they live. Duff's communitarian view of
law implies on the other hand that no society whose communal life
is guided by a legal system can avoid imposing on all those governed

75

by the legal system a view of the common good. How can a state claim to respect the value sovereignty of its citizens, while at the same time claiming the right to punish them if they fail to respect the moral values around which its legal system is built?

Duff's response is twofold. A legal system can be said to respect the value sovereignty of individuals only if it seeks to win their compliance through a process of rational argument and persuasion. This in turn requires that in punishing those who fail to comply with the law's demands the state's aim must be persuasion and not manipulation. Throughout, the goal of the state must be to win respect for the view of the common good around which the law has been shaped on the part of all those required to obey it.

It is this which gives rise to our second major criticism. As with many contemporary theorists who endorse some version of the value sovereignty principle, Duff is committed to the view that respect for value sovereignty is justified at least in part by the fact that no system of values can be shown in the end to be rationally compelling or alternatively morally superior to all rivals. It follows that some moral disagreements cannot be resolved through rational debate. It also follows that, however coherent or sound the vision of the common good captured by a particular legal system, there may be some who reject those values for good and valid reasons.

How then can the state justify punishment where it has failed to convince those who have broken its laws that they were wrong in doing so? How can punishment fail to be manipulative where the dispute with the law breaker is fundamental and objectively unresolvable, and where as a consequence rational persuasion is beyond reach?

Duff's only apparent concession to this fundamental dilemma posed by his account is to suggest that conscientious objection be admitted as a defence in criminal trials in some cases. This concession, however, does not resolve the dilemma. First, principled legal disobedience seems in practice to be perceived by judicial authorities and others as a greater threat to the legal system than unprincipled disobedience.[24] Second, the range of reasons that might lead people to disobey the law that Duff's position allows for is much broader than that range of disputes traditionally captured by the notion of conscientious objection. It would seem to extend even to those who simply refused to sacrifice their personal interests to those of the community.[25] On this interpretation, the mere fact of recidivism might be taken to imply fundamental and therefore rationally unresolvable disagreement on the part of the recidivist with the values imposed by the legal system. What purpose could punishment then be said to have?

It would seem to follow that, in the absence of an argument designed to show that a society is morally justified in imposing a set of common values on its members even where equally valid optional sets of values are available, punishment of those who reject the vision of the common good captured by the law can have no legitimate point, since there is no reason for assuming that the state's view is more soundly grounded than the position of the person who has come into conflict with the law. Under these circumstances, punishment cannot be justified as a part of a rational process of persuasion. If it is then imposed and results in a change in attitude on the part of the offender, its success cannot be attributed to a rational process of persuasion. We must assume, therefore, that punishment that succeeds under these conditions succeeds for prudential reasons, in which case punishment has operated as a deterrent pure and simple. But this is to give to punishment a utilitarian role that Duff argues persuasively must undermine individual autonomy, not enhance it.

It might also be argued that Duff is committed to the position that the state is justified in imposing punishments even where it has no rational grounds for assuming that persuasion can accomplish its legitimate objectives. However, if this is the conclusion to which the account leads, it is surely indistinguishable from a purely retributivist view that punishment of those who break the law is justified for its own sake.

Concluding comments

If the discussion of this chapter is sound, we have learned a great deal about the justification of punishment, in spite of our rejection of the two most promising hybrid theories. First, any satisfactory justification of punishment will have to evaluate the practice of punishment from within the context of a working legal system. It will also have to show the relationship of punishment to dominant social practices and values, like the protection of individual liberty and respect for value sovereignty and moral autonomy.

Punishment has political and social dimensions. Its use implies a belief that the community has a right to enforce laws that unavoidably reflect values that may not be universally shared. Indeed, the very need for laws formally imposed implies disagreements about what values should guide social conduct. It would seem, therefore, that an adequate account of punishment must establish the moral grounds for state coercion and define at least in broad terms the limits to that power. Further, it must do so in a way that neither places unrealistic demands on those creating or those implementing the law nor ignores the practical realities of morally pluralistic societies.

It might be argued that our discussion to this stage simply underlines the impracticality of our search for a justification of the practice of punishment in modern pluralistic democratic societies. No such society, it might be argued, could possibly generate the kind of morally coherent legal system that any justification would seem to require. There are options, however, which we have not yet explored. To do so will carry us beyond the range of theories traditionally canvassed. However, the failure of modern systems as well as contemporary theories of punishment combined with the persistence of the view that, in spite of the lack of coherent justifications, the practice of punishment is an unavoidable feature of modern societies, suggests that moving beyond the boundaries of traditional theories may now be justified.

4

THE FUNCTION OF LAW AND THE NATURE OF LEGAL OBLIGATION

With this chapter we move beyond the critical evaluation of those accounts of punishment which have at one time or another seemed convincing. In some respects that means starting again. In other respects it means building on what has already been learned. However, before we move too far in that direction, we need to remind ourselves of the practical importance of our quest. Finding an adequate justification of punishment does pose an intellectual challenge. Trying to understand a practice as deeply entrenched as punishment is an unavoidably significant challenge for moral, political and legal theorists. However, it is the practical expression of punishment which poses the most pressing concerns. As we begin to rebuild an account of that practice, it is worth reminding ourselves of the nature and importance of those practical concerns.

Why do we need a sound justification of punishment?

In assuming the legal right to punish, the state assumes a formidable power, the power to control and direct the lives of its citizens. Equally important, there are no natural or obvious constraints on the use of this power. The desire to punish when expressed collectively has no natural point of satiation. There is no obvious formula which says clearly when enough is enough. History presents ample evidence of this fact. One needs only a limited knowledge of the history of penal practices to know that, up to the present day, instruments of punishment have been and are still being used to inflict unimaginable suffering on people for a wide variety of perceived misdeeds. Less dramatically, in our contemporary world, the use of punishment varies enormously even among countries that share common values and systems of government.[1]

A central need, therefore, is an account which explains and justifies punishment in a way which identifies its proper uses and limits.

Retributivism, the theory that over the history of discussions on the topic has appealed to many as answering this need, cannot in fact do so. Retributivist accounts can provide criteria for identifying who should be punished. They can also provide guidance in controlling punishment by insisting that like cases be treated alike. And, as we saw in our discussion of vengeance, this element of control can be very significant. What retributivist theories cannot do, however, is to establish limits to the kinds of punishment a state is justified in imposing on those who break its laws. Retributivist accounts can insist only that punishment be limited to those who are morally responsible for breaking the law and that punishment be handed out in an even-handed way. Neither requirement sets limits to the harshness or cruelty of punishments imposed.

It is not surprising, therefore, that retributivism has historically been seen by its advocates as consistent with a wide range of barbaric and cruel practices. In this sense, retributivism has not for the most part been an effective instrument of reform.[2]

The most effective penal reforms have been accomplished in modern society by shifting the focus of sentencing from punishment for reasons of desert to punishment as a means of rehabilitation and reform. Reform-oriented sentencing does provide criteria at least of a negative variety for limiting punishment. It is not overwhelmingly difficult to convince people today that physical disfigurement, maiming, the worst forms of corporal punishment, physical neglect, torture, and the like are inefficient or counter-productive instruments for the reform or rehabilitation of offenders. It is not surprising, therefore, that, over the century and a half in which forward-looking accounts of punishment have increasingly dominated the theory and practice of sentencing and corrections, significant reforms in penal practices have been achieved.

Paradoxically, forward-looking accounts of punishment taken by themselves are now thoroughly discredited at the level of both theory and practice. The result is a vacuum in the fields of sentencing and corrections that is increasingly being filled by a return to the notion of just retribution. However, from the point of view of penal reform, retributivist accounts cannot fill and have not filled the gap left by the collapse of confidence in reform- and rehabilitation-oriented sentencing criteria, namely determining acceptable limits to the severity with which a society is justified in responding to crime. This has meant that governments faced with unsettling social change, sensational crimes, rising crime rates, and genuine public fear have few grounds for resisting public pressure to institute harsher and harsher penalties.

Against this backdrop, it is not surprising that current trends in most liberal democracies are toward longer and harsher sentences, reduced emphasis on rehabilitation, elimination of parole and early release programmes, and increased reliance on incarceration for a wider and wider range of offences.[3] Neither is there any obvious end to the process. Harsh sentencing practices move to a perverse logic. Where sentences are imposed with a view to deterrence or with a view to demonstrating the strength of community revulsion to particular kinds of behaviour, failure to reduce the incidence of crime is invariably treated as an indication that the system is too lenient. What this means in practice is that the failure to control crime with any given set of punishments simply whets the public appetite for harsher sentences. Over the past two decades this is the pattern that sentencing 'reform' has followed.

What kind of theory do we need?

What has already been said suggests that, if the practice of punishment is to be restrained and disciplined, it must be guided by an account that identifies its function and thereby defines its legitimate uses and limits. What else can be said about the kind of theory for which we are searching?

Evaluation of classical accounts of punishment suggests strongly that punishment cannot be justified independently of an understanding of its place in functioning legal systems. Both of the hybrid accounts that we have examined look at punishment in this broader context and in doing so advance beyond the classical backward- and forward-looking accounts.

Our discussion to this point suggests strongly that the account we are looking for must also attempt to clarify the relation between law and morality. If, as legal positivists suggest, law has no necessary moral content, then it would seem to follow that a general moral justification of the practice of punishment in legal contexts is out of reach. That is, it is hard to see how we could generate a moral justification of punishment quite independently of any consideration of the moral character of the laws being enforced.

The supposition that there exists a strong connection between law and morality, a view that implies that the function of law is to enforce morality, also generates dilemmas. The simple fact that actual legal systems do not seem to have this function cannot be ignored. Whether or not one is under a legal obligation to obey the law does not seem to vary with the moral quality of the law in question.

What we are looking for, then, is a third possibility, an account which rejects both legal positivism on the one hand and natural law accounts on the other.

Finally, our account should also attempt to understand the relation of punishment to other values that have come to play a significant part in our collective lives. Freedom and autonomy have already been mentioned. There are others as well: forgiveness, mercy, compassion, social justice, to name the more important. Once again, the hybrid theories examined in the previous chapter go some distance in this direction. One test of the value of any alternative account of punishment, then, is whether it can clarify and justify a place for these values more effectively than classical or hybrid theories are able to do.

Previous discussion suggests that outlining the nature of the relation between law and morality would seem to be an unavoidable first step in an account of punishment. This, then, will be our task in what remains of this chapter.

Law and the legal point of view

Lon Fuller (1969) describes law as 'the enterprise of subjecting human conduct to rules.' As Hart points out (1961: 190), the most central kinds of rule are those designed to protect life and limb. Without rules of this sort, all other rules would be otiose. More than this is required, however. Rules that govern the exchange of property are needed to create a social context in which there is some point to accumulating those things needed to sustain life and render it less onerous.

The law provides both sorts of rules. It also provides a vehicle that allows a society to channel resources in the direction of institutions and practices thought to be important for the improvement of the human condition.

It has been suggested that a legal system is necessary for the pursuit of all these goals. This seems not to be true. Societies have existed and flourished after their own fashion without formal legal structures.[4] What can be said is that the law accomplishes these goals in a manner peculiar to legal systems.

Although there are many different accounts of the defining characteristics of law, the most influential analysis is that offered by Hart in *The Concept of Law*. Law, he suggests, is marked by three essential characteristics. First, in any system of laws, there will be both primary and secondary rules. The primary rules will be directed to everyone falling under the law's jurisdiction and will describe the rules of conduct prescribed by law. These laws will be validated by secondary rules of three types. There will be a 'rule of recognition' whose function is to set out 'a conclusive identification of the primary rules of obligation' (Hart 1961: 92). There will be 'rules of change' whose function is to identify those people who have the authority to introduce new primary rules and eliminate old ones (Hart 1961: 93). And finally, 'there will be secondary rules empowering individuals to make authoritative determinations of the question whether, on a particular occasion, a primary rule has been broken', that is to say, 'rules of adjudication' (Hart 1961: 94).

Second, a system of rules can properly be called a legal system only if its rules are systematically enforced and generally obeyed (Hart 1961: 113).[5]

Finally, at least some of the officials responsible for administering the system must voluntarily accept that the law is binding on themselves and others over whom the law claims authority.[6] To accept voluntarily that the law is binding is to take what Hart describes as the internal view of law and what I shall describe as the legal point of view.

A system of rules having these three characteristics is properly described as a system of law and will give rise to binding legal obligations.

What then is the legal point of view? It is the view that the law is a system of overriding rules, rules that take precedence over competing obligations or desires where there is a conflict. From the legal point of view, individuals are not free as individuals to decide: what the law is; what interpretation of the law shall prevail when the law is applied to particular cases; and whether to do what the law requires.

To commit oneself to the legal point of view, as Nicola Lacey points out (1988: 90), is to accept a limitation 'of one's freedom to decide for oneself what one ought to do in a wide range of situations'.

It is to accept, as Joseph Raz puts it, that being required by law is a 'sufficient reason for [doing] the [legally] required act'; further, that the law provides 'exclusionary reasons for disregarding reasons for non-conformity' and that 'non-legal reasons do not justify deviation from a legal requirement except if such justification is allowed by a specific legal doctrine' (Raz 1979: 30–1).

Law, morality, and the moral point of view

Given our description of law as by its very nature formal in character – formal laws, formal courts, formal enforcement – it is clear that laws are not a necessary feature of social life. The cooperation needed to overcome human vulnerability can be achieved in other ways, ways that do not require a formal state apparatus for their implementation.

We can say, however, that cooperation does require respect for rules: rules that prohibit murder and physical assault as acceptable means for accomplishing individual or group objectives; rules that regulate the transfer of property, thereby prohibiting theft and deliberate misrepresentation, among other things; and rules that coordinate access to the social resources that cooperation generates and requires. The rules providing the framework for cooperation might be grounded on custom, morality, religion, or even habit. But they will have functions similar to those of their legal counterparts.

Morality finds its place within the matrix of informal rules. Normally, the moral values of individuals and communities will coincide with, support, and reinforce related systems of rules. However, this is not inevitable. Clashes can occur. In these cases, where moral considerations are ignored or overridden, the moral objections that have been ignored will either be argued to have been without substance, or the offending conduct will be viewed with disapproval.[7] From a moral perspective, then, moral rules are overriding.

Morality has a second significant characteristic. Moral systems by their nature do not require secondary rules whose function is to identify who has the authority to make, interpret, and enforce the rules. Moral authority may be conferred by custom or religious practice or even conceded by virtue of acquired habits of obedience.[8] However, the judgement that someone is a moral authority whose directives ought therefore to be respected is itself by its very nature always a substantive moral judgement. That is to say, to view someone as a moral authority is to accept that that person is someone whose moral judgements are worthy of respect.

It is this feature of morality that Plato appeals to in arguing that moral belief must in some fundamental sense be independent of religious belief, in as much as any religious pronouncement is itself always subject to moral appraisal.[9] Socrates makes the same point when he argues in *The Crito* that each person ought to take responsibility for the moral character of her life since determining what is morally required is something which in the last analysis cannot by its very nature be delegated to others. The opinions of the gods or of the many should be respected only if they are worthy of respect. In particular, their being worthy of respect cannot derive simply from the fact that they are the opinions of the gods or of the many.

Let us describe this perspective as the moral point of view. It is a point of view that makes the individual the final authority in determining her own conduct. That is to say, from the moral point of view individuals have a responsibility to determine: what the content of morality is; how particular values or principles apply in particular situations or cases; and then to act on their own assessment of what, morally speaking, they ought to do.[10] To take the moral point of view is to assume the status of an autonomous moral agent.

Legal obligation and the moral point of view

Our description of the legal and moral points of view now brings us up against a striking difficulty; the two points of view seem logically incompatible. The moral point of view requires of those assuming it that they assess what, morally speaking, is required of them, and then act in a manner consistent with that assessment, even where doing so will bring them into conflict with non-moral rules or values. The legal point of view requires instead that individuals respect their legal obligations even where to do so clashes with their moral obligations. Thus to assume the legal point of view requires that one relinquish one's freedom to be guided by moral considerations where morality and law diverge.

There seem to be three possible responses to this dilemma. The first is to accept that the two points of view are incompatible, that the moral point of view is overriding, and that as a consequence the legal point of view is morally unacceptable. This response builds on the assumption that, other things being equal, all human beings have the capacity to become moral agents. Becoming a moral agent requires that one accept responsibility to direct one's own life. The law, on the other hand, appears to put one under an obligation to do what the law commands just because the law commands it.[11]

If the legal and the moral points of view are incompatible, then there can be no general justification of the practice of legally sanctioned punishment. This view of the matter, however, creates profound difficulties, not the least of which is the way in which it challenges common sense. Human experience does not suggest that as individuals we must choose between law and morality. On the contrary, law seems often to provide the social conditions in the absence of which the exercise of moral autonomy might well become impossible.

I take it, however, that this first response would be defeated if we could show that the legal and moral points of view are neither logically nor morally incompatible. Since this approach is more in keeping with our central task, it is this path that I propose to follow.

A second response to the apparent incompatibility of the legal and moral points of view is to suggest a strong connection between law and morality. Only when the law commands what morality either requires or permits should people understand themselves to be under an obligation to obey the law. It is this view which is implied by natural law accounts of legal obligation. However, as we have already seen, it too is unsatisfactory.

Is a third response available? Common experience would suggest that there must be. Law is a central feature of contemporary human life and has been for many centuries. Over that period, the moral point of view has not atrophied. Indeed, the commitment to the pursuit of moral autonomy is a widely shared objective of modern life. That is not to say that morality and law have always coexisted easily. On the contrary. On the other hand, it is not a feature of our experience that the moral point of view is in some fundamental way incompatible with its legal counterpart. If anything, experience would suggest that each relies in important ways on the other.

That being the case, might there be reasons for thinking that under certain conditions moral considerations might justify shifting from a moral to a legal point of view? Hart in *The Concept of Law* offers some useful guidance in this regard. Although he rejects the view that law and morality are logically related, he does see a core of good sense in the natural law view. There are five features of human life, he suggests, that point toward a need for law (Hart 1961: 189).

Although Hart himself does not point this out, these features fall into two distinct categories.

First is the fact of human vulnerability: the fragility of human life; the limited capacity of individuals to satisfy their need for food, clothing, and shelter in the absence of the assistance of others. Vulnerability creates the need for cooperation and for rules designed to make cooperation possible. Both moral and legal rules have a role in achieving this goal.

Second is a series of three factors that identify a need not simply for rules but for coercion. Human beings, Hart points out, are approximately equal in strength, have a limited capacity to understand the impact of their actions on others, and are often tempted to put their own interests first, even though they are capable of genuine concern for the welfare of others. For these reasons, those who respect the rules are vulnerable to those who do not. It is these factors to which formal instruments of coercion are a response.

This account is valuable but incomplete. In particular, it implies that the reason law has come to replace morality as a way of resolving disputes is because law offers a more efficient or effective way of ensuring compliance with rules designed to block the free use of force. This is at least partially true. However, it is not the use of formal instruments of coercion that sets formal and informal rule systems apart.[12] Rather, law deviates from morality not in the matter of coercion where law and morality have a good deal in common, but in its manner of settling disputes. Unlike informal rule systems, a necessary component of legal systems is rules of adjudication designed to bring disputes to an end by rendering a decision that is authoritative and final. Hart marks the importance of this fact as follows:

> It is obvious that the waste of time involved in the group's unorganized efforts to catch and punish offenders, and the smoldering vendettas which may result from self help in the absence of an official monopoly of 'sanctions' may be serious. The history of law does, however, strongly suggest that the lack of official agencies to determine authoritatively the fact of violation of the rules is a much more serious defect; for many societies have remedies for this defect long before the other.
> (Hart 1961: 91)[13]

What needs to be accounted for is why formal adjudication should be thought to be so necessary.

Moral agency, security, and the problem of violence

Human beings have substantial needs that are not easily satisfied. They are vulnerable to attacks causing death or physical injury. Their property is easily taken. Patterns of social cooperation are open to disruption. What this means, as Hobbes saw so clearly, is that where there are no restraints on the free use of force to accomplish human objectives there will be:

> no Arts; no Letters; no Society; and which is worst of all, continuall feare, and danger of violent death; and the life of man, solitary, poore, nasty, brutish and short.
>
> (Hobbes 1952: 85)

The free use of force, it would seem, threatens not simply human life. It attacks the capacity of human beings to live human lives.

Violence, the Oxford English Dictionary tells us, is the 'exercise of physical force so as to inflict injury on or cause damage to persons or property'. It is disruptive for two reasons. First, where there are no rules governing the use of force, or where there are people whose behaviour is unrestrained by such rules, the occurrence of violence will be unpredictable. Second, the effects of force used with a view to causing harm are equally unpredictable. Even where harm is not intended, force used coercively can have an unpredictably violent outcome. This is why our society insists that even legally sanctioned uses of force by law enforcement officers must be carefully controlled.[14]

For these reasons, those harmed by the free use of force are unlikely to be harmed in ways consistent with any variety of justice. It follows that violence has a *prima facie* immoral character.

What is less frequently noticed is that violence also has what I shall describe as an *anti-moral* character. That is to say, violence, by virtue of the way in which it does harm, can, and frequently (though not always) does, impact on the capacity of those affected to act as responsible moral agents. This feature of violence is rarely explicitly identified. But paradoxically, it is implied by much of what is said in justification of the use of force. For example, one widely shared view is that those threatened by violence have a moral right to respond using violence if necessary just because violence itself threatens fundamental rights. This view implies that those who use violence to achieve their goals both ignore and undermine the moral status of those on whom their violence impinges.[15] Political theories that identify a state of nature in Hobbesian terms imply that individuals acquire moral status and the capacity to act as moral agents only in a social setting in which explicit mechanisms are put in place to protect those entering into the social contract from violence.[16]

What is it about the nature of violence, then, that justifies the assertion that violence by its very nature can threaten the moral status of those against whom it is directed? First, moral agents act in the context of rules and are concerned for the consequences of their actions. Violence has a disrupting effect on the context in which it is present. It reduces the ability of those affected by it to plan, to assess the consequences of their actions, or to predict how their actions will be understood by those affected by them. For example, under conditions of civil disaster, background assumptions that normally condition responses to the presence of people who are strangers are easily undermined. Natural disasters, civil war, riots, war itself provide endless examples of this phenomenon.

These considerations lead to a second observation. Violence undermines the capacity of those affected to act as responsible moral agents by threatening their security and thereby forcing a shift to a self-interested perspective. This is glossed by arguments that seek to justify the right to self-defence using force if necessary. The concerns of someone forced into a posture of self-defence are inevitably self-regarding. While morality does not ignore questions of self-interest, its focus is not the interests of the agent alone. Violence gives an urgency to self-interest that, if it comes to dominate, severely inhibits the capacity of agents to assume a moral point of view.

Finally, because of the harm that violence can do to individuals, it can be used to coerce changes in the structure of values that guide action. Violence and threats of violence are frequently used in this way. Thus governments use the threat of violence to coerce the acceptance of political regimes, policies, actions, and so on. States use war and threats of war to coerce changes in the behaviour of other states. Torture is a tool of political repression. And so on. These uses of violence are designed to force changes in values in ways that negate the moral status of those against whom these tactics are directed. When encountered in this extreme form, the anti-moral character of violence is explicit.

Violence and the moral point of view

Violence creates a serious dilemma for the moral point of view. To begin with, disputes about what morally speaking is required in a particular situation are always in principle possible. Hence, although in practice they do not inevitably occur, when they do occur, the potential for irresolvable disagreement is always present.

Second, it is widely assumed that individuals have a right to use force to resist actions on the part of others that they regard as seriously immoral. If this were not true, adopting a moral point of view would imply endorsing a pacifist outlook. But not only is pacifism widely rejected, it is argued by some to be incoherent. Thus Jan Narveson argues in 'Pacifism: A philosophical analysis' that individuals have a right to their own security. Furthermore, such a right is of no value if it is not combined with a right to intervene in defence of one's own security. For, 'a right just is a status justifying preventive action'. The right to self-defence, it is frequently argued, extends particularly to defence against violence. Thus Narveson goes on to ask: 'What could that right to their own security which people have, possibly consist in, if not a right at least to defend themselves from whatever violence might be offered them?' (Narveson 1970: 72).

This brings us to a third point. Violence is both immoral and anti-moral. Yet it would seem that morality can justify recourse to the use of force in defence of moral principle or of what moral values identify as being of deep moral significance, human life for example. And although the use of force does not inevitably cause violence, it often does, particularly when it is resisted by those against whom it is directed.

Recourse to force is one obvious indication of moral disagreement. Moral disagreement may be of two sorts: there may be disagreement about the moral quality of the action, situation, or event which is the focus of the disagreement; or there may be a disagreement about whether the use of force is justified by the action, situation, or event in question.

Finally, from the point of view of morality, might does not make right. If it did, all disputes would be resolvable both in theory and in practice. Yet it seems that individuals are justified in using force to resist force, when force is being used to resolve a dispute. When this happens, the side that prevails will be the side that can muster the strongest force, which in turn suggests that, in practice at least, might makes right.

To summarize, it would seem that morality can be and frequently is used to justify a method of resolving disputes that is implicitly both immoral and anti-moral.[17] To resort to violence is not only likely to have immoral consequences but is self-defeating in as much as it undermines what it is designed to defend. This is obviously a serious defect. Is a remedy available?

Law, morality, and the resolution of disputes

Informal methods of resolving disputes can be highly effective. However, informal systems can and do break down for a wide variety of reasons. The result may be a loss of confidence in the rules themselves, an abuse of self-help enforcement practices, or a loss of confidence in those occupying dispute-settling roles.

The law, too, is a social mechanism for resolving disputes. It fulfils this role by formalizing and centralizing the tasks of making rules, adjudicating disputes, and imposing sanctions. Those assigned these tasks derive their authority from the rules themselves. The result is a dispute resolution system that lifts from individuals the right to decide: the rules by reference to which disputes will be adjudicated; how those rules will be interpreted; and whether they will respect the outcome.

Legal systems accomplish this last objective by shifting authority to use force in settling disputes from private individuals to the state. This is important because it is access to coercion that ensures that the verdict rendered by the law is final and thus brings disputes to an end. Since a legal system cannot continue to exist where the decisions of legal authorities are widely ignored, the right to use force to coerce compliance where compliance cannot otherwise be obtained would appear, therefore, to be a necessary feature of legal systems.

Law, morality, and the paradox of coercion

The law imposes a decision procedure on those caught up in disputes. The function of coercion in legal contexts is to ensure that disputes are settled in accordance with law. However, the fact of coercion gives rise to a series of problems.

Where the resolution of disputes or the enforcement of law requires the use of force, the subsequent resolution is a function of superior physical strength. But the power of the state to coerce respect for the law cannot give the law either moral or legal legitimacy. Neither in law nor in morality is there a necessary connection between the power to impose a solution and the justifiability of the solution imposed.

To begin with, the capacity of an 'official' to force compliance with a directive cannot in itself generate a legal obligation. Someone can be said to have a legal obligation to act in a particular way only where there are rules which have themselves been established in accordance with law and which the individual can see impose a particular legal obligation, or which have been followed by a legal authority in issuing a decision or directive.

Neither can the capacity of someone to enforce compliance with a set of decisions or directives confer moral legitimacy on those directives, even when they have been arrived at in accordance with law. Might does not make right. Power cannot confer moral legitimacy. What is more, as we have already seen, it is widely believed that individuals have a fundamental right and obligation to resist with force, if necessary, any use of force designed to coerce compliance with directives thought to be fundamentally immoral.

Law's apparent independence of morality is also relevant in this context. The legal point of view is self-sufficient. The law does not permit appeals to non-legal rules or values to override one's obligation to obey the law except under conditions and in ways that are themselves specified by law. Hence, individuals cannot free themselves from their legal obligations by claiming that the law is in conflict with other important obligations.[18] One reason that they cannot free themselves, of course, is the capacity of legal systems to enforce the law. The apparent independence of law from morality rests in part, therefore, on the power of coercion.

Finally, laws comprise a *system*. There is no way in which the law can tolerate refusal to obey a particular law or set of laws without thereby having its authority undermined. This characteristic of legal systems is nowhere better illustrated than in the common law offence of contempt of court. A person is in contempt who refuses to be guided by a decision of the court on any matter. The credibility of the law is undermined if even one person is able to defy an order of the court with impunity. From a legal point of view, therefore, the law comes as a system of rules.[19]

Taken together, these considerations imply two things. First, the power to coerce compliance is a necessary characteristic of legal systems.[20] But it is a secondary characteristic, something the law must be able to fall back on. That is to say, the obligations the law generates cannot be grounded exclusively or even primarily on coercion. Second, if there is a moral justification for the enforcement of law, the focus of that justification must be the legal system itself, not individual laws.

The moral justification of law: first approximations

We have already seen that both legal and informal rule systems offer ways of resolving disputes. Dispute settlement that rests on informal mechanisms, however, may be unable to resolve disputes fairly[21] or efficiently.[22] Neither can the use of force, whether formally or informally administered, guarantee a morally acceptable resolution of a dispute. There is no reason to assume that, in a contest of strength, the best solution, morally speaking, will result.

It would seem to follow, therefore, that *a shift to the legal point of view would be justified where it could be shown that approaching the resolution of disputes from a formal, i.e. legal, perspective rather than an informal one would reduce the level of violence to which those affected would otherwise be exposed.* A legal system that had this result would be justified in imposing a legal obligation to obey the law, it might be suggested, because it satisfied the necessary conditions for social order more efficiently and facilitated cooperation more effectively than available alternatives.

This first attempt at finding a moral justification for law, however, is flawed. The need for protection from violence is a central moral concern, as we have seen. But it is not the only concern. It is conceivable that a system of law could meet this test for moral acceptability even though it achieved its goal through brute intimidation. And, as we have seen, such a system would by its nature of operation imply that might makes right, thus undermining the moral status of those required to obey it.

This criticism of our first formulation suggests a second. *A shift from the moral to the legal point of view would be justified where it could be shown that approaching the resolution of disputes from a formal, i.e. legal, perspective rather than an informal one would reduce the level of violence to which those affected would otherwise be exposed, by winning widespread voluntary compliance with the legal system thus put in place.*

This formulation is an improvement on the first so long as we understand that voluntary compliance does not include voluntary obedience won by the threat of punishment. However, it is still defective because it is exposed to the argument that it is possible for legal systems to attract voluntary compliance quite independently of their moral character. Calculations of long-term interest, unreflecting, inherited, or traditional attitudes, or the mere wish to do as others do have all been suggested as reasons that might lead people to comply voluntarily with the law. This in turn implies that the legal point of view might attract voluntary compliance in spite of conclusive evidence that the system in question was deeply immoral.[23]

I do not propose to challenge this view here, though I think it a good deal less plausible than it might appear on first encounter. For, even if it could be shown that no set of non-moral considerations could provide a coherent reason for accepting the authority of the law, it remains possible that those accepting the law might do so for reasons that were in the end unsound or even repugnant from a moral perspective. The law, it might be argued, would still exist for all of that because at least some of the key officials responsible for administering the law accepted that they had an obligation to do so in accordance with the law and the law was generally obeyed.[24]

The moral justification of law

With these criticisms in mind, let us try once more. *A shift from the moral to the legal point of view would be justified*, I shall argue, *where it could be shown that approaching the resolution of disputes from a formal, i.e. legal, perspective rather than an informal one would reduce the free use of force that would be morally justifiable otherwise.* We need now to look carefully at what this implies.

It might be thought that the ideal legal system from this perspective would be one which paralleled morality in content. The appearance here is deceiving for many reasons already explored. In particular, in most modern societies moral pluralism is a social fact. In practice, an ideal morality would have to be imposed if disobedience, motivated by moral considerations, was to be overcome.

Rather, in a pluralistic society, the only potentially attainable ideal would be a system of law that approximated the characteristics of a system of voluntary binding arbitration. Under these conditions, the criteria for resolving disputes that might otherwise erupt in violence would be seen by those involved as fair, or alternatively as fair as possible in the circumstances, and therefore worthy of respect. They would by definition be the kinds of criteria and standards that they would be prepared to accept voluntarily to achieve a non-violent resolution of a dispute in which they were involved.

It is certainly arguable that this is an ideal to which at least western democracies are implicitly committed. It is an ideal that focuses attention on procedural fairness, a notion that is basic to common law, for example. It might then be argued that, where disagreements on questions of substance occurred, the fairest procedure for ending disagreement would be by majority vote, an approach to dispute resolution which again is essentially procedural in content. This approach, too, is basic to notions of fairness and justice embedded in democratic institutions.

However, even here difficulties with the ideal are apparent. Majorities are not necessarily right. Indeed, history is replete with examples of democratic governments creating morally obnoxious laws. Neither are all democratic regimes equally committed to notions of procedural fairness. Hence, the ideal is not a sound standard for assessing the justifiability of shifting to a legal point of view. Rather, what the proposal suggests is that any formal system that was seen as conducive to solutions that were, on balance, more acceptable from a moral point of view than solutions likely to result from available informal alternatives would meet the test. In particular, any system that was less arbitrary in its outcome than a system relying on the exercise of brute force, deception, and manipulation would meet the test where the option was one or the other.

Even interpreted in this way, however, this test is a significant one for several reasons. Clearly, some regimes would not satisfy it. It has in addition the clear virtue, as we shall see, of providing criteria for evaluating proposals for legal reform. It is also realistic. It does not imply that taking the legal point of view would be justified only if legally grounded directives and decisions were better than available alternatives in all respects or in every case. Rather, it implies that the legal point of view would be justified where, on balance, given available alternatives, to have a legal system in place would reduce the vulnerability of those under its authority to the justified use of force and thereby provide improved opportunities for cooperation in the pursuit by individuals of their various goals.

Morality and the enforcement of law

As we have seen, the virtue of formal as opposed to informal dispute resolution is the capacity of a formal system to bring disagreements that might otherwise be settled by recourse to violence to a final arbitrated resolution. Since there is no reason to believe that the solutions arrived at in accordance with law will always win voluntary compliance, the right to use force to ensure compliance is a necessary feature of formal legal systems. It follows that the legal point of view commits those who endorse it to law enforcement and, by implication, to the use of force should that be necessary.

The fact that coercion will normally play a role in the enforcement of law has a number of implications for our understanding of the law and the moral foundations of the legal point of view.

1 Assuming the legal point of view would be justified only where those responsible for enforcement understood themselves to be under an obligation to minimize the use of force in obtaining compliance with the law.[25] In the absence of constraints on the use of force, a legal system could not be expected to reduce justified recourse to violence to which those subject to it would otherwise be exposed.

This requirement has significant implications for legal reform. It implies, for example, that a basic test of the effectiveness and efficiency of a legal system is the extent to which it must rely on coercion to accomplish its ends. It also explains the force of arguments designed to demonstrate that the use of force relied on by a given legal system was excessive, or could be reduced without undermining the law.

This account is thus consistent with principles regarding the use of force and helps to explain why they have come to have a central place in modern discussions of law enforcement. For example, the code of ethics contained in the Council of Europe's 'Declaration on the Police' assigns to police a moral obligation to oppose violations of the law but requires that: 'In performing his duties . . . [a police officer] *may never use more force than is reasonable*' (Alderson 1984: 172). The declaration also requires that:

Police officers shall receive clear and precise instructions as to the manner and circumstances in which they should make use of arms.[26]

(Alderson 1984: 172)

These principles are echoed in the 'United Nations Code of Conduct for Law Enforcement Officials'[27] and find concrete expression in modern criminal codes, for example the Canadian code, where law enforcement is explicitly assigned to *peace* officers'.[28]

2 If the function of law is to reduce recourse to the morally justifiable use of force, it follows that the use of force has a place, but only a secondary place, in law enforcement. This in turn implies that the use of force to ensure compliance is morally justified only where the law recognizes that its primary task is to win voluntary compliance, that is, compliance not compelled by fear or coercive threats.

This principle too is widely recognized, as we shall see in more detail in the next chapter. To use just one example, J. Alderson, former Chief Constable of Devon and Cornwall in the United Kingdom, writes in a police instruction manual commissioned by the Directorate of Human Rights of the Council of Europe:

Ideally, police should aim to achieve their objectives without the use of force at all. By striking the correct attitude it is often possible to achieve these by persuasion.

(Alderson 1984: 27)

He derives this view from the Council of Europe 'Declaration on the Police' and specifically from the minimum use of force principle on which the declaration is built.

3 Legal systems by their nature confer on officials both the power and the obligation to enforce the law.[29] They also remove from officials the right to decide in accordance with non-legal values which laws should be enforced. This means that those who disobey the law risk bringing themselves into conflict with the authorities to whom the state has assigned responsibility for implementing the law.

Those who refuse to acknowledge their obligations under the law undermine the legal point of view by implying that compliance is a matter of choice. To disobey the law intentionally, then, is to invite a coercive response. To resist attempts by officials to enforce the law is to invite violence. Because of the anti-social and immoral character of violence, avoiding the kind of conflict that is a virtually inevitable consequence of refusing to acknowledge the authority of the law itself becomes a moral obligation where the law is adequately grounded from a moral point of view.

This conclusion illuminates what was referred to earlier as the paradox of coercion in a special way. We have already seen that the capacity of the state to force compliance with the law cannot in itself confer moral status on the law. On the other hand, the capacity of the state to use force to compel compliance is itself a reason for accepting the authority of the law just because defying the law invites a coercive and potentially violent response.

This is particularly true where defiance rests on an appeal to moral principle. To refuse to obey the law for reasons of moral principle is a direct threat to the legal point of view, because it implies that people have a moral right to choose which laws they will obey. A legal system cannot exist where this view is widely shared. Thus morally motivated disobedience poses a serious challenge and invites a strong reaction from those to whom responsibility for enforcing the law has been delegated.

What is here being argued is well illustrated by cases which involve the criminal offence of contempt of court. To refuse to obey a directive or decision of the court is to be in contempt. It is, in effect, to challenge the court's authority to enforce the law.

This is well illustrated by Justice Farris, Chief Justice of the Supreme Court of British Columbia, in *R. v. Poje* where he argued:

> Once our laws are flouted and orders of our courts treated with contempt the whole fabric of our freedom is destroyed. We can then only revert to conditions of the dark ages when the only law recognized was that of might. One law broken and the breach thereof ignored, is but an invitation to ignore further laws and this, if continued, can only result in the breakdown of the freedom under the law which we so greatly prize.
> (6 Western Weekly Reports, New Series, 473: 478)

Hence too, Chief Justice Brian Dickson felt constrained to say in an important Canadian Supreme Court judgment:

> It is still my opinion that 'no system of positive law can recognize any principle which entitles a person to violate the law because of his view that the law conflicted with

98

some higher social value'. . . . Such a doctrine could well become the last resort of scoundrels and in the words of Edmund Davies L.J. in *Southwark London Borough Council* v. *Williams et al.* (1971) Ch. 743, at page 746, it would 'very easily become simply a mask for anarchy'.

(*Perka et al.* v. *The Queen.*
[1984] 13 Dominion Law Reports [4th]: 14)

Finally, in a recent case in which anti-abortionists refused to abide by a court injunction requiring that they not block access to a Vancouver abortion clinic, the presiding Supreme Court Justice, Judge Wood, pointed out that it is not the function of the court 'to rule upon the morality of abortion, nor is it for this Court to legislate to fill any void that may be seen by some to exist in present law'. Rather 'it is the duty of this Court to act upon and to apply the law as it now exists, and to do so fairly and impartially to all in accordance with legal precedent'. Judge Wood concluded that:

The breach of an order of this Court is . . . an attack upon [the court] itself – that institution which alone stands between the rule of law and anarchy. The inherent jurisdiction of the Court to punish for contempt . . . is the sole device by which the Court can ensure its own continued effectiveness in the struggle to preserve the rule of law. Thus it is that the more serious the contempt the more serious the threat to the rule of law. In the whole spectrum of conduct classified as contemptuous, there can be none more sinister or more threatening than that of organized, large scale, deliberate defiance of an order of the Court.

(*Everywoman's Health Centre Society etc.* v.
Kenneth Lloyet Bridges et al.)

4 This now leads to a final point. Reliance on legal systems generates its own kind of vulnerability. No matter how reprehensible, laws create their own patterns of conduct. The fact that rules promulgated by a legal system are respected for whatever reason creates predictability and thus provides a basis for planning and for cooperation. Thus legal systems create conditions for cooperation and pattern the ways in which people can produce and enjoy those goods that cooperation makes possible.

Reliance on legally inspired patterns of cooperation creates two forms of vulnerability. First, no matter how skewed the law, rapid or revolutionary social change or the collapse of a legal system will expose people to varying degrees of insecurity. It is therefore not surprising that resistance to rapid change or to revolution is often strong even amongst those who are badly treated by the status quo, since what little they do have they cannot afford to lose.

Second, a legal system creates its own patterns of dependence, thereby exposing those who respect the law to being harmed by people who do not. It also allows people to calculate the advantages that might be gained through manipulation or fraud or bribery or through illegal use of force and so on. Furthermore, by abrogating to itself the exclusive right to enforce the law, a legal system makes people vulnerable to the way in which this function is performed. Lax, uncertain, manipulative, or corrupt enforcement will emphasize vulnerability and increase a sense of insecurity. Even-handed, effective enforcement will have the opposite effect.

Punishment, coercion, and the legal point of view

The account we have now developed illustrates why the compulsory character of law, formally insisted upon, is an essential characteristic of legal systems. Without this, the law is not binding and hence not law. Legal systems *must* remove from individuals the right to choose not to obey the law even (one might well say particularly) on moral grounds and must be prepared to compel compliance where compliance will otherwise not likely occur. Otherwise they cannot fulfil their function.

Reliance on the law also leads people to perceive morally inspired lawless behaviour as a serious threat to their security for the same reasons. Those who reserve the right to disobey the law *and to resist the state's attempt to bring them to justice for their action* are effectively repudiating the legal point of view by implying that they have no moral obligation to obey, with all that this implies for the capacity of the law to fulfil its function.

Those who take the view that their moral obligations are more fundamental than their legal obligations generate what appears to be a fundamental conflict between the legal and the moral point of view. However, because law rests on moral foundations, the conflict is resolvable by an appeal to the moral point of view. That is to say, because of the immoral and anti-moral implications of any appeal to the use of force to resolve conflict, the use of force to compel compliance of even those who refuse to obey the law on moral grounds is justified where imposing the legal point of view will function to reduce recourse to the justified use of force. This being the case, there is no fundamental incompatibility, though there may be serious tension, because the claim not to have an obligation to obey the law is subject, in principle at least, to moral resolution.[30]

Although it may not be immediately obvious, the foundations for an analysis of punishment are now in place. However, the account remains incomplete. It points to the justifiability of coercion but does not describe in detail the forms it might legitimately take. What is needed is a detailed account of the implications of the view we have developed for the use of coercion in the enforcement of law. It is to this task we now turn.[31]

5

THE ENFORCEMENT OF LAW

PART I: THE FUNCTION OF ENFORCEMENT

The account set out in the previous chapter suggests that the function of a legal system is to facilitate cooperation, by requiring that disputes to which the need for cooperation gives rise be resolved by adjudication in accordance with law using force or coercion to secure compliance where that is necessary. We have also argued that, because the use of force to accomplish individual or group objectives is potentially both immoral and anti-moral, the use of force to obtain compliance with the law is justifiable only where its use reduces recourse to what would otherwise be morally justifiable uses of force.

This principle is a valuable one for our purposes. A legal system cannot exist where those subject to it are free to choose whether or not they will obey the law and which laws they will obey. Neither can a legal system exist unless it is generally obeyed. A test of any legal system, therefore, is the extent to which force is needed to obtain compliance.

In fact, the enforcement of law in modern democratic legal systems does not rely directly on coercion. Thus, appeals to private law usually result in the resolution of disputes without recourse to coercion, something which is also true for constitutional interpretation and the interpretation of regulations. It is also the case that most people are prepared to comply voluntarily with the judgments arrived at by the courts.

No modern legal system, however, could rely simply on voluntary compliance. There are many reasons for this.[1] Self-interest is one. So is the fact of moral pluralism. In some areas, consensus on what values the law should reflect is simply impossible. Where the behaviour of those subject to the law is motivated by these factors, voluntary compliance may not be forthcoming. That being the case, when is recourse to force justified?

There is one principle of enforcement that flows directly from previous discussion. It is *the minimum force principle*, which implies that to use more force than is required to accomplish legitimate enforcement objectives is morally unjustifiable. This is not an insignificant principle, as advocates of penal reform are only too well aware. However, it leaves the objectives of enforcement unspecified.

What, then, is the goal of enforcement? Is the function of enforcement to ensure compliance with the law? Is this a feasible or morally legitimate objective? If so, is the law justified in using whatever force is necessary to ensure compliance? If the goal is compliance, should the objective be simple compliance, or is the law justified in coercing changes in the values and attitudes of those whose cooperation cannot be secured in other ways? What is the role of punishment in the enforcement process? Are corporal punishment or indefinite incarceration acceptable?

The problems these questions raise are difficult enough in their own right. They are rendered even more difficult when we recall that the legal system whose laws are to be enforced is likely to be an imperfect one. Law and morality do diverge. The laws may be unjust. The procedures set out by law for determining the law's proper application may be inadequate, or unfairly biased, and so on. What implications does this have for the enforcement of law?

Enforcement, punishment, and the notion of an ideal legal system

One view that has been vigorously defended in the past is that we can come to a clear understanding of the purpose and justification of the punishment component of enforcement only if we begin with an ideal legal system. The fact that the laws sometimes enforced are less than ideal is a seriously complicating factor. This problem can be avoided, or so it is suggested, by determining the proper function of punishment in an ideally just legal system. The resulting account can be used to evaluate the practice of punishment in actual imperfect legal systems of the sort found in the real world.[2]

To approach the justification of punishment in this way would seem to be a mistake for three reasons. First and most important, the world in which we live is an imperfect world. Our legal systems mirror this reality. Even in those societies that have made remarkable contributions to the development of law, the law itself has often been a powerful vehicle for the enforcement of prejudice, discrimination, and social injustices of many kinds.[3]

It is within the context of imperfect systems that punishment is inflicted. How, then, can a system of punishment, devised and justified within the context of an ideal legal system, be expected to provide guidance for the considerably less than perfect world in which offenders are actually sentenced and punished?

Second, punishment is just one component of enforcement. It is true that it attracts a good deal of public attention. Nevertheless, the practice of punishment works in partnership with policing and the adjudicative or trial process to accomplish the enforcement goals of the law. There are many reasons for looking at punishment as one part of a more general process, as we shall see. For our immediate purposes, however, there is a particular value to setting punishment in this wider context.

The adjudicative process is clearly one component in law enforcement. Our understanding of the purpose of a trial and the values that should guide it has developed pragmatically and in direct response to the imperfections of human nature and the imperfections of the legal process itself, combined with an appreciation of the enormous power that the enforcement process places in the hands of the state. For example, the law of evidence that has evolved in common law was not devised in response to speculation about the function of a trial in an ideal world of just laws and unfailingly honest officials. To the contrary, it developed in response to an awareness bred of experience of the kinds of safeguards required to ensure a just outcome for an accused faced with the need to defend himself in a court of law guided by imperfect officials in an imperfect world.

The same could be said about the way in which our understanding of law enforcement by the police has developed. Our conception of the appropriate use of police power has evolved in light of actual experience with policing and the need to control and direct the powers which the law grants to the police.

Why, then, should punishment be thought to be different? One reason is that punishment is inflicted only on those who have been found guilty of an offence. The police, it might be argued, interact with those who are law-abiding as well as offenders and are not always in a position to know the difference. Caution is required to protect the innocent. Similarly, the purpose of a trial is to identify beyond a reasonable doubt (in the case of a criminal trial) the guilt of an accused. Until such time as the outcome is certain, the court must treat all alike.

Offenders, on the other hand, have been found guilty in a court of law. They have set themselves apart by their own actions. Society is therefore justified, or so it might be argued, in treating offenders differently. This would suggest that the administration of sentences imposed by a criminal court can be legitimately distinguished from other aspects of law enforcement.

What is odd about this argument is that all the factors that have led society carefully to define appropriate uses of state power apply equally to sentencing and the administration of sentences. Abuses in the use of power, the capacity for error, the potentially harmful impact of coercion on those who experience it, are present at every stage of the enforcement process. Building an understanding of the role of punishment in light of known abuses and failures would seem as appropriate here as elsewhere.

Third, there is something very misleading in talk about ideal systems of justice. To begin with, law is needed, at least in part, to facilitate the peaceful resolution of disagreements. If we had available to us a comprehensive and homogeneous view of morality, our whole perception of the need for law might well undergo substantial changes. Such a view, however, is not only distant, it may well be suspect as a moral vision. Our contemporary world is deeply pluralistic. Inevitably, therefore, there are disagreements about what a consistently just legal system would be like. What this means is that punishment, if used, will be imposed in a world of individuals with differing conceptions of the nature of justice. Our task in part is to find a justification of punishment that reflects this fact. Utopian visions seem inadequate in this context.

Finally, focusing on punishment in an ideal legal system can have the effect of placing certain assumptions about the nature and function of law enforcement in a context where they are hard to test empirically. For example, discussions about punishment in ideal settings project the view that the function of enforcement is simply the identification and punishment of offenders. In practice, however, this is not so. The police spend only a small fraction of their time in this role. What is more, the exercise of police power requires an extensive use of discretion. Finally, there is little evidence that the identification and punishment of offenders actually results in a reduction of crime.[4] All of this suggests that, if enforcement is restricted to the identification and punishment of offenders, it has little prospect of achieving its goal, which is securing that the law is obeyed.

The same is true of the trial process. Many of the protections which restrict the ways in which evidence of criminal activity can be obtained and introduced in court serve quite explicitly to frustrate the ability of authorities to bring culprits to justice. Rather, they have to do with a vision of human dignity and the need to protect the innocent, even at the sometimes considerable cost of allowing the guilty to go free.

All of this suggests that law enforcement is a much more complicated process than might appear to be the case. Our task in what follows is to unravel some of those complexities and to attempt to understand their implications for the practice of punishment.

Let us return, then, to an examination of law enforcement within the context of societies of the sort we are familiar with, and address the following questions. Should law enforcement be a priority in contemporary society? If so, what are appropriate law enforcement goals and what principles should guide the pursuit of those goals?

Why enforce the law?

There is a sense in which this question has now been answered. At any rate, we have seen what we have argued to be a moral justification for enforcing the law. A morally justifiable reason for enforcing the law is to reduce morally justifiable recourse to the free use of force in the resolution of disputes.

This response provides the foundation for our discussion. However, as it stands it is too general and abstract to provide us with a detailed understanding of the function of law enforcement. What is needed is a more careful look at the reasons that specific groups in a community might have for wanting the law enforced. We also need a more detailed account of what counts as law enforcement, what, that is to say, law enforcement consists in.

Why enforce the law: the victim's perspective

There is something of a paradox in asking why, looked at from the perspective of a victim, the law should be enforced. The victim, after all, is a victim because the law was not successfully enforced in the first instance. Looking at the question from the victim's perspective, however, can help us identify a number of things. First, it can help us to identify the kinds of harm that successful enforcement can prevent. Second, it can illustrate the fact that law enforcement is a complex process both in terms of its goals and in the ways in which it is carried out. Finally, it can help us to identify what it is that sets the criminal law apart from civil law, what it is about some actions that justifies the imposition of sanctions because they are contrary to law.

The effect of crime on its victims is not uniform. Not all crime is violent, or involves loss of property. Some crimes are very serious, for example murder, some quite minor, for example minor traffic infractions or the theft of small sums of money. Nevertheless, criminal behaviour is harmful in typical ways.

To begin with, criminal behaviour can result in direct material harm to victims. Physical assault resulting in bodily harm is an example, as is murder, or theft or vandalism. Where there is direct material harm, something is taken that the victim would otherwise have been able to enjoy, something to which he was entitled under the law.

The harms caused when people are deprived of material assets like physical health in legally unjustified ways can alter their lives in dramatic ways. However, in and of itself, unjustified material deprivation does not and cannot justify the imposition of sanctions. Serious harm can be caused by many things: natural disasters, breach of contract, civil harms or torts, and so on. Consequently, if punishment is justified, it must be for a reason that goes beyond the simple fact that criminal behaviour can cause unjustified material harm.

There is a second kind of harm that can result from criminal behaviour. Criminal activity can be the source of unfairness. There is the unfairness experienced by a victim who has been directly harmed, the unfairness of the pain, discomfort, disruption, and disability that result from physical injury, for example. There is also the unfairness that occurs when some enjoy benefits they have not earned through tax evasion, or theft and so on. Here, the victims are the people who, as a consequence, are required to carry more than their fair share of the costs.[5]

Once again, however, the fact of unfairness does not in itself justify imposing sanctions. There is much about life that is unfair. Some people are by nature endowed with good health, some are not; some are the victims of accidents, others are not; some are the fortunate beneficiaries of the law or government action, or economic developments, some are not. And some are victims of unfair treatment that happens not to be contrary to the law.[6]

Thirdly, criminal activity may undermine the moral and legal status of victims. It can have the effect of interfering with a victim's ability to pursue his goals and interests, thus undermining his autonomy. This is obvious where the victim is directly and seriously affected. The victim of a murder is thereby deprived of autonomy in an absolute sense. Other harms may have a less decisive but nevertheless real impact. A person who is physically disabled by an attacker will be restricted as a consequence in the activities in which he can subsequently participate. The loss of physical possessions removes the choices that their possession would otherwise make possible.[7]

Victims also experience secondary or indirect harms as a consequence of their victimization. The experience of victimization can and frequently does alter the victim's attitudes and feelings in a number of ways. The Canadian urban victimization survey found, for example, that 'many of the victims of break and enter . . . experience some form of crisis reaction quite apart from the suffering caused by their actual material loss. This invasion of one's home often produces a heightened concern about and fear of crime more generally' (Solicitor General of Canada 1983: 2–3). The urban victimization survey also showed that victims are somewhat more likely to believe their neighbourhood crime rate is high than are non-victims and are more likely to consider the crime problem in their neighbourhood to be serious. For example, while 56 per cent of the women residents in the urban areas surveyed felt unsafe walking alone in their neighbourhoods at night, the percentage rose to 65 per cent for women who had experienced some type of violent victimization (Solicitor General 1984a: 10).

Many crimes, particularly those that are violent, create fears of retaliation and result in a sense of intimidation which in turn can affect personal relationships and reduce the ability of those affected to seek the protection of the law.[8]

Victimization can also cause harm by undermining a victim's perception of his legal status. There are two reasons for this. A person who breaks the law implies by his own behaviour that he does not respect his victim's rights under the law. The fact that the victim's legal rights have not been respected may also imply that they are illusory, thus undermining the victim's confidence in the ability or willingness of the law to provide protection.[9]

Victimization can harm a victim's perception of his moral status. People who trample on the rights of others show contempt for those they offend against. They imply by their actions that their victims are not worthy of respect. Their actions also suggest that the law has failed to protect their victims because it does not care about them or does not see them as worthy of protection. As Hume puts it: 'men always consider the sentiments of others in their judgements of themselves' (Hume 1896: 303).

Jean Hampton makes a similar point in a discussion of 'Forgiveness, resentment and hatred' when she points out that:

> When someone wrongs another, she does not regard her victim as the sort of person who is valuable enough to require better treatment.
>
> (Murphy and Hampton 1988: 44)

Jefferie Murphy argues:

> One reason we so deeply resent moral injuries done to us is ... because such injuries are ... messages. They are ways a wrongdoer has of saying to us, 'I count but you do not', 'I can use you for my purposes' or 'I am here up high and you are there down below.'

He goes on to say:

> Intentional wrongdoing insults us and attempts (sometimes successfully) to degrade us .... It is a moral injury, and we care about such injuries.
>
> (Murphy and Hampton 1988: 25)

One thing that victims of crime need, then, is 'help to restore their dignity and self-respect' (Randle 1985: 19).

Once again, however, it is clear that none of these harms is unique to victims of crime. They may result from the actions of friends, employers, colleagues, school-mates, and so on. Neither are the moral harms caused by criminal acts by their nature more serious or threatening than those resulting from actions not criminal in nature. In some instances, of course, they are a deep threat. Sexual assault, family violence, threats to one's life are virtually always very traumatic. But not all crimes fall into this category. Theft of small sums or items, and many traffic offences, are examples. Equally, actions that we have not criminalized can be deeply disturbing; divorce, disloyalty, hypocrisy can all cause deep wounds.

It follows that we need to look further for the key to the distinction between those harms for which public sanctions are justified and those for which they are not.

There is a fourth and, as it turns out, decisive harm which criminal behaviour causes, namely the undermining of confidence in the legal system itself. Creating a legal system, we have argued, is one way for human beings to respond to their vulnerability to violence and manipulation by those stronger than themselves. The law prohibits people from exploiting each other's weaknesses in particular ways. Its prohibitions create legal obligations that the law is committed to enforcing.

The experience of victimization undermines confidence in the capacity of the law to provide the protection it sets out to offer. It does so in two ways. First, it underlines the victim's vulnerability to the aggressive actions of others. This in turn can create fear and thus undermine the victim's sense of security, which in turn may prevent him from doing what he might otherwise choose to do.

The law also creates its own sort of vulnerability. It requires that individuals delegate important aspects of their own protection to the law. It requires that they follow rules that also make them vulnerable in particular ways, rules pertaining to the possession or use of weapons, for example. The law compensates for this by offering protection and by creating opportunities that otherwise would not be available. It requires, for example, that rules about the exchange of property be respected. It requires that grievances be resolved in particular ways and prohibits recourse to self-help remedies that would otherwise be available. And so on. Those who respect the law do so on the assumption that others will as well. In the absence of this assumption, the law cannot provide the benefits it promises. That is to say, those who obey the law expect that others will as well and rely on the truth of that assumption as they interact with others.

Traffic laws provide a graphic example here. The use of auto-mobiles has led to the creation of a complex system of traffic laws without which car travel would be either very dangerous or impossible. Drivers assume that others will respect those laws. In the absence of that assumption, individuals would not know on which side of the street to drive, how to proceed at traffic lights, when to yield the right of way and so on. That is to say, as individuals, we rely on others respecting the rules that we respect. This makes us vulnerable in ways that would not otherwise exist. Because we assume that other drivers too will respect the rules, we become vulnerable to those who do not do so. The result can be as minor as simple inconvenience or as serious as physical injury or death.

The experience of victimization can undermine the victim's confidence in the law in three ways. It can undermine the victim's assumption that he is justified in assuming that for the most part others are law-abiding. That this is a real consequence of victimization is evidenced by the results of urban crime and victimization surveys. Second, the experience of victimization can also undermine confidence in the commitment of those responsible for enforcing the law to fulfilling their obligations. Finally, victimization can undermine victims' confidence in the capacity of those responsible for enforcing the law to do so.[10]

Law enforcement, then, is needed to maintain and build the confidence of victims that the harms they have experienced are acknowledged by others as real harms, that there is a commitment to fairness in the way the law is enforced, and that, as individuals, they and others like them do have the moral and the legal status that the law purports to give them.

It is therefore for victims a matter of considerable importance that the law be enforced.

Why enforce the law: the offender's perspective

It might seem perverse to ask why someone who has broken the law would or should want the law enforced.[11] The paradoxical character of the question is relieved in part by recognizing that offenders can also be (and frequently are) victims.[12] They are vulnerable in all the ways we have already described. For the most part, they have no special protection from criminal acts. And where the special protection they may sometimes have, perhaps as a member of a crime syndicate, may reduce their vulnerability in some respects, it may well increase it in others. For example, they may become vulnerable to the exercise of power which is itself relatively unrestrained by law on the part of the group of which they are a part or its leader.

It is also true that much crime is parasitic on the law. Theft, for example, would not be possible if there were no laws defining the rights of ownership. Thus, if thieves did not believe that their possession of what they stole would be respected, there would be no point to theft. These observations, however, do not relieve the sense of paradox engendered by our question. Would it not be more appropriate to say of offenders that their behaviour implies a desire on their part that the law should be enforced except in their own particular case?

Once again, the truth of this general observation has to be qualified. The offender is involved in a contest which he may well lose. He knows that the legal system is committed to preventing him from breaking the law. In breaking the law he takes the risk that he will be found out. The risk is substantial in as much as he is confronting the power of the state. If he does lose, he is drawn into an unequal contest in which he is vulnerable to the misuse of power on the part of the representatives of the state. Offenders do occasionally benefit from the arbitrary use of state power. However, for most offenders most of the time, the law is their best defence against the kind of victimization to which all human beings are vulnerable. Even when incarcerated (one might appropriately say, particularly when incarcerated), the rule of law is better than the rule of the jungle.

Why enforce the law: the authorities' perspective

Those who break the law set themselves above the law. They imply by their actions that the law does not apply to them. In so doing, they challenge the authority of the law. For, if the law does not apply to those who break it, it does not apply to anyone. Those who break the law also raise questions about the capacity of the authorities to enforce the law and challenge the law's moral authority in requiring compliance.

Those who break the law imply by their behaviour a kind of contempt for the law and those assigned responsibility for its administration and enforcement. It is not surprising that 'contempt' is the word used by courts when their directives are ignored or disobeyed.[13] The same language is equally appropriate where the directives of other officials with responsibility for enforcing the law are concerned.[14] It follows that the status of those who act on behalf of the state in administering the law is dependent on the extent to which their decisions and directives are accepted as authoritative and followed.

Why enforce the law: the public's perspective

Members of the public are for the most part rarely the direct victims of even minor criminal offences. Neither are most members of the public likely to find themselves accused of being offenders. Nevertheless, the public's perception of law enforcement is very significant. The law builds patterns of trust and reliance on the part of individuals. It prohibits recourse to the free use of force in settling disputes. It coordinates social behaviour, thus encouraging some patterns of cooperation and discouraging others. Finally, it structures the ways in which social goods are shared.

Confident of their personal security, members of the public can engage in tasks that otherwise they would not risk. Knowing what patterns of cooperation are legally sanctioned, individuals can plan their activities with some confidence about the response their activities are likely to evoke from others. Knowing the rules governing how the goods that result from social cooperation will be distributed, individuals can gauge their efforts, calculate their interests, and anticipate their returns.

A legal system can be said to exist, we have argued, where two conditions are satisfied: there must be widespread public compliance with the law, and at least some officials responsible for administering the law must endorse the legal point of view. If these are necessary conditions and widely understood as necessary conditions, it would follow that confidence that the law can be relied on to fulfil its various functions will be built on a widely shared belief that compliance with the law is widespread and that key officials responsible for law enforcement have the capacity to enforce the law and are committed to doing so.

As we have seen, victimization does undermine the confidence of victims in the ability of the law to protect them. Victimization can also have a direct impact on the confidence of the wider public in the ability of the law to offer reliable protection. Personal experience and media reports of community reactions to criminal activity provide evidence of this. People who believe that there has been an increase in crime in their neighbourhood will begin to take special precautions to protect themselves. This will often include demands for improved enforcement. It is also clear that fear of crime can reduce in significant ways the willingness of people to do things that they might otherwise do.

Crime impacts on the public in several ways. Results of the

Canadian urban victimization survey suggest that, for example, '[r]epeated exposure to threatening situations, vulnerability to the aftermath and consequences of violence, and the lack, real or perceived, of adequate avenues of redress all influence perception of risk, and therefore fear' (Solicitor General 1985a: 1). The response of the elderly to crime illustrates this point. Available research indicates that, although the elderly are the least likely of all groups to be victimized by crime, 'where one older person is victimized, the whole elderly community tends to identify with the victim. The result can be fear and a tendency for many seniors to isolate themselves from the community' (Randle 1985: 21).

Those who break the law may harm their victims in specific and often very damaging ways. However, as we have seen, it is not the private harm that justifies inflicting sanctions on offenders. What then is the public harm?

Victimization underlines personal vulnerability and raises questions about the capacity of the law to offer the protection it promises, as we have seen. Evidence of victimization raises questions for members of the public, whether they have experienced victimization directly or not. The belief that the law can be broken with impunity can lead people to question whether most people are law-abiding. It can also lead people to question the capacity or willingness of enforcement officers to perform their duties.

To raise doubts of this sort is to raise doubts about the legal and the moral authority of the law. Loss of confidence in the ability of the law to fulfil its function occasions fear and a growing sense of vulnerability and injustice. This phenomenon is frequently reported in the popular press. For example, fear, anxiety, depression, a sense of vulnerability are often cited by reporters where the authorities are unable to solve violent crimes. News stories in Canadian newspapers following the capture of the person thought to have perpetrated a series of murders over a period of several months following his escape from a penitentiary illustrate this well. One paper, *The Globe and Mail*, carried the following headline: 'Killer's capture ends nightmare for New Brunswick town'. The lead paragraph of the story which followed spoke of the 'relief and joy' that 'swept through the Mirimichi community . . . at the news that escaped murderer Alan Legere had been captured . . . .' One of the residents of Mirimachi is reported as saying: 'Now we feel free, we feel so good. . . . We were sleeping with a gun in our bedroom. We were really terrified' (*The Globe and Mail*, November 25, 1989: 1). In a similar vein, the business pages of many papers attributed a lack of small investor involvement in the stock market over 1989 to the spectacular revelations about illegal insider trading by New York stockbrokers.

This loss of confidence in turn undermines the ability of the law to fulfil its function. For example, the *Report of the Canadian Committee on Corrections* comments that 'police cannot *effectively* carry our their duties with respect to law enforcement unless they have the support and confidence of the public' (Ouimet 1969: 41). This view is echoed by the United States National Advisory Commission on Higher Education for Police Officers, which pointed out that '[t]he way the public treats the police clearly affects the ability of the police to accomplish their objectives' (Sherman 1978: 28).

The findings of the Canadian urban victimization survey help us to understand why this is so. The survey shows that the police depend on the public to report crimes, since only about 3 per cent of crimes are known because police were actually on the scene when they occurred. Unless crime is reported, the police cannot do their job. However, fewer than 50 per cent of crimes are reported.[15] One of two significant reasons for this phenomenon is a judgement by victims who fail to report offences that the police would not have been able to do anything about it anyway (Solicitor General 1984a: 2–3). This finding is confirmed by American studies. The National Advisory Commission on Higher Education for Police Officers reports in *The Quality of Police Education* that: 'Research on criminal victimization has consistently found that many citizens, up to half in some surveys, do not even bother to tell the police about the crimes committed against them often because they believe that there is little the police can do' (Sherman 1978: 29).

Police corruption is a problem for much the same reason. The National Advisory Commission reports that '[p]olice organizations in which corruption is widespread tend to be inefficient in providing basic police services' (Sherman 1978: 27). They go on to point out that '[r]evelations of corruption clearly undermine public respect for the police and may even undermine public respect for the law itself' (Sherman 1978: 28). That is to say, inefficient law enforcement undermines confidence in the legal and moral authority of the law.

Those actions we call crimes, then, do have an important public dimension to which private remedies do not provide an adequate response. Indeed, civil law remedies for private disputes are possible only if those who bring their disputes to the court for resolution can be confident that the law as interpreted by the court will be enforced. For this reason, failure to follow the decisions and directives of civil as well as criminal courts has the character of a criminal offence.[16]

It does not follow from what has been argued that evidence that some people do not respect the law must lead inevitably to a loss of confidence in the ability of the law to fulfil its various functions. If it did, no legal system could exist for long, since in modern legal systems the law is frequently broken.[17] Rather, evidence that there are some people who are not prepared to obey the law can undermine confidence in the law only if it is taken to imply that those responsible for enforcement are not committed or willing to fulfil their responsibilities in a conscientious way, or alternatively if it is taken as evidence that the people with whom they are likely to come into contact cannot in fact be trusted for the most part to obey the law.

The function of law enforcement

If what we have argued is true then the task facing those responsible for enforcement is to provide convincing support for the assumption that, while not everyone is prepared to obey the law all the time, nevertheless it is the case that people generally can be trusted to obey the law most of the time.

How would we expect a legal system to accomplish this task? That is to say, how would we expect authorities, whose goal was to demonstrate to those subject to the law that public confidence in the law was justified, to go about the task of enforcement?

First, we would expect enforcement authorities to seek to demonstrate that the law was in fact widely respected, if indeed this was the case. We would also expect them to provide evidence that for the most part people were in fact prepared to obey the law and could be trusted to do so. Finally, we would expect them to provide evidence that the authorities were committed to carrying out their duties in accordance with law and had the support of the public in so doing.

The evidence needed to justify continuing confidence in the law would not be convincing unless the public also believed there was a commitment on the part of the authorities to detecting offences and bringing those found guilty of breaking the law to justice, since the law could not fulfil its function where those who disobeyed it did so with impunity. Further, if the account we have given is correct, we would expect that public confidence would be undermined if the force used in the enforcement process was more than was thought to be necessary or appropriate to ensure that those guilty of breaking the law were identified, and tried in accordance with law.

In short, the first task of a system of enforcement committed to sustaining public confidence in the enforcement would be to *demonstrate* that the law was widely respected and that those charged with the responsibility of enforcing the law were committed to fulfilling their responsibilities in a lawful manner.

Second, we would expect enforcement to be oriented toward *persuasion*, since *persuading those under the law's authority that the law ought to be obeyed would be one way of ensuring that it generally was obeyed.* Further, given the account we have developed, we would expect the process of persuasion to be oriented toward identifying the role of the law in reducing recourse to the use of force in settling disputes and the importance of this for those affected by it for protecting individual and collective security and enhancing the possibilities for cooperation.[18]

Finally, an important task for building confidence in the capacity of the law to fulfil its function would be enablement, a feature of enforcement that is often overlooked. The law will not be obeyed where people do not have the assistance they need if they are to obey it. For example, fear of retaliation,[19] simply not knowing what the law required, involvement in a dispute from which one could not seem to extricate oneself for whatever reason might all impede compliance. We would normally expect that efficient enforcement would involve removing those impediments and assisting people to obey the law who might not do so in the absence of that assistance.

What our account of the function of enforcement implies, therefore, is that enforcement involves three tasks: demonstrating that for the most part those under the law's authority are prepared to obey the law, that those responsible for enforcement are able and willing to fulfil their responsibilities in a lawful way; persuading those who might not otherwise do so to obey the law; and, finally, enabling those who might not otherwise be able to do so to obey the law.

Testing the theory

Earlier it was suggested that enforcement had three components, policing, adjudication, and sentencing and sentence administration.

If enforcement has the functions described, we should expect to see this illustrated in the ways in which enforcement was carried out. Our next task, then, is to show that this is the case by examining briefly the policing and adjudication functions of law, as they have evolved in modern democratic countries. A clearer understanding of what efficient enforcement requires for policing and adjudication on our account of the matter should provide us with the grounding we need to move to an analysis of the role of sentencing and sentence administration in the enforcement process.

PART II: THE PRACTICAL DIMENSIONS OF ENFORCEMENT – POLICING AND ADJUDICATION

The function of police work

It is a common misperception that the police are primarily concerned with the task of identifying and bringing to justice those who have committed offences. However, time studies of police work show that between 75 per cent and 80 per cent of a police officer's time is spent in community activities not directly related to criminal investigations. J.A. Blake, in a discussion of 'The role of police in society', describes these community activities as 'non-enforcement functions', though they include: 'intervention in family quarrels, work with juveniles, rescue and paramedical emergency work and crime prevention' (Blake 1981: 78). Lawrence Sherman refers to a study done of calls to the Syracuse Police Department that found that 'only 10 per cent of them afforded a potential opportunity to enforce the law' (Sherman 1978: 21).

The fact that police spend as little time as they do in the detection and prosecution of crime is significant. It is also significant that commentators typically take the view that these other activities are not enforcement tasks. Blake and Sherman are not exceptions in this regard. This common view, however, is not consistent with police practice, police manuals, or empirical studies of the enforcement practices of the police.

How, then, are the functions of the police normally described by commentators and police manuals? And are those descriptions consistent with the view that the three dominant tasks of enforcement are: demonstrating that the law is generally obeyed; persuading those who might not otherwise do so to obey the law; and enabling

118

people who might otherwise find it difficult or impossible to obey the law to do so?

According to Blake, 'most police manuals state that the primary functions of the police are (1) to prevent crime; (2) to detect crime and apprehend offenders: (3) to maintain order in the community; and (4) to protect life and property' (Blake 1981: 77). Sherman identifies eight principal policing objectives:

1　To prevent and control conduct widely recognized as threatening to life and property (serious crime).
2　To aid individuals who are in danger of physical harm, such as the victim of a criminal attack.
3　To protect constitutional guarantees, such as the right of free speech and assembly.
4　To facilitate the movement of people and vehicles.
5　To assist those who cannot care for themselves: the intoxicated, the addicted, the mentally ill, the physically disabled, the old, and the young.
6　To resolve conflict, whether it be between individuals, groups of individuals, or individuals and their government.
7　To identify problems that have the potential for becoming more serious problems for the individual citizen, for the police or for government.
8　To create and maintain a feeling of security in the community.

(Sherman 1978: 22)

What then do these accounts imply for the function of enforcement as we have described it?

The role of the police and the demonstration function

Both these accounts identify prevention as the primary task of law enforcement. This view has an impressive history. In *On Crimes and Punishments*, Beccaria argues:

It is better to prevent crimes than to punish them. This is the chief aim of every good system of legislation . . . .

(Marin 1981: 19)

Beccaria's dictum was heeded in one of the first directives issued to the Metropolitan London police in 1829, which observed:

119

It should be understood, at the outset, that the principal object to be attained is the prevention of crime. To this goal, every effort of the police is to be directed. The security of person and property, the preservation of public tranquillity and all the other objects of a Police Establishment will thus be better effected than by the detection and punishment of the offender, after he has succeeded in committing the crime.

(Marin 1981: 20)

Sherman, speaking of the American experience with law enforcement, points out that '[p]reventive patrol consumes the greatest portion of police resources and is the most expensive item in the criminal justice budget' (Sherman 1978: 23). J.W. Cooley, a Royal Canadian Mounted Police inspector, suggests in a discussion of 'police discretion and public attitudes' that '(t)he law is best enforced, its aim is best achieved, when the prime responsibility of the police is the prevention of violations' (Cooley 1981: 188).

If the primary function of enforcement is to maintain or build public confidence in the capacity of the law, by demonstrating that the law is generally obeyed, then it is not surprising that crime prevention is so widely regarded as one of the central tasks of enforcement. There can be no more effective way of demonstrating that public confidence in the law is warranted than the absence of the kind of behaviour the law is put in place to discourage.[20]

Prevention effectively carried out can help to demonstrate that public confidence in the law is warranted. However, no modern society could expect preventive measures to secure universal compliance. General compliance, of course, is compatible with defiance on the part of some individuals. If breaches of the law elicited no response either from the public generally or from those charged with responsibility for enforcing the law, it is unlikely that respect for the law would or could remain stable. Demonstrating commitment to enforcing the law must entail, therefore, a commitment to detecting offences and apprehending offenders.

This reality is reflected in the descriptions of the functions of police by both Blake and Sherman. Sherman gives detection a less dominant role than Blake, who identifies it as one of four functions. Neither list, however, suggests that detecting crime and apprehending offenders is or ought to be the highest priority of law enforcement. Our discussion of the adjudicative component of law enforcement will confirm that the same is true at the trial stage as well. Nevertheless, crime detection plays an important role in demonstrating police commitment to law enforcement.

The need to demonstrate a commitment to *conscientious* enforcement is also reflected in the oath that police officers are frequently required to take on appointment to a police force. For example, The Royal Canadian Mounted Police Act requires that each officer on joining the force swear that he or she will 'faithfully, diligently and impartially execute and perform the duties required . . . as a member of the Royal Canadian Mounted Police and will truly obey and perform all lawful orders and instructions . . . without fear, favour or affection of or towards any person. So help me God.' J.W. Cooley, points out that this oath is similar to the oath taken by most Canadian police officers and, by implication, officers in other countries as well (Cooley 1981: 187).

Although many professions have codes of ethics, the requirement that practitioners take an oath before assuming their duties is quite restricted. That police officers should be required to make a public commitment is therefore significant, particularly since police work is not widely regarded as a profession. The function of an oath is to provide public evidence that the person taking the oath understands what is expected of him and understands himself to be under a moral obligation to fulfil his obligations. An oath cannot guarantee that those responsible for enforcing the law will do so in accordance with law. On the other hand, it is one way of underlining the nature of the commitment that police work requires. And it is a way of demonstrating that those responsible for law enforcement have a moral as well as a legal obligation to fulfil their duties conscientiously.

The role of the police and the function of persuasion

If the existence of law depended on general compliance with the law, and if preventing crime were the most important objective of police work, then we would expect that persuading people to obey the law would play a central role in law enforcement. Studies of police work show that this is indeed the case. Persuasion is an important part of that 80 per cent of police work that does not involve the detection of crime and the apprehension of offenders. Virtually all studies of police work have pointed to the important role played by the police in dealing with personal problems and disputes. For example, 'one study of telephone calls to a metropolitan police department . . .

121

found that over half of the calls appeared to be requests for help with personal or interpersonal problems, seeking police assistance as philosopher, friend, and guide' (Sherman 1978: 20).

Police are frequently called to deal with domestic disputes, where their function is to negotiate a non-violent solution acceptable to both sides. The fact that the police have in the past been widely criticized for their lack of expertise in this regard simply serves to underline the importance of this kind of 'conflict management' in police work.[21]

Work with juvenile offenders offers another excellent example where coercion is normally a last resort. Issuing warnings, talking to parents, persuading those involved to seek the assistance of community groups and agencies are all activities that are typical of police work with juveniles. A similar role is played in dealing with people who are distraught, mentally disturbed, angry, intoxicated, frustrated and so on.

One of the points at which persuasion is a clear option is where the police are called on to exercise discretion. This is an aspect of law enforcement to which we shall return below. However, it is important to examine its significance in the context of this function.

For the most part, literal application of the law is not possible. As one commentator has pointed out: 'A chief constable who decided to prosecute every ascertainable breach of the law would exhaust his force, overload officers of the courts, and be an appalling nuisance' (Cooley 1981: 189). Faced with a possible offence, a police officer must decide whether to lay a charge and what charge to lay. If preventing crime is a central goal, then asking whether proceeding with a formal charge is the best way of achieving this goal is unavoidable. In many situations it will not be. Taking a juvenile home to his parents, convincing a potentially violent spouse to spend the night with a friend or in a hotel, taking an intoxicated person to a hostel might all be more conducive to winning compliance with the law than laying a charge. In each case, persuading the individuals involved to resolve their problem in a manner that is compatible with the law is an obvious option.

The role of the police and the enabling function

The role of the police in prevention and persuasion is frequently ignored. The enabling function of the police is even less visible.

Yet it is central to a good deal of what the police do. If we return to the eight objectives of police work set out by Sherman and quoted earlier, it becomes clear on examination that most of them, namely 2, 3, 4, 5, 6 and 7, are enablement activities. This too should not be surprising if the function of enforcement is as we have described it.

Studies of how the police actually allocate their time show that there is a widespread consensus about what some of their enabling functions are. In domestic disputes, for example, one central function of intervention is to enable those involved to resolve their differences in non-violent ways. This might mean transporting family members to a shelter, or persuading an abusive parent to give up a child to a child welfare worker and so on. The police are also called on to help people caught in a violent conflict by persuading them to use peaceful means to sort out their problems, or by removing them from conflict situations involving or threatening violence, to allow for a cooling-off period. Police are also required to ensure that individuals are assisted in finding medical help where accidents have occurred or where individuals are in obvious need of medical attention.

Recent trends in police work also illustrate the importance of the enabling function. Developing programmes designed to encourage and assist people to live within the law is now widely acknowledged to be an appropriate police function, as programmes like neighbourhood watch, school visits, block parents' houses and public education initiatives demonstrate. The role of the police in answering queries about the law is another important enablement activity.

To see that one of the three principal tasks of law enforcement is to assist people to obey the law is to see law enforcement in a new light. It is also to add an important dimension to our understanding of how the law can accomplish the goal of reducing the justified use of violence in the resolution of social disputes. Finally it links to our earlier claim that the function of law is to reduce vulnerability to violence, facilitate cooperation, and structure the sharing of the benefits of social goods. Enabling people to obey the law serves all three purposes.

Adjudication

The second component of enforcement is adjudication. A criminal trial normally has two tasks. The first is to determine guilt or innocence, the second to ensure that those found guilty are sentenced in accordance with law. It is the first of these two functions that will be the focus of the discussion in this section. The second will be discussed in detail in the next chapter.

The simple view of the function of the first phase of a trial is that its purpose is to ascertain the guilt or innocence of the accused. However, such a view provides little help in understanding the complex rules and procedures that govern the conduct of a modern trial. The publicity of trials, the right to counsel, the provision of counsel where serious crimes are at issue, the practice of entering a plea of not guilty where the accused refuses to enter a plea on his own behalf, the rules that govern the introduction of evidence, formal constitutional protections for those accused of offences, all suggest that the role of judicial proceedings is something more than simply determining the facts of the case.

Formal mechanisms of adjudication play an integral role in formal systems of law. Disputes or conflicts cannot be resolved fairly unless the facts relevant to those disputes are known and the rules applying to the disputes are fairly applied. Discovering the facts and applying the rules are therefore essential purposes of adjudication. Nevertheless, accomplishing these two goals is only part of what is required. As is well known, it is not enough that justice be done. It must also be seen to be done.

Enforcement, I have suggested, has three functions. Understanding the role of adjudication is facilitated by examining each of these functions in turn.

Adjudication, and the demonstration function of enforcement

The first is to demonstrate that the law is widely respected and conscientiously enforced. There are three aspects to this process of demonstration. The first is providing information. It is not insignificant in this regard that one of the earliest and perhaps the most basic right or constitutional protection in the common law system is *habeas corpus*,[22] whose sole purpose is to require the authorities to demonstrate publicly the legality of a decision to take someone into custody. The fact that the most pressing demand of victims is that they be kept informed about the response of the law to their victimization is also significant in this regard.

It is obvious that adjudication cannot fill the need for information in believable ways unless it is public. However, more than this is required. Adjudication must proceed in accordance with rules designed to ensure that all of the relevant information is brought before the court in a fair way. It is equally important that those responsible for enforcing the law fulfil their responsibilities in accordance with law. A public trial requires those bringing a charge to prove that the charge is justified by introducing their evidence and explaining how the evidence was obtained.

A system of adjudication that ensures that the public is well-informed about the operation of the legal system also has the effect of informing the public about attitudes toward the law. Effective adjudication can proceed only with the cooperation of the public. An uncooperative public makes the task of discovering and presenting evidence to the court difficult and sometimes impossible. A public trial, therefore, reveals public attitudes toward the law. It also provides significant information about the attitudes of those responsible for enforcing the law, since failure to prosecute and the way the prosecution proceeds with a case serve as tests of the commitment and competence of law enforcement authorities.

Adjudication and persuasion

That persuasion is central to adjudication is so obvious that it frequently goes unnoticed. Adjudication requires persuasion. One obvious task of all participants is to persuade an impartial adjudicator and, where serious offences are concerned, an impartial jury to accept a particular point of view or conclusion. Judicial impartiality is important because it ensures that the process of persuasion is not short-circuited. An impartial judge is one who has not made up his mind on the case prior to hearing it in a court setting and who has no personal interest in the outcome. Then, having come to a conclusion, the court has the task of persuading those who have participated that its findings are based on a fair assessment of the evidence presented and a sound understanding of the law. Persuasion, then, is central to the adjudicative process.

The persuasive component of adjudication has important implications for all those on whom the law places legal obligations: offenders, victims, the authorities themselves, and the public at large. Where a court is dealing with a criminal offence, it has two tasks. The first is to ensure a just trial. However, as is reflected in the aphorism 'justice must not only be done, it must be seen to be done', the court's task is not simply to do justice. It must also seek

125

to persuade all those concerned that justice has been done. This is true not simply of the public at large. It is also true of the accused. We have argued that persuading those who might not otherwise do so to obey the law is an important enforcement task. Convincing offenders that officials are committed to conscientious enforcement is an important step in this process.

Demonstrating that an accused has received a fair trial is one of the court's central tasks. Only if this is done will the verdict be accepted as credible. Hence, this is one of the informative functions of the adjudicative process. A trial also provides the court with an opportunity to explain the law and to explain why the law must be respected. In so doing, the court is providing those who are on trial with reasons for cooperating with the court and by implication with the law more generally.[23]

Law enforcement requires the cooperation of the public. Cooperating with law enforcement requires effort and exposes those involved to the risk of retaliation. Where the adjudicative process functions well, those whose cooperation is required will have good reasons for voluntary participation. A properly functioning system will enhance individual and collective security and will also provide evidence supporting the assumption that for the most part people are prepared to live within the law.

Winning the compliance of those subject to the law is the primary goal of the enforcement process. This is particularly true of offenders. A trial provides the law with an opportunity to persuade those who appear before it that the law is committed to principles of justice. It is also an opportunity to persuade those appearing before it that the law must be enforced and that the court has an obligation to see that this is done. A trial is, therefore, a dialogue whose purpose is to explain why the law should be obeyed. If the court succeeds in that task, it will have provided additional support for the assumption that people generally can be trusted to obey the law most of the time.[24]

Adjudication and enablement

Enablement is also important in adjudication. The law is of no value to those who are unable to have their grievances heard. *Habeas corpus* is a good example. Bringing a detainee before a judicial authority creates an opportunity for that person to make representations and claim his rights. One of the early steps in the creation of Roman law was a publication of a court formulary whose purpose was to establish when complaints could be brought before the court, thus enabling citizens to present their grievances and defend their rights. This development also illustrates the central role of enablement in the adjudicative process.

Access to adjudication enables people to defend important interests. Many of the rules governing the trial process are directed to this goal. The right to hire counsel, to examine and cross-examine, to call witnesses, are all examples. So too are procedures that allow individuals to get relief from harassment, or abuse, or the many other reasons that might lead someone to petition the court. In all these respects, the court functions to enable individuals and the state to solve disputes in lawful ways.

PART III: ENFORCEMENT, REFORM, AND THE CONCEPT OF DIVERSION

The function of enforcement and the justification of reform

Our suggestion that the policing and judicial components of law enforcement comprise the three functions described is strengthened by an examination of the kinds of criticism that are typically offered of legal systems in the pursuit of their reform. I have already pointed to two significant reforms in the development of Roman and common law and the function that those reforms were designed to serve. More recent criticisms of our legal systems offer many other examples. As many commentators have pointed out, one of the most significant weaknesses of most contemporary western systems of law is their treatment of victims. Realization of this has created a demand for more effective ways of keeping victims informed of the law's response to the harm they have experienced.[25]

Legal aid, the right to a trial without undue delay, access to bail, the use of evidence illegally obtained, the strengthening of provisions allowing spouses to secure support payments, the requirement that those whom the police propose to detain on suspicion that they have committed an offence be informed of their rights are all issues around which efforts at reform have focused. The goal of some reforms is relatively unproblematic from a legal point of view. Legal aid is a good example. When individuals are not properly represented by counsel, the power of the law to persuade an accused who is not properly represented, as well as interested onlookers, that he has been treated fairly in accordance with law is undermined. Finally, the ability of those who are not represented by counsel to ensure that their rights are respected is reduced. Providing legal aid to those without the means to hire legal counsel is therefore clearly desirable.[26]

Other suggested reforms are less straight-forward. Many have argued that all modern systems of law should prohibit the use of evidence illegally obtained in the conviction of offenders. The arguments in favour point to the desirability of ensuring that the police work within the law. Since one of the functions of law enforcement as I have described it is to demonstrate that those responsible for law enforcement are committed to obeying the law, this reform has obvious point. Yet allowing those who are known to have broken the law to escape the censure of the court undermines the capacity of the law to bring those who are known to have broken the law to justice. The functions of law enforcement are complex and not always easily harmonized. The analysis offered above helps to explain why this is so.

Law enforcement and the role of discretion

A central and controversial component in law enforcement is the exercise of discretion. Describing its role will allow us to complete the general account of law enforcement being developed.

Although discretion is a ubiquitous feature of law enforcement, its role usually goes unscrutinized, even though it operates at every level of the legal process. To begin with, whether the law is invoked depends in the first instance on a decision to report a crime. Ninety-seven per cent of cases in which the police become involved are initiated by a request from the public generally or a victim in particular. The decision to report a crime is an exercise of discretion. The fact than fewer that 50 per cent of crimes are reported to the police emphasizes its importance at this basic level of the legal process.

Discretion also plays a central role in police work. Where initial contact with the police is by phone, the telephone operator must decide how to respond. If the call is passed to a dispatch officer, he must decide what priority to give to the problem. Should an officer be dispatched immediately or are other problems of higher priority? Police officers in turn operate with a high degree of autonomy. The

Canadian Criminal Code, for example, specifies that an officer *may* make an arrest where there are reasonable and probable grounds to believe that an offence has been committed; but he is not required to do so. Empirical studies show, furthermore, that a majority of the problems encountered by the police are resolved through mediation, warnings, or in some other way. For example, American studies indicate that officers make arrests in fewer than one-third of encounters in which it is a clear option. Further, of those arrested, not everyone is charged. A Canadian study of the youth bureau of a large urban police force revealed that only 13 per cent of youths apprehended by the police were charged after they had been arrested.[27]

The adjudicatory process leaves much to the discretion of key participants as well. Griffiths and Verdun-Jones point out that 'the Canadian prosecutor enjoys a formidable degree of discretion in carrying out his or her duties in the court process' (Griffiths and Verdun-Jones 1989: 251). Discretion exists in selecting cases for prosecution, picking the appropriate charge, varying or withdrawing charges, delaying or staying proceedings, and plea bargaining.[28]

The exercise of discretion and the problem of justice

There can be no doubt that the use of discretion in the enforcement process raises serious issues. Discretion allows for the differential treatment of offenders. It raises problems of fairness. People whose behaviour is in essential respects similar may through the exercise of discretion be treated differently. One person might find himself in court while another is simply cautioned. Hence, the exercise of discretion can lead to questions about equality of treatment.

These concerns are clearly not purely hypothetical. Plea bargaining, for example, is available only to those who have access to a lawyer. Research in Canada suggests that natives 'are less likely to gain any advantage from this process than their white counterparts' (Griffiths and Verdun-Jones 1989: 264). Use of discretion thus opens the door to racial discrimination and differential treatment based on economic status, themes that have been explored at length in public inquiries and Royal Commissions, or their equivalents, and by commentators.[29]

What is more, the use of discretion in enforcing the law is often disguised. It is not easy for those responsible for the administration of the law to explain or justify proceeding with an arrest in some cases but not in others, or laying charges in some cases or not in others. And how is a plea bargain compatible with the pursuit of justice or fairness, implying as it does varying sentences in return for a plea of guilty?

The unavoidability of discretion

These questions raise serious difficulties. Yet it is clear that discretion is an unavoidable feature of law enforcement.[30] No system of rules can long withstand literal application. In labour disputes, for example, one form of harassment of management is working to rule. In law enforcement, laying charges in all cases where they are appropriate under the law and eliminating plea bargaining would, taken together or even apart, bring legal systems to a grinding halt.

Discretion in law enforcement is unavoidable for two related reasons. First, applying rules in concrete cases requires the use of judgement. While some cases will obviously come under a rule, others will not. Rules are subject to interpretation. When is someone exceeding the speed limit: at 0.1 miles per hour in excess of what is posted; at 1 mile per hour; at 5 miles per hour? Human actions are also subject to interpretation. Someone is accused of assault. Did he really intend to strike his opponent? Was there a misunderstanding? Was the action a product of careless but not criminal negligence or recklessness? What really motivated the action?

There is a second important factor that must also be considered. The existence, importance, and use of discretion suggest that law enforcement is not restricted to detecting crime and assessing guilt or innocence. Law enforcement serves the much wider functions of demonstrating that the law is widely respected, and persuading and enabling individuals to comply with the law. None of these functions could be efficiently pursued in the absence of the wide use of discretion that empirical studies confirm is a clear feature of our legal systems. Were police officers required to lay charges whenever they had reasonable and probable grounds to believe an offence had been committed, their freedom to explore other, perhaps more effective, ways of winning compliance with the law would be truncated. The aggressive behaviour of an adolescent who has just discovered alcohol, or a spouse who has learned that he is to be laid off, or friends after a night on the town, or someone with a history of aggressive behaviour would all have to be treated in the same way. Yet each case is relevantly different from the perspective of law enforcement.

What this suggests is that the nature of law enforcement is inevitably influenced by the understanding that those charged with responsibility for enforcing the law have of its goals.

The exercise of discretion: public attitudes

Although the exercise of discretion is not easily discussed by those directly responsible for law enforcement, and is sometimes the source of public criticism, its central role is widely acknowledged by those called on to evaluate its use. In England, it has long been recognized (and confirmed by the 1962 Royal Commission on the Police) that the police have discretion in deciding whether to prosecute. Lord Denning in *Regina* v. *Metropolitan Police* said:

Although the chief officers of police are answerable to the law, there are many fields in which they have a discretion with which the law will not interfere. For instance, it is for the Commissioner of Police of the Metropolis, or the chief constable, as the case may be, to decide in any particular case whether inquiries should be pursued, or whether an arrest should be made, or a prosecution brought. It must be for him to decide on the disposition of his force and the concentration of his resources on any particular crime or area. No court can or should give him direction on such a matter. He can also make policy decisions and give effect to them, as, for instance, was often done when prosecutions were not brought for attempted suicide.[31]

A commission looking into allegations that the Toronto police were favouring certain citizens in issuing traffic tickets said:

This commission will not discourage the use of discretion by any officer when it is believed that a citizen of this community is deserving of consideration.

(Saxton 1981: 175)

The Report of the Canadian Committee on Corrections points out:

[T]he element of the exercise of police discretion cannot be separated from law enforcement and ... its complete elimination would not advance the ends of justice.

(Ouimet 1969: 45)

Finally, a study by J.W. Cooley, undertaken in Ottawa in 1981, showed that 82 per cent of the public and 83 per cent of the police disagreed with a statement that the police should charge everyone who commits an offence, regardless of the nature of the offence and other circumstances surrounding it. That same study revealed that the public felt that the total circumstances surrounding a particular offence should be examined by the police in their decision making (Cooley 1981: 194).[32]

Discretion and the principle of diversion

Although by common agreement it cannot be eliminated from law enforcement, discretion can none the less be the source of unfairness and discrimination. Does it follow that justice must be imperfect where the exercise of discretion is unavoidable? If discretion is unguided by principle and exercised by individuals in morally arbitrary ways, the answer to this question will be 'yes'. However, the exercise of discretion need not be morally arbitrary. What is required is an exploration of the principles by which it should be guided.

We have already argued that the goal of law enforcement is to build public confidence in the law by demonstrating that the law is widely respected, and persuading and enabling people to obey it. We have also seen that using minimum force is an important principle that ought to guide law enforcement. And finally, we have argued that reducing recourse to the use of force is important because violence can and frequently does undermine the moral autonomy of those caught up in it.

Coercion introduces a morally arbitrary component into a process designed to obtain compliance with the law. The less coercion used, the less arbitrary the requirement that one comply will seem. Respect for individual autonomy requires, therefore, that as much room as possible be made for voluntary compliance.

These deliberations now allow us to add a second principle with which to approach issues of sentencing and sentence administration, what I propose to call *the principle of diversion*.

Diversion represents restraint in the use of force. The principle of diversion implies that, when faced with the need to resolve a dispute or end conflict, an authority ought to use the least coercive method available of ensuring compliance with the law. For example, if faced with an altercation between juveniles involving the use of alcohol, assuming the role of mediator, undertaking to persuade those involved to end their dispute peacefully, issuing a caution, intervening with parents, seeking social support services for assistance, would all be preferable to arrest, other things being equal. If an arrest was called for, arrest and release, rather than an arrest followed by a charge, would be preferable, other things being equal, and so on.

When are other things equal? We have argued that maintaining public confidence in the law is the function of law enforcement. We have also seen that effective pursuit of that goal will inevitably require the exercise of discretion on the part of those assigned responsibility for law enforcement. The need to use discretion occurs where there is more than one way of accomplishing the objective of law enforcement. The principle of diversion is a guide to the use of discretion, directing those responsible for law enforcement to seek out the least coercive way of achieving the underlying goal of enforcement.

Diversion, and the pursuit of justice

It should be clear that the principle of diversion is quite compatible with the goals of persuasion and enablement. Indeed the tools of diversion are persuasion and enablement. If the police can obtain compliance with the law by helping a person get to a place where he can more easily cope with his physical or emotional state in a lawful way, then the police have succeeded in helping that person to obey the law, while avoiding the need to place him under arrest. If a person can be persuaded to appear in court without imposing bail, then the process has achieved its goal of compliance without imposing a financial penalty.

Diversion is also compatible with the goal of demonstrating that the law is widely respected. An official who succeeds in obtaining compliance without the use of force thereby demonstrates his authority in a way the use of brute force cannot. Recourse to force carries an ambiguous message. The very fact that it is needed demonstrates that the law is not respected. Any use of force carries with it the danger of escalation where coerced compliance is the goal. Both the use of force and any subsequent escalation are a concrete demonstration that the law has not secured the voluntary compliance of those against whom it is directed, and awareness of this fact may well serve to undermine the sense of security that the law seeks to instil.

Diversion does not subvert the law. Rather, it seeks the least coercive method of ensuring compliance with the law. Neither does the principle of diversion clash with principles of justice. Justice requires respect for principles of fairness and equal treatment. Justice requires that officials not discriminate between people in morally arbitrary ways. The principle of diversion is not morally arbitrary. Its purpose is to provide guidance in the task of achieving the goal of law enforcement with the minimum use of force. Applied consistently, diversion becomes a principle of justice, a way of treating like cases alike.

It is also clear from what we have already said that the principle of diversion does in fact now have an informal, though largely unacknowledged and inchoate, role in law enforcement in modern democratic legal systems, a role that is implied in the use to which discretion is frequently put.

The pursuit of justice and other virtues

One of the striking features of systems of justice is their apparent inability to accommodate other virtues. Justice, it is widely thought, is incompatible with forgiveness, or mercy, or even compassion. Those required to administer justice must ensure that their judgement is not distorted by inappropriate emotions, like human affection, which might introduce bias. Real justice has a remorseless, almost heartless, quality that requires that principles be set ahead of people. Justice is blind. It judges actions not people. Justice is impersonal. It is also deaf. It cannot accept special pleading.

At the same time, these images of justice are unsettling. They attribute to justice an imperialistic quality that is somehow not in keeping with common experience. Justice in the treatment of children is widely thought to be a parental virtue. Yet parents are also expected to exhibit love and affection for their children. We speak of social justice as a reflection of fellow-feeling. And we rebel at Kantian images that make punishment an obligation even when no good can possibly come of it.

It is clear that the relation of justice to other values is a troubling one. However, two other things are also clear. In everyday discourse, people do distinguish legal administration and enforcement that is humane from that which is not. Further, there is a more substantial place for humanitarian values in law enforcement than popular mythology or cursory analysis sometimes allow. If we can discover where these values have a role and how they are related to the pursuit of justice in policing and adjudication, we shall perhaps have a better understanding of their potential role in sentencing and sentence administration.

We need to begin our search by acknowledging three things. First, values like love, forgiveness, mercy, and compassion can be expressed in ways that do interfere with the pursuit of justice. Socrates identifies some of those ways in his own trial. He rejects the custom of bringing wife and family into the judicial arena to plead for support as incompatible with the purpose of a trial. On this he is surely right. To argue that on compassionate grounds alone someone should not be charged with a serious offence he has clearly committed is special pleading for which justice quite rightly has no 'ears'.

Second, there are many who believe that legal justice has an imperialistic quality that renders it incapable of responding to or accommodating other values. This fact is seen by some as grounds for moving beyond justice, with its emphasis on desert, guilt, and liability, to responses reflecting assessments of need. Indeed, in many areas of social life, our society has done just this. Workers' compensation plans are a good example, as is universal medical insurance. In these and other areas, justice models have been deemed to be inadequate, in large part because of the way they seem to exclude other values.

Finally, our legal systems do sometimes allow appeals to values like compassion and mercy to override justice. The head of state does in most countries have the power to grant pardons. People who are terminally ill are sometimes released from prison on compassionate grounds. And so on.

All of this makes it clear that virtues like mercy do have applications that put them in conflict with justice and require that priority be given to one or the other. However, the fact that values can come into conflict does not prove that conflict defines their normal relation. To the contrary, there is much room for the expression of a range of values in the pursuit of justice. We can see that this is the case if we shift our attention from why the law is enforced to *how* the law is enforced. In fact, people are very sensitive to a wide range of values in law enforcement, for example, honesty, courtesy, and respect for individual dignity. Even *kindness* and *gentleness* may on occasion have their place. The law can also be interpreted in mean-spirited ways. It can be applied literally, with harsh and counter-productive results.[33]

It should be clear, on careful appraisal, that there is a good deal of room for the expression of a wide variety of values, both negative and positive, in how the law is enforced. This is because law enforcement requires the use of discretion. Further, while principles of justice and fairness require consistency in the way discretion is employed, as we have already seen, there remains a good deal of room for other values. We can see that this is the case by returning to a consideration of the notion of diversion.

Let us use an example. A police officer is called to the scene of an accident, where he finds a collision between a car and a commercial vehicle. Damage is extensive but there are no injuries. The driver of the car is an elderly man whose actions can be interpreted in a number of ways. He may have been careless in turning into the path of the truck. Or his hearing and sight may simply have let him down. All losses are insured. How does the officer proceed? He could lay a charge of careless driving. The personal costs that the driver would bear in such a case would certainly be substantial, with the loss of driving privileges the likely outcome. Alternatively, he could negotiate with the driver with a view to his taking a series of tests designed to determine whether he should continue to drive. Or he could negotiate with a view to gaining the driver's agreement to give up his licence. Each of these actions would likely issue in the same result. From the point of view of the driving public whose protection the law serves, there is nothing to choose among them. It is clear that the path chosen will have to be determined by other values. We might describe an officer who laid a charge in these circumstances as insensitive or uncaring, and the officer who chose to negotiate or mediate wise or understanding. But whatever the outcome, some such description would be clearly appropriate.

The law functions to encourage and structure cooperation, reduce violence, and build or maintain public confidence in the capacity of the law to fulfil these goals. To accomplish this end requires the wide use of discretion and judgement. Where discretion is guided by values consistently applied in ways that build confidence in the law and encourage cooperation, its exercise cannot conflict with principles of justice. Justice is compromised by inconsistency. Values like compassion or mercy can intersect with law enforcement in unjust ways. However, they can also intersect with enforcement in ways that complement and reinforce law enforcement. When this happens, justice is enriched not subverted.

Respect for legal justice conditions, limits, and shapes the role of other values in the enforcement of law. In law enforcement, justice is the dominant value, the value that must prevail where values conflict. However, because law enforcement requires the exercise of discretion, it can be shaped and guided by a wide range of values. How actions and evidence are interpreted requires judgement. Exercising judgement wisely strengthens the enforcement process. Wisdom in the exercise of discretion requires the interplay of many virtues: understanding, sensitivity, prudence, courage, honesty, to name but a few. When, in the course of enforcement, a plea for sympathy or understanding leads to mediation or negotiation rather than arrest, both justice and mercy have found expression. Where legal intervention is followed by mediation and then reconciliation, law enforcement has made room for forgiveness. Where a family is allowed to deal with a disturbed member privately without disgrace, the law has shown compassion.

6

TOWARDS A THEORY
OF SENTENCING
Responsibility, Guilt, and the Idea
of a Criminal Offence

An overview

It is probably true that, in the popular mind, law enforcement is closely linked with the idea of punishment. The association is based on common sense. Most of us most of the time seek to avoid actions that will hurt us. When people act foolishly and are hurt in the process, we see the results as a warning and the resulting self-inflicted hurt as a kind of penalty. When innocent bystanders are harmed, a dimension of blame is added. When parents lay down rules, they frequently accompany the prohibitions with warnings of the consequences of disobedience. The 'penalties' alluded to may be 'natural' consequences of prohibited behaviour. 'Don't cross the street without looking both ways, otherwise you might be hit by a vehicle and badly hurt.' The penalties may be imposed. 'If you are not in by 12 o'clock, you will lose driving privileges.' In either case, unpleasant consequences are seen as directly associated with the conduct which breaks the rules.

When governments establish laws, we gauge their intentions by the penalties attached to them. A government that requires that drivers wear seat-belts or states that it wishes to regulate the disposal of waste, but attaches no penalties to the laws created for this purpose, will be widely seen as hypocritical or insincere. The same could be said of institutional and organizational rules, the rules of games, and so on. The suggestion that those who break the law should be punished appears, therefore, to have the character of a truism. However, where the punishment of offenders is concerned, what seems clear and uncomplicated on the surface is often a good deal less clear on careful examination.

Some examples help to illustrate this. As we have seen, fewer than 50 per cent of crimes are reported to the authorities. Careful and independently administered research in Canada, the United States, and Great Britain shows that, when people are presented with detailed information about offenders and their offences, harsh judgements are frequently modified and non-punitive options often endorsed.[1] Finally, crime surveys suggest that a common reason given by those who do not report serious crimes, for example aggravated and simple assaults, family crime and consumer fraud, is that they regarded the offence as 'a private matter' or, alternatively, that 'they did not want to harm the offender'.[2]

Punishment has traditionally been assigned the central role in sentencing by theories of punishment, as we have seen. However, here too, apparently unequivocal endorsements of punishment seem less substantial on careful scrutiny. Desert-oriented theories are problematic for a number of reasons, which are emphasized when set in a context where fewer than half of all criminal offences are reported and, of those reported, fewer than 10 per cent result in convictions, where the poor and members of minority groups are much more likely to be punished than others, and where no reliable system for eradicating these injustices is available.[3]

Most of us believe that punishment is a deterrent. For many, this is its *raison d'être*. Yet careful empirical studies have failed to establish that those punishments that modern societies typically rely on for serious offences – imprisonment and, not infrequently, capital punishment – are effective deterrents. Thus, the Canadian Sentencing Commission could not avoid the conclusion after extensive research and a careful review of the literature that:

> Such factors as the rate of recidivism, the relative success of early release from custody and the 'undeterability' of certain groups of offenders have called into question the possibility of achieving with any significant degree of success the goal of individual deterrence.

Further:

> there is little or no evidence to sustain an empirically justified belief in the deterrent efficacy of legal sanctions.
> (Archambault 1987: 135–6)

Finally, as we have already seen, the experience of the last few decades has virtually eliminated confidence in rehabilitation-oriented punishment.[4]

Two false starts

The range of difficulties with punishment in practice has led some commentators to conclude that the central problem is with punishment itself. This idea is not a new one. Arguably, it has dominated penal reform movements throughout most of the twentieth century. Some commentators have argued that punishment as a response to crime should be abandoned in its entirety because of its association with moral wrongdoing. Typically, those defending this view have suggested that moral paradigms for understanding illegal activity be replaced with health paradigms. Lady Barbara Wootton (1963) is a good example. We have already canvassed this option in some detail and concluded that to follow this advice would require that we restructure in a very significant way our understanding of the nature and moral foundations of human relationships.[5] At the same time, there is enough truth in this proposal to prevent easy dismissal. The relation of law to morality is complex and often tenuous. Further, as already remarked, those who become enmeshed with the law are often people with serious handicaps. For example, a very high percentage of those in our prisons can neither read nor write with any facility, have rarely if ever held regular employment, and are the victims of drug addictions.

A second approach that has been seriously debated in some circles in recent years would replace punishment with mediation, reconciliation, restitution, and social reparation. This approach has become particularly popular with church and advocacy organizations discouraged with the possibility of rehabilitating punishment. Punishment, they argue, is destructive. It breaks down human relationships, where what is needed is their restoration. It deepens wounds, where healing is called for. It encourages the marginalization of its victims. Indeed, it does not solve enforcement problems, it exacerbates them.

A related school of thought that has become increasingly influential in this regard has advanced the thesis that formal systems of justice of the sort found in modern industrial societies have in effect 'stolen' offenders from the community, isolated them from the pushes and shoves of everyday life, and rendered justice an alienating exercise in abstract formalities and debilitating penalties. On this view, punishment should be returned to the community by reintroducing the conflict resolution techniques of non-modern societies and simple communities, where disputes are handled face to face by those directly involved in the dispute. The goal of such proposals is to allow conflict to be mediated in a way that promotes healing and reconciliation.[6]

These proposals have considerable merit, as we shall see. Indeed, community-based responses to crime and to offenders have over the past few decades come to have an important if minor place in our criminal justice systems. Victim/offender reconciliation programmes (VORP) and community service orders, to take but two examples, are now familiar sentencing options.

However, taken by themselves, they generate serious problems. First, the rejection of punishment often disguises loss of confidence in formal legal systems. Returning punishment to the community implies removing it from the jurisdiction of formal courts of law. The proposal is not an incoherent one. Formal dispute-settling mechanisms are not an essential feature of social life. On the other hand, it is a serious mistake to see informality as inevitably benign or by its nature less punitive or more humanitarian.[7] Indeed, it is the defects to which informal systems of social control are prone that provide some of the most persuasive reasons for creating formal legal systems.[8]

Community-based sanctions pose a second difficulty. Coercion and punishment are not inventions of formal legal systems. They are recurring features of social life. Formal legal systems are set apart from informal systems only in the way in which coercion and punishment are organized. We have argued that formalizing dispute-settling mechanisms is justified where its effect is to reduce reliance on force to settle disputes. We have also pointed to a good deal of evidence that suggests that reducing recourse to the use of force in settling disputes is a goal of modern legal systems. This in itself suggests that informal community-based methods of resolving disputes are not always successful and may have to give way to formally organized alternatives. In this sense, the existence of formal legal systems is evidence that informal alternatives have been found wanting. Accounts of sentencing and the administration of sanctions must take this into account.

Finally, the proposal that we return to a simpler time, though appealing, is surely unrealistic. Modern societies are complex and frequently pluralistic. No doubt, shared values provide the basis for social cooperation. But with the growth of large nation states, immigration, religious pluralism, international commerce and so on, the need for formal institutions for coordinating human interaction and resolving disputes, which are seemingly an inevitable feature of human life, would seem to be a virtual necessity.[9]

What emerges from this discussion is by now a familiar difficulty. Punishment, it would seem, is very hard to justify, yet seemingly impossible to abolish. Faced with this impasse, one approach would simply accept punishment as an inevitable feature of modern legal systems and seek to limit its harmful side-effects.[10] An alternative approach is to try to reconceptualize the problem. If, as our discussion and that of many other commentators suggest, punishment is both deeply entrenched but also very puzzling, perhaps there is a serious difficulty with the traditional philosophical assumptions and justifications.

If punishment is so hard to justify, perhaps we should set aside attempts to justify it. This is not the same as arguing that it should be abolished. However, what it does suggest is that we should seek to understand the function of sentencing in other terms. If we succeed in that task, perhaps we shall have discovered a somewhat different way of explaining the persistence of the practice of punishment.

PART I: THE NATURE OF THE TASK

Trust, reliance, and social interaction

The extent to which human relationships rest on trust is not always noticed. We rely on others in a wide variety of ways. That reliance is in large measure a matter of faith. We assume, sometimes tacitly, sometimes explicitly, that those with whom we deal can be trusted to respect basic rules. This feature of human relationships is most often emphasized when we are dealing with the professions. When we turn to doctors, we assume that they are competent and can be relied on to provide good medical advice. A city that employs a firm of engineers to design a bridge assumes that, when the bridge has been constructed, it will carry the traffic for which it has been designed. Viewers watching the evening news assume that reporters are honestly reporting the events which are being described.

The relation of trust need not be a naive one. We all know that it is wise to check credentials and obtain references. There are charlatans who are prepared to defraud the unwary. Trust is therefore not automatically conferred. Where it is not conferred as a matter of course, it has to be earned. Professionals, business people, and mechanics earn the confidence of their clients. Nevertheless, though we may check carefully to see whether trust is warranted, the process of checking will come to rest at some point on the assumption that those to whom we turn for advice are trustworthy. Insisting on infallible proof of reliability before acting must in the end be self-defeating. In a complex society, when we ask for proof of graduation or certification, we cannot avoid relying at some point on the integrity of those who have issued the certificates. When we ask for letters of reference, we shall often be unable to avoid relying on the honesty of those whose evaluation we seek.

Trust is not restricted to professional relationships. It plays a central role in social interactions of all forms. We rely on our friends to keep us in mind where our interests are concerned. We rely on employers to ensure that our safety is protected. We assume that the city will ensure a clean water supply and that the power company will keep the power coming when we need it. We rely on shopkeepers to tell us the truth about their products and mechanics to do the work needed to keep our cars running and not perform unneeded repairs.

Inevitably we are let down. We discover that: a product advertised as having certain qualities does not; our family physician has been giving us unreliable advice on a serious health matter; corruption has crept into city hall and health standards have suffered; our accountant does not have the skills she said she had; a friend has treated us unscrupulously; a business partner has been feathering her own nest; and so on.

When our trust in those with whom we deal is shaken, the relationships in question are damaged. If we lose faith in someone who has been offering us professional services, we look for another adviser. If we discover that a drug manufacturer has allowed safety standards to drop, we stop buying the product. If a friend lets us down, we re-evaluate the friendship. Re-evaluation may result in a permanent rupture, or an effort may be made to win back the confidence lost or undermined.

How badly relationships are damaged is a function of the harm that has been caused. There are two aspects to this. When we rely on others, we expose ourselves to direct harm. Bad or incompetent professional advice can lead to exactly those harms we sought to protect ourselves from by seeking the advice in the first place, or to even worse harms. However, there is a second and more indirect harm that may also result. The dishonesty of one car sales person may lead us to question the honesty of everyone involved in the sale of cars. A series of stock market frauds can lead to a loss of confidence in all stockbrokers. Much of the motivation for professional disciplinary committees and carefully constructed codes of ethics can be traced to the way in which confidence in a profession can be damaged by the actions of single individuals.[11]

The damage caused when trust is undermined need not be permanent, though it may be. Compensating victims can help to overcome the loss of confidence in question as can careful effort to ensure that the actions in question do not recur. Sometimes, repairing the damage can be achieved in relatively short order. Sometimes it will require sustained effort over an extended period. The length of the healing process and the effort it will require will again vary with the harm that has been sustained.

The law has a strong influence on patterns of human interaction. It establishes rules that people are required to obey. It channels the ways in which people can solve their problems or pursue their interests. This in turn builds assumptions in the public mind about how things are to be done. The very existence of law is evidence, as we have already seen, that people generally are prepared to live within the law. This in itself shapes expectations in powerful ways. People are prepared to entrust money to a bank because they believe that the laws governing financial interactions will be observed. People are prepared to use the roads because they believe that, for the most part, the rules of the road will be respected by other drivers.

Virtually all our relationships are heavily influenced by the assumption that others are prepared to obey the law. As a consequence, when confidence in the law is undermined, patterns of behaviour are affected. Urban crime surveys provide striking examples of this fact. So does the daily newspaper. Losing confidence in the capacity of the law to protect people from physical assault affects one's mobility. Property values drop in those neighbourhoods where vandalism is common. A business can be destroyed by evidence that it has dealt dishonestly with a customer and so on.

As we saw in the previous chapter, the person who breaks the law may cause direct harm. This is not inevitable, since not all offences will have direct victims. An offence may also cause indirect harm by undermining public confidence and the confidence of the victim in the law. That is to say, an offence may be taken as evidence by the victim or the public generally that the law is not widely respected or that confidence in the law enforcement process is unwarranted. This, too, is not an inevitable consequence of criminal activity. Again, crime surveys show that victimization does not necessarily result in a change of attitudes on the part of those affected. For example, the Canadian urban victimization survey discovered that the group most likely to be the victims of crime are young men. The survey also showed that, in spite of this fact, of all groups young men are the least concerned about crime and the least affected by victimization. The elderly, on the other hand, are the least likely to be victimized. Yet, the experience of victimization, as well as the knowledge on the part of the elderly that people like them have been the victims of crime, often have a seriously harmful impact on their confidence in the capacity of the law to offer protection.[12]

To these two harms we can add a third one. An offence can damage an offender's relationships with those with whom she would normally interact. The harm here is to the offender, who may find that she has become a victim of the distrust her actions have caused. A shopkeeper cannot help but be uneasy when she spies a known shoplifter in her store. School authorities are duty bound to react differently to the visit of a known paedophile than to the visit of a local citizen. When someone is known to have told a lie, it will become more difficult to take her at her word.

What this suggests is that, by breaking the law, an offender jeopardizes important assumptions that underpin normal social interaction. As is the case more generally, the effect is to undermine the offender's relationships with those with whom she comes into contact. The extent of the damage will depend on the seriousness of the rules and the harm, both potential and actual, that the breach of rules caused or might cause. Where the damage is slight, little will be needed to overcome it. Where the damage is serious, loss of confidence will be severe and rebuilding trust will be difficult or perhaps impossible.

Sentencing and the treatment of offenders

What then are the appropriate remedies to these harms? How should offenders be treated? And can the analysis of the functions of enforcement offered in Chapter 5 help to structure our understanding of what is required? Let us address this question by looking at the general implications of that analysis for sentencing.

The fundamental justification of law, we have argued, is to reduce the use of force in settling disputes. The law cannot accomplish this goal unless it is widely believed that most of those falling under the law's authority are willing for the most part to obey the law voluntarily. Seen in this context, the function of enforcement is to sustain this belief.

What responses does this require? First, the law must demonstrate that the offender's willingness to break the law is not widely shared or condoned, and that the harms suffered by victims are genuine wrongs from which actual and potential victims have a legal right to be protected and which the law is under an obligation to correct. Second, the law must undertake to persuade the public generally and offenders in particular to obey the law. Finally, effective enforcement will involve assisting people in general and offenders in particular to live within the law.

We have already seen that the demonstrative, persuasive and enablement functions of enforcement explain and justify a wide range of activities in policing and adjudication. In sentencing, however, all three functions become a part of a single focused action or process directed as a rule at a single individual. Can a sentence perform all three roles?

To begin with, a sentence is itself an expression of public views that can reflect public attitudes in three ways: first, by the penalties that are attached by law to particular types of offences; second, by the penalties decided on by sentencing authorities in particular cases and the way in which those sentences are justified; and third, by public reactions to the sentence imposed.[13] Hence a sentence can be used to demonstrate public support for the law and its enforcement, to demonstrate that the behaviour of the offender is not widely condoned, and to acknowledge the harm inflicted on the victim by the offence. Requiring that an offender serve a sentence can be seen as a form of compensation for an offence, a repaying of a debt to society. Further, sentences can be vehicles for directing compensation to victims. They can also be imposed with a view to persuading and assisting offenders to live within the law.

It is clear, therefore, that, just as demonstration, persuasion, and enablement have a place in policing and adjudication, they also have a potential role in sentencing.

Previous discussion also identified three constraints on the pursuit of enforcement goals, those arising from the minimum use of force principle, the importance of respect for moral autonomy, and finally, the diversion principle. It is clear that each of these constraints has a potential role in sentencing as well.

How to proceed

We need now to step back and review our progress. In the previous chapter, we saw that the function of law enforcement can be seen as maintaining or building public confidence in the law. That analysis of the function of policing and adjudication as two components of enforcement was then evaluated in two ways. First, we asked whether it fitted with widely shared understandings of the role and function of policing and adjudication and argued that it did. Second, we looked to see what the implications of the approach suggested were for understanding the need for reform. Again a careful review indicated that understanding the function of enforcement in the way suggested was consistent with principles of reform that have a recognized place in public policy discussions in contemporary democratic societies.

Our preliminary discussion of the nature and function of sentencing suggests that it, too, fits the account that has been emerging. This presents us with three questions. First, does the account we have been developing describe the function of sentencing and corrections as they are currently practised in modern democratic countries? Second, what are the implications for our understanding of sentencing and corrections of requiring that they function in this way? Should sentencing and corrections be understood as having the functions we have described? And, finally, what are the implications of this approach for developing a philosophy of punishment and an understanding of the nature of crime?

Any theory of sentencing has three tasks. It must provide criteria for identifying those against whom sanctions should be directed. It must provide criteria for evaluating the relative seriousness of offences. And it must provide guidance on the sentencing of offenders. In the remainder of this chapter, I propose to address the first two tasks. The final task will be undertaken in Chapter 7.

PART II: THE PRINCIPLE OF RESPONSIBILITY AND THE CONCEPT OF GUILT

Against whom should sanctions be addressed?

Let us assume for the moment that any response on the part of the court to an accused who has been found guilty of an offence is appropriately called a sanction. We must then decide what behaviour should be regarded as requiring a response by the court. What is it that turns an action into an offence? Answering this question requires that we determine what kinds of behaviour undermine relationships of trust.

What is it about an action that undermines trust? The answer would appear to lie in how it impacts on the legitimate expectations of others. Legitimate expectations are created in many ways: by rules, customs, commitments of a variety of kinds, institutions, roles and so on. Some examples will help to illustrate the point.

Part of what it means to be a friend is to take the needs and expectations of one's friend into account in one's day to day decisions. Someone who refused to respond to a friend's appeal for help for no apparent reason would likely damage that friendship and cause hurt and anger. For, by her actions, she would be revealing attitudes inappropriate for friends.

A professional adviser who expressed through her actions no particular concern for the interests of a client would not likely retain her client's confidence, since professional advisers are expected to offer advice in the best interests of those who seek it. A person who loans money on a promise that it will be returned will expect to be repaid as agreed upon. Those who fail to live up to their promises can expect questions to arise about their reliability.

We assume that our legitimate expectations will be met in the normal course of events and are disappointed when they are not. However, failure to meet legitimate expectations does not always evoke censure. This is because the legitimacy of an expectation is a function both of its content, what it requires, and of the capacity of those toward whom it is directed to live up to it.

The content of expectations is set in a number of ways, as already suggested. Whether it is legitimate to expect certain things will depend on whether the expectation is justified. To say it is justified is to say it ought to be met. Whether it ought to be met may require evaluation, and in some cases moral evaluation. For

148

example, whether the expectation that someone work overtime without remuneration is legitimate may well be a function of the responsibilities she has assumed, the job description under which she works, the conditions under which she was hired, and so on. All of this may also be subject to moral assessment. Expectations that may be seen as legitimate from one point of view may not be legitimate from another. To return to our example, someone's agreement to certain job requirements may have been obtained under duress. Or they may not have been clearly understood. This might well have a bearing on their legitimacy.

The legitimacy of expectations, however, is also a function of capacity. To say that an expectation is legitimate, as we have said, is to say it ought to be met. However, 'ought implies can'.[14] We do not normally expect people to 'do the impossible', or ignore other commitments, or take unreasonable risks, and so on.

Normally our confidence in others is undermined only when we believe that they could have done what was expected of them, but chose not to. We do not judge people negatively when they fail to meet legitimate expectations through no fault of their own. We lose confidence in others only when we begin to suspect that meeting their obligations is not something to which they assign a high priority.

Expectations set the context in which social interaction occurs. We are normally not surprised when friends act as friends, or lawyers fulfil their responsibilities, or bank employees direct our funds into the right accounts, and so on. Failure, on the other hand, is surprising. Normally we expect it to be justified. The manager who is responsible for producing an annual report must explain its absence. The child who is expected home right after school must justify being late. The friend who lets us down owes us an explanation.

Because expectations are legitimate only when those toward whom they are directed have the capacity to meet them, there are a number of standard excuses. Accident is one. Mistake is another. A person who accidentally knocks over a lamp while visiting a friend would not normally be blamed for failing to exercise the care someone would usually be expected to exhibit toward the property of others. Someone who mistakes the date on which she has agreed to help a friend would normally expect that it would not be held against her. A professional who provides unsound advice through no fault of her own would not normally attract censure from her client. Equally, a client who pursued a complaint under these circumstances before a professional ethics committee, for example, would not be likely to succeed.

Finally, when what are regarded as legitimate expectations are not met, social relationships are strained or ruptured. Feelings of disappointment, anger, a sense of betrayal, and so on are a natural outcome.

The law, too, creates expectations. Authorities expect as a matter of course that the law will be obeyed. So do those who are subject to it. When products are required by law to meet certain standards, consumers will normally expect that, if something is offered for sale, it meets the standards in question. Where there are laws prohibiting theft, people will normally assume that others will not take their property without permission. And so on.

The legitimacy of expectations that are grounded in the law is a function of their content and the capacity of those to whom they are directed to fulfil them. They are legitimate as to content where they reflect a sound understanding of the law. As to capacity, they are justified only when directed toward voluntary actions, that is, those actions for which someone can be legitimately held responsible. In this regard, legal expectations are no different from those which arise in other contexts. Only by their voluntary actions do people signal their attitudes toward the law. Hence, it is only voluntary actions that can cause the kind of harm to which a sentencing authority has an obligation to respond.

Mens rea, excuses, and the problem of strict liability

The idea that people should be held responsible in criminal law only for things they could have avoided doing has a fundamental role in modern legal systems. In common law jurisdictions it takes the form of the doctrine of *mens rea* and requires that only actions that are done intentionally, knowingly, recklessly, or negligently should attract the censure of criminal law.

On our account, it is clear why a principle of responsibility (e.g. the common law *mens rea* requirement) should be given a fundamental role in the determination of guilt. Only those actions that someone could have avoided are capable of undermining a belief that people can, on the whole, be trusted to do what the law requires of them. A person who breaks a law knowingly or intentionally implies by her behaviour that she was not prepared to obey the law at least in this case. Someone who acts recklessly or negligently implies that, on at least that occasion, the interests of others had a lower priority for her than her own desires. A person who breaks the law intentionally, knowingly, recklessly, or negligently, cannot help but give rise to questions about her willingness to respect the law.

Modern legal systems, then, do give the notion of responsibility a central role. However, they also give a prominent place to the notion of strict liability. This raises serious problems for the account being developed for two reasons. First, strict liability offences comprise a significant proportion of criminal offences in modern criminal codes.[15] Second, to hold someone strictly responsible for their actions would seem to be unjustifiable if we maintain that what gives an offence its public, and therefore criminal, character is its capacity to undermine confidence in the law. We need to examine carefully, therefore, why strict liability has come to play the role it now does play in modern systems and whether the role it has come to play is compatible with the account here being developed.

Strict liability laws require that a person be held responsible simply for performing the prohibited act, whether she did so voluntarily or not. The Canadian case of *Pierce Fisheries Ltd* is a good example. The accused was charged with being in possession of undersized lobsters in contravention of Lobster Fishery Regulations. The company in question had taken precautions to ensure that it did not purchase undersized lobsters. However, some twenty-six undersized lobsters in a load of 50,000 pounds had gone undetected and the company was subsequently charged with a breach of the regulations. The trial magistrate and the Nova Scotia Court of Appeal refused to convict the accused on the grounds that the offence required a guilty mind (i.e. *mens rea*). The verdict was overturned by the Supreme Court of Canada on the grounds that, if the Crown were required to establish that the accused had an evil intent in committing the offence, the regulation could not fulfil its purpose. It would simply be too easy to escape conviction.

It is clear that in modern societies many of the personal and commercial activities that take place carry with them serious risks of harm to those engaging in them and to bystanders. Strict liability has come to play the role it now does in modern legal systems because of the need to regulate those activities. Driving is a good example. We know that drivers pose serious risks to others. Those risks are magnified if, for example, a driver is under the influence of alcohol. Making drivers strictly liable for driving while under the influence of alcohol is an effective way of reducing the risk that people will drink and drive.[16] That is to say, strict liability laws shift the responsibility for ensuring that they are acting in conformity with law onto those engaging in activities that have been identified as needing careful regulation.[17]

Are strict liability laws incompatible with the view that the proper concern of the criminal law is only with actions that undermine confidence in the law? The answer would appear to depend on how the notion of strict liability is interpreted. If its purpose is to provide protection by shifting the onus of proving that the person in breach of a law undertook carefully to avoid breaking it, then there is no incompatibility. A fundamental function of the law is to protect those subject to it from harms to which they would otherwise be exposed. Many activities in our world pose severe risks. The function of regulatory offences is to reduce those risks.

What is inconsistent with our account is any provision that would hold people legally responsible for performing a prohibited action, whether they tried conscientiously to avoid doing so or not. For, by trying to avoid breaking the law, a person implies that she is one of those who is prepared to obey the law. Hence her actions could not reasonably be construed as undermining the law.

Holding people responsible for their actions regardless of the care they took to avoid the prohibited act is now commonly referred to as absolute liability. It should be clear that, on the view being developed here, it is absolute, not strict, liability that has no place in the criminal law. What is not clear is what is to be achieved by imposing absolute criminal liability. A person who conscientiously tries to avoid a prohibited act in engaging in a regulated activity has done all in her power to reduce the risk that she will break the law. If the law is broken under these conditions, then by implication the breach could not have been avoided, except by not engaging in the activity in question. But if the goal is to reduce the risk to zero, the activity in question should be banned. To use the lobster fisheries case, if taking undersized lobsters is so harmful that it must be prevented at all costs, the answer is to ban lobster fishing. While this is an apparently absurd solution in the case of the lobster fishery, it might be more convincing where the control of particularly toxic chemicals was involved.[18]

It would seem, therefore, that the view that it is the capacity of an offence to undermine confidence in the law that makes it a criminal offence is compatible with at least one important aspect of modern sentencing practice. It also helps us to understand why modern legal systems have in practice resisted the sometimes strident claims that strict liability and the principle of responsibility are incompatible. It is clear on our account of the matter that there is a place for both.

The role of excuses and the concept of legitimate expectations

In a law-governed society, events take place against a background of expectations that are created by the law. People subject to those laws will normally assume that those with whom they deal will be law-abiding. That being the case, we would expect that failure to meet those expectations would not be a matter of public concern where that failure carried no implications for the willingness of those involved to live within the law. We would also expect that to establish that an enforcement response was appropriate or required would require evidence that the person involved could have obeyed the law, had the matter been of sufficient importance to her.

In the common law, these expectations are captured by the doctrine of *mens rea*, as we have already seen. Their importance is also reflected in the role played by excuses. As Hart has pointed out, '[i]n the criminal law of every modern state responsibility for serious crimes is excluded or "diminished" by . . . "excusing conditions"', which come under the general heads of mistake, accident, provocation, duress, and insanity (Hart 1968: 31).[19] It is for this reason that 'a criminal trial may involve investigations into the insanity of the accused; into what he knew, believed, or foresaw; or into questions whether or not he was subject to coercion by threats, or provoked into passion, or was prevented by disease or transitory loss of consciousness from controlling the movement of his body or muscles' (Hart 1968: 31).

Asking whether an accused could have lived within the law had she so chosen has analogues in informal social relations. Excuses play a central role in assessing culpability wherever responsibilities are assessed against a background of social expectations. Consequently, the excusing conditions that apply in law apply equally in informal relations. It is also true that whether someone might have met the legitimate expectations of others in particular cases had she assigned sufficient importance to doing so must frequently be a matter of controversy. Mistakes and accidents are more easily accepted as excuses than are what are sometimes referred to as defects of will (Hart 1968: 33). The law is justifiably sceptical of the person who claims that her judgement was incapacitated by anger, just as instructors are justifiably sceptical of students who seek to be excused for failing to meet important deadlines because their capacity to concentrate has been destroyed by news of some misfortune.

The parallel between the law's treatment of failure to meet legitimate legal expectations and our reactions to the failure of someone to meet legitimate informal expectations extends also to the fact that the more serious the consequences of failing to meet the expectations in question, the more stringent the evaluation of proffered excuses will be. A family emergency may suffice to excuse someone for missing an appointment or convince a police officer not to issue a ticket for a parking offence. It is unlikely to suffice where serious harm is involved, for example, the loss of an important contract or involvement in an automobile accident. The more serious the harm threatened, the more determined the effort we are normally expected to make to live up to our informal and our legal obligations.

The parallel extends also to ignorance of the law as a defence. One of the general expectations that permeate social life is that those adults with whom we deal will have a competent understanding of common expectations. We don't accept pleas by friends that they did not know they were expected to help out in times of distress, or by parents that they did not know that they were responsible for ensuring the welfare of their children. Learning what is expected of one in various situations just is one of the expectations that people generally are expected to live up to. The same is true of the law. Legal systems impose obligations that are overriding. A legal system cannot fulfil its function unless those who are subject to it are prepared to observe its requirements for the most part. To do so requires a knowledge of the law. Hence, the law generates not only those specific expectations associated with specific laws but the general background expectation that those subject to the law take some care to learn what their responsibilities under the law are.

Not surprisingly, the more complex the law the less force this background expectation has. Expecting that people know themselves to have legal obligation not to commit murder is uncontroversial. Expecting that people know the intricacies of income tax law and meet all its requirements when filing their income tax returns is another. Mistakes of the latter sort are excusable in any fair legal system. Mistakes of the former sort almost never are.

Legitimate expectations and hard cases

To find someone guilty of breaking the law, then, is to identify her as someone who failed to obey a law she could have chosen to obey. Such people are brought to account because their actions raise doubts about whether they can be trusted to live up to their legal obligations. One of the ways in which this question is answered is by looking to see whether there were excusing conditions in operation at the time the law was broken. On this view, culpability is a function of capacity, the capacity to obey the law. Where capacity is lacking, there can be no finding of guilt.

What, then, are we to say of three categories of persons: children, the mentally ill, and those who are handicapped in ways that render it difficult, if not impossible, to participate in normal social life? Children present a difficult case. What can legitimately be expected of them? Living within the law has to be learned. It also requires judgement and sufficient strength of character to be capable of identifying priorities and choosing within them in accordance with a scale of values. Children are normally thought to be deficient to varying degrees on all counts. We do not expect very young children to know what is expected of a mature member of society. They have not lived long enough, are not sufficiently mature to understand what they have learned, or may simply not have formed an adequate system of values. On the other hand, they may have formed attitudes that mark them clearly as people who have no intention of living within the law.

Clearly, our relations with children are structured by expectations. One of the most fundamental is that they undertake to learn to live within the law. Juvenile delinquency thus poses a special challenge. A juvenile cannot be treated like an adult. Yet her actions in concert with other evidence might well suggest that she is not at this stage of her life one of those who can be trusted to do as the law requires. Because of immaturity, we may not be willing to assign culpability. Yet she may pose a substantial threat to others.

The dilemma posed by children in applying the law illustrates an important dimension of the notion of responsibility. Only those who could have obeyed the law had they so chosen are properly held responsible for their actions. However, the ability to live within the law has to be learned and can be acquired only with effort and support from others. Society expects children to acquire this ability. That being the case, then presumably it also has an obligation to provide children with the means to acquire the knowledge, understanding, and the maturity that responding to those expectations demands. As it turns out, providing support and guidance is a recognized responsibility of parents, schools and other community groups.[20]

Children pose a second dilemma as well. Clearly they have the capacity to cause many of the harms from which the law is intended to provide protection. Their actions are therefore capable of undermining public confidence in the capacity of the law to fulfil its function. Failure on the part of the law to provide protection from the actions of juveniles is a real failure. Furthermore, the actions of juveniles often reflect attitudes toward the law and values which, if widely shared, must undermine the basic assumptions on which the law rests.

Children and adolescents therefore pose real difficulties for the law. They are capable of breaking the law intentionally, knowingly, recklessly, and negligently. Yet, because they are not yet adults, we are not justified in assuming that they have had the time and opportunities required to learn what is expected of them, to understand those expectations, and to acquire the ability and the maturity to respond to them in acceptable ways. They have, that is to say, an excuse that we are not justified in ignoring in responding to their behaviour. What the account illustrates, therefore, is why it is not legitimate for the law to treat children and young offenders as it treats adults.[21]

Insanity and mental illness also pose a test for the view we are developing. People who are mentally ill are capable none the less of causing the harms which the law is designed to prevent. Yet it is doubtful that it is always legitimate to expect such persons to live within the law of their own volition. Why this is so is not easy to explain and cannot be explored at length here.[22] However, a few comments are needed to establish the bearing of mental illness on the matter of culpability.

One of the deeply disturbing aspects of mental illness is its effect, in at least some of its manifestations, on the capacity of those afflicted by it to respond in a normal way to the expectations of those around them. The more severe the incapacity, the less capable are those afflicted by mental illness to live normal lives. It is clear that, on the account we are offering, the less able someone is to identify and respond to the expectations of others, the less justification there is to hold them legally responsible for their actions.

A person who steals to enhance her prestige within her peer group is responding to perceived expectations, her own and others. Those who exceed the speed limit demonstrate their capacity to respond to the expectations created by traffic laws by the way they drive and how they respond to the police. Mental illness impacts on questions of responsibility before the law when it exhibits itself in an incapacity or a diminished capacity on the part of those afflicted by it to respond in similar ways to the expectations of others. Hence, mental illness ought to be and is, to some degree in most jurisdictions, recognized as a defence against criminal charges and a relevant consideration in the sentencing process.

Diminished capacity to respond to the expectations of others does create severe problems in a society where human relationships are structured around expectations, however. Hence, a response on the part of the law to those who are seriously mentally ill is justified. What is not justified, however, is a response that fails to acknowledge the disfunctionality that mental illness can bring in its train and what that implies for what others can legitimately expect from them.

Many of those in serious trouble with the law in modern societies are people who are handicapped in ways that render it difficult, if not impossible, to participate in normal social life. Recent studies in Canada suggest, for example, that a very high proportion of those in Canadian prisons are illiterate, suffer from debilitating drug and alcohol dependencies, lack elementary social skills, have little job training, are often unable to engage in sustained work of the sort required to hold a job in a modern economy, and so on.[23]

The capacity to live within the law is not an abstraction that can be defined solely in terms of the absence of impediments. Rather it involves the capacity to meet the expectations of others with whom interaction is inevitable. A person is not free to work if she has none of the requisite skills. A person cannot up-grade skills if she cannot read instruction manuals or operating instructions. Those who are not capable of responding emotionally to others cannot build relationships that allow significant participation in the world around them.

Does it follow, therefore, that those who are severely handicapped in these ways do not have the capacity to live within the law in the requisite sense? What, for example, distinguishes such a person from a child, or someone who is seriously mentally ill? The answer again lies in the notion of legitimate expectations. Just as the law rests on an assumption that for the most part people are prepared to obey the law, so too it must rest on an assumption that it is reasonable and legitimate to expect them to learn how to do so. It is legitimate to expect a child to learn. It is equally legitimate to expect an adult *to have learned*.

For example, the law assumes that in the normal course of events adults will have the capacity to deal with drugs and drug dependency in lawful ways. Those who fail to do so fail to live up to those expectations. Hence even seriously debilitating handicaps of the sort being discussed cannot excuse those afflicted by them from obeying the law.

On the other hand, the brute fact that compliance with the law requires not simply an absence of negative restraint but also resources in the form of knowledge, skills, and character development must impact on how the law responds to those found guilty of illegal behaviour. What impact it should have will be explored in the next chapter.

Determining guilt

Earlier we suggested that the response of the law to an apparent breach of the law depends on the answers to two questions. First, are the actions in question, taken by themselves or in conjunction with other evidence, likely to suggest to those affected by them that the law may not be able to fulfil its function in general or some particular area? Second, do they undermine confidence in the trustworthiness of the particular offender? Answering this second question requires in part that the court determine whether the person on trial could have obeyed the law had she wished to do so, for only actions that reflect the intentions, attitudes or values of an accused can undermine confidence in the willingness of the accused to obey the law. Guilt is therefore quite appropriately tied to the notion of responsibility. In this respect, the account being developed here coincides with modern legal practice. It also implies a rejection of absolute liability.

The notion of responsibility we have defended coincides with what is required by retributivism. However, it is not a retributivist account. It does not rest on the view that the law is justified in responding punitively to those who voluntarily break the law because in so doing they have committed a moral wrong, though they may indeed have done so. Rather it rests on the view that, in breaking the law, an offender ignores the legitimate expectation that she will do as the law requires and, in doing so, raises doubts about her willingness to live within the law, as well as about the capacity of the law to fulfil its function. It is because only voluntary actions can have this effect that guilt is a function of an individual's control over her own actions. Hence, the account we are developing captures the essence of the retributivist notion of responsibility but avoids any direct connection to notions of desert.

The account being developed here is also in an important respect forward-looking. Sanctions must have a point if they are to be justified. They are justified only where an offence taken by itself or in conjunction with other evidence suggests that the offender is not a person who is prepared voluntarily to obey the law. However, although forward-looking, the account is not vulnerable to the criticisms typically raised against forward-looking sentencing theories. Previous argument shows that a legal system that undertook to enforce the law in a way that ignored or undermined the moral status of those or a subgroup of those subject to its authority would in the process undermine its own authority. Equally, a legal system that allowed officials to deviate from principles of justice reflected in the law for utilitarian reasons would undermine its function as a legal system by weakening the capacity of that system to maintain public confidence. Respect for basic moral values is one of the conditions which determine how effectively a particular legal system is capable of fulfilling its primary function. For this reason, soundly conceived reform-oriented criticism of the law can have considerable force.

Our account would seem, therefore, to have a number of strengths. It captures a notion of responsibility that is seen by many to be an essential component of a just legal system and it does so in a way that helps us to understand why cases that modern law finds to be hard cases are indeed hard cases. Further, it coincides with retributivist claims that to punish those who could not have obeyed the law they are accused of breaking is unjust and it does so in a way that disentangles the notion of responsibility from the notion of desert. Finally, it incorporates the utilitarian insight that the law should not impose penalties except where some social benefit will result without undermining the doctrine of responsibility or requiring that the function of enforcement is deterrence.

Thus we have answered our first question. What actions should be regarded as offensive from the law's perspective? The answer: only those actions that a person could have avoided had she so chosen.

PART III: WEIGHING THE SERIOUSNESS OF OFFENCES

How should the seriousness of offences be gauged?

What an offender does that requires a response, then, is to break a law she could have obeyed had she so chosen. Not to respond to actions of that sort would undermine confidence in the law.

But what is it specifically about the actions of those who break laws they could have chosen to obey that requires a response? The account we have been developing suggests three elements.

First, social interaction occurs against a background of expectations. Ignoring or overriding those expectations inevitably gives offence and disrupts the capacity of those affected to cooperate. However, not all expectations are of equal significance to those who hold them. For example, we may expect those we deal with to keep their appointments. However, we also distinguish between arriving late and not showing up at all. Again, most people expect those with whom they deal to tell the truth. However, a minor inaccuracy will not have the weight of a serious distortion or misconstruction.

The law has the same character. Offenders choose to ignore laws that those responsible for creating them have concluded are needed to protect interests they have identified as requiring the protection of the law. The importance of some of those interests will be obvious. Human beings are particularly vulnerable to violence. For that reason, violence threatens fundamental interests. Using force to accomplish goals is by its nature implicitly violent. Hence, controlling the use of force is bound to be a central function of a legal system. To use force to override the law is therefore to give serious offence.

However, not all laws are directly concerned with prohibiting violence. Some of the interests protected by the law will be matters of convenience, and the harms threatened by non-compliance may therefore be relatively minor. Parking regulations are a good example. The interests involved may be thought to be of sufficient importance that they warrant protection by law. However, overriding the expectations they create may hold only minor significance for those affected.

It follows, therefore, that the seriousness of an offence will be a function in part of the nature of the offence itself. However, the impact of an offence is also in part a function of the attitudes it reflects. People fail to meet the expectations of others for many reasons. How those failures are interpreted will depend a great deal on those reasons. A failure may be simply a matter of communication. Or it may have a more upsetting source. Thus, we would expect the reactions of an employer, who discovered that an employee had failed to lock up the cash before taking a break because she did not understand clearly what was expected of her, to be shaped by that knowledge. If it turned out that the employee had already been warned about the problem, we would anticipate yet another reaction. And if it turned out that the employee simply attached no importance to meeting her employer's expectation that she treat cash carefully, yet another reaction would be called for.

Offenders, too, break the law for a variety of reasons. It may be that an opportunity which could not be resisted simply presented itself. The theft of a purse left unattended in an open car might well provide such an occasion. Or an offence might be motivated by anger or a perceived slight. Or it might reflect careful planning.

Those who break laws they could have obeyed raise doubts about their attitude to the law. Whether an offence was the product of careful planning or alternatively a spontaneous response to a temptation would normally be understood as relevant to shaping an appropriate response. Knowledge that an offence had been carefully planned, that it was one of several that an individual had attempted, and that she had attempted to involve others would normally play a role in determining whether she could in the future be trusted to live within the law. Hence, one element of an offence that requires a response is the intentions and attitudes of the offender committing it.

The actual harm caused is a third element of any offence that requires a response. The law is put in place to protect interests that those creating it think important. However, not all offences of the same type have equally harmful consequences. Someone through carelessness may leave a fire alarm unrepaired. If the error is detected before a fire occurs, little harm will have resulted. If, on the other hand, the error results in delay in detecting a fire, the consequences might well warrant serious criticism.

But is this fair? Why should we react one way to someone whose actions by good fortune caused no direct harm and another way to someone who was less fortunate, though her action was identical?

There are several reasons for taking the harm actually caused into consideration in evaluating the nature of an offence. In general, when legitimate expectations are ignored with harmful results, the outcome underlines the importance of the rule or practice generating the expectation. The harm caused may also give rise to a serious grievance on the part of the victim. Responding to the offence now requires responding to that grievance. The greater the harm, the more effort that will be required to deal with it. Finally, the harm caused makes it more difficult to avoid asking whether the offender should be trusted in the future.

A question of fit

How does this account of how to determine the seriousness of an offence fit with the operation of legal systems? And what implications does it have for law reform?

The fit appears to be a very good one. The criminal law is divided into various categories of offence. And what might be described as the law's view of the generic seriousness of those offences is signalled by the penalties attached to them. At the same time, most legal codes leave a great deal of room for sentencing discretion, either by specifying the range within which a penalty for a specific type of offence must fall – a minimum of two and a maximum of ten years' imprisonment, for example – or by giving maximum penalties only. What is more, the penalties attached to offences are widely interpreted by the public as indicating the seriousness with which a given offence is regarded by the authorities. Thus, as attitudes toward drinking and driving have altered, the severity of penalties attached to drinking and driving offences has been increased. The same is true of environmental protection laws. Those who want environmental protection taken more seriously invariably argue for increased penalties, a change which their opponents invariably resist.

It is clear too that legal systems respond carefully to what offenders have in mind in committing offences. This is reflected by the role played in sentencing of mitigating and aggravating factors, a role which at the present time is important and universal but still relatively unstructured.[24] A recent study commissioned by the Canadian Sentencing Commission of appeal court sentencing decisions in Alberta and Quebec identified nineteen mitigating and seventeen aggravating factors which influence the court in determining an appropriate sentence for specific offenders. Mitigating factors included: plea of guilty, cooperation with the police, presence but no use of weapon, role of offender, drugs/alcohol, spontaneity, attempts, no record, good work record, age, amount and type of substance, no violence, low intelligence, education, good reputation in community, remorse, rehabilitation, marital status, and family background. Identified as aggravating factors were: use of weapons, seriousness of offence, amount and type of substance, degree of sophistication, frequency of crime in society, violence/harm, vulnerability of victim, drugs/alcohol, premeditation, leader, criminal record, work record, age, violent propensity, good family history, professional criminal, and status at time of offence (Benzvy-Miller 1988: 32).

After a study of court records and other sources, Leslie Wilkins (1984: 100ff) compiled two lists as follows:

Aggravating factors
  Relating to the offender
    Offender continued criminal activity after arrest
    Offender showed erratic/irrational behaviour in the offence
    Offender showed bizarre/depraved behaviour in the offence
    Police state arrest was difficult
    Offender under the influence of drugs at time
    Offender under the influence of alcohol at time
    Offender a person of high status in the community
    Offender a person of no fixed abode
    Instant offence repeats an earlier
    Instant offence is of different type than earlier
    Military record shows proven military crime
    Offender does not express remorse – e.g. found guilty but pleaded not guilty
  Relating to victim
    Victim was particularly vulnerable
    Injury to victim was unusually extensive
    Damage to property was unusually extensive
    Multiple injuries to the victim
    Victim is/was friend
    Victim is relation
    Victim presses for heavy penalty
  Relating to crime
    Evidence of planning of the crime
  Relating to the environment
    Much similar crime in district lately

Mitigating factors
  Factors relating to the offender
    Offender is younger than usual for this crime

163

Offender offers restitution
Offender assisted law officers in solving other crimes
Offender has exceptionally good employment record
Offender had been drinking at the time
Offender of low intelligence
Offender's spouse a serious problem/family difficulties
Prior mental treatment
Physical handicap of offender
No arrests or convictions
No arrests or convictions except as juvenile
No previous crimes of same kind
No previous crimes, but only arrests
Relating to victim
   Provocation seems likely
   Victim is/was friend of offender
   Victim asks for leniency
   Political motive for crime
Relating to the crime
   Others involved apparently leaders
   Property recovered by the police
Relating to situation/other
   Prison would cause exceptional hardship to offender's dependants

Neither of these studies could be said to provide a definitive categorization of mitigating and aggravating factors. What they do show is widespread agreement that the intentions, attitudes, and values of offenders, as reflected in their actions, are important in gauging the seriousness of an offence.[25] This should not be surprising. Remorse, the offering of apologies, belligerence, maturity, and so on do, in the normal course of events, influence reactions to actions that fail to meet legitimate expectations. That being the case, one would expect these same factors to influence the sentencing process. In shaping an appropriate response to what someone has done, whether it was part of a pattern or an isolated case, whether it was a result of immature judgement or a formed personality, whether the offender showed remorse or regret, and so on play a role in interpreting her action and what it implies about her attitude toward the law.

These studies also point to the importance of the impact of an offence on its victims in assessing its seriousness. Our account suggests two basic reasons for this. In the normal course of events, the more harm done by someone in the pursuit of her objectives, the more significant the impact of her actions will be and the more difficult it will be to ignore what has taken place. Harming others creates grievances. The greater the harm, the more substantial the grievance. To ignore this factor is to leave the grievance unaddressed.

Implications for sentencing reform

An important test of a theory of sentencing is its implications for sentencing reform. In this case, the test is particularly important because concern with sentencing practices is a major reason for current interest in the philosophy of punishment.

The practical problems which sentencing theory must address are substantial. There is to begin with a growing concern among the public, as well as those charged with the responsibility for administering the criminal justice system, with the phenomenon of disparity. Numerous studies have shown that sentences handed down by judges do vary sometimes quite substantially from judge to judge, from one region to another, from country to country, and so on.

Why is disparity a problem? There are two principal reasons. First, fairness has traditionally been thought to require equality of treatment before the law. When great disparities in sentences for similar crimes begin to appear, equality of treatment is the obvious victim. Examination of the data also suggests apparent disparity in the treatment of various groups. In Canada, for example, there are a disproportionate number of native people in prison. In the United States and Great Britain, racial and ethnic minorities are also over-represented.

For some commentators, sentencing discrepancy is a natural consequence of judicial discretion. Appealing to a just deserts model, they urge the elimination of judicial discretion through the use of fixed sentences specified by law, based on criteria whose focus is equality of treatment. Following this reasoning, some jurisdictions, particularly in the United States, have introduced mandatory sentencing guidelines that leave judges with little or no room for the exercise of discretion, flat sentences that specify the amount of time that an offender must serve, the elimination of parole (because of its discretionary quality), and the elimination of earned remission.

We have already seen, however, that a single-minded pursuit of just deserts can create only the illusion of justice. We have also seen that discretion is a factor in the enforcement process at every level. To seek to eliminate it at the sentencing stage cannot avoid having procrustean implications. Interpreting the behaviour of others is unavoidably complex and requires the exercise of judgement. The meaning of people's actions is not easily discerned. If judges are prohibited from exercising judgement, responsibility for this task will simply shift to other authorities – the prosecutors or the police – where it is less visible and therefore less easy to control.

Discrepancy in sentencing creates a second significant problem, that of uncertainty. Where sentences range widely for similar offences, the capacity of individuals to predict their treatment at the hands of the law is greatly diminished. This has both moral and practical implications. The greater the uncertainty, the more arbitrary and the less fair or just sentencing will appear to the public or offenders. This sense that sentencing practices no longer follow predictable patterns lies at the heart of recent attempts to find an appropriate place for sentencing guidelines in the criminal justice process. It may also have contributed to public demands for more consistently harsh sentencing practices. Yet studies show that imposing harsher sentences has little effect on the incidence of crime.[26]

The suggestion that a sentence is a response to three things – the nature of the crime committed, the offender herself, and the harm caused by her offence – together with the suggestion that its proper role is to provide assurance that continued confidence in the law is warranted, does not, taken by itself, imply a definitive theory of sentencing. It is sufficiently rich, however, to justify the rejection of some of the more popular proposals for sentencing reform. To begin with, if what is required is a response to the offence itself, the offender herself, and the harm actually caused, then exclusive focus on either the offender or the offence will be unsatisfactory in ways that would be immediately apparent were either approach to be applied in parallel but non-legal areas of life. The law must respond to offenders as individuals, their intentions, attitudes, and values (all of which play a central role in how actions are interpreted by others). It must also, and inevitably does, respond to what they did. Finally, the law cannot ignore the nature of the harm offenders actually cause.

This implies a number of things. First, it is clear that any system that lays down mandatory sentences for specific types of offence will in practice be unjust. Mitigating and aggravating factors do play a role in human behaviour and in our interpretation of human actions, in both formal and informal settings. It is equally obvious, on the account we have set out, that indeterminate sentencing will also be the source of serious injustice for similar reasons.

However, the fact that the law is justified in responding to those who voluntarily break the law, and that an adequate response must address the three elements of an offence identified, says little in a positive way about what response is required. We can complete the picture only by turning to a discussion of sentencing and corrections.

Before we go on, however, let us look briefly at three worries to which our account might be thought to give rise. First, if a key element in responding to offenders is what their behaviour implies about their willingness to live within the law, why should the authorities wait for an offence to be committed to intervene? Why should the law not intervene when confidence has been undermined for whatever reason?

If we see sentencing as an isolated component in the enforcement process, this question will be a difficult one to answer. However, if we see it as a part of an enforcement process guided by common principles and objectives, then it is clear that the law should not and, in the normal course of events, does not wait for offences to occur before it intervenes. The process of demonstration, persuasion, and enablement is a continuous one. The law can and does quite legitimately intervene in a variety of ways designed (with more or less skill) to secure its observance. On the other hand, to use any component of the enforcement process inappropriately can only undermine efficient and effective enforcement.

Those who by their actions and words indicate they are not to be trusted to obey the law pose severe problems for any society. Earlier, in our discussion of juveniles and the mentally ill, we explored some of those problems. However, to confuse the challenge people of this sort pose with that posed by those adults who have broken laws they could have chosen to obey is to ignore factors that normally play a central role in our response as human beings to the actions of others. It is, in short, to treat people as manipulable things and not as persons. And it would be to ignore and confuse matters which should, on our account of the matter, be carefully distinguished.

Second, if what is at issue is confidence or trust, is there any limitation on the kind of evidence that can legitimately be introduced? The

167

lists of mitigating and aggravating factors provide a good example. It seems an empirical fact that people are influenced in deciding on the reliability of others by a wide range of considerations – education, ethnic background, place of residence, work record, social status, and so on. Are these factors all equally legitimate in shaping a response to an offence? If not, which factors have a legitimate place in the process and which do not?

Any theory of sentencing in which judgement and interpretation have a role will have to face this question. The account being offered here is no exception.

Assessing the implications of an action for ongoing social relationships may invoke considerations that over time come to be seen as morally unacceptable. Legal systems have discriminated against individuals and groups. They have judged such things as race or religion to play a role in assessing reliability. And in doing so they have been mistaken. The account here being developed does not require that criteria for interpreting behaviour be taken at face value or accepted uncritically. Individuals and culture may well give inappropriate weight to considerations that bear little or no relationship to trustworthiness. Identifying and weeding out those considerations is one of the ongoing tasks of a morally sensitive society and a well-functioning legal system.[27]

Finally, if we accept that the function of a sentence is to reassure the public, does this not expose offenders to the whims of the majority? Might it not mean, for example, the reintroduction of capital punishment and harsher sentences generally, given prevailing moods?

This is indeed a fundamental question. However, providing a sound response requires that we provide a more detailed account of the role of sentencing and corrections as a component of law enforcement. It is to this task that we must now turn.

7

SENTENCING AND THE IDEA OF RESTORATIVE JUSTICE

PART I: TWO PRELIMINARY SENTENCING OPTIONS

If the account we have been developing is correct, sentencing, like enforcement generally, has three functions: to demonstrate widespread willingness to obey the law, conjoined with commitment to conscientious enforcement; to persuade those who might otherwise not obey the law to do so; and to enable those who might not otherwise obey the law to do so. We have seen that to approach sentencing this way not only allows us to link sentencing to a broader set of enforcement principles, it also fits with and allows us to explain the commitment of modern legal systems to the principle of responsibility in determining guilt and the role of mitigating and aggravating circumstances in assessing the seriousness of offences. But does it fit modern sentencing and correctional practices? Investigating this question is our task in this chapter.

Popular views of the function of sentencing and corrections

There is much about contemporary and historical approaches to sentencing that suggests that the analysis we have developed captures widely shared understandings of the function of sanctions. This is true at the level of both theory and practice. It is not uncommon for judges to describe a sentence as demonstrating the court's view of the seriousness of an offence. The idea that a sentence is a device for persuading offenders not to repeat their act is also a common aspect of sentencing. Sanctions whose goal is either specific or general deterrence have this as an explicit objective. So, too, sanctions are

169

often justified in common parlance for their educative value, a theme as old as punishment itself. Finally, the theme of enablement has dominated corrections in the twentieth century under the rubric of rehabilitation.

These themes have also played prominent roles in theories of punishment. One of the functions of punishment on retributivist accounts of the matter is to express public condemnation of moral wrongdoing.[1] Traditionally, both retributive and utilitarian theories have highlighted the educative (i.e. persuasive) function of punishment.[2] Finally, many theories have emphasized the need in responding to crime for rehabilitation, the need, that is, to assist offenders to learn how to live within the law.

On the other hand, there is much about the history and the theory of punishment that conflicts with the account we have been developing. For example, the idea that the underlying themes of sentencing should parallel those of policing and adjudication is not a common feature of traditional or current discussions of punishment.[3] More important, it has become increasingly clear that there is no common unifying theme running through the sentencing practice or theory in contemporary legal systems.[4]

Finally, although it is common for reform proposals to call for the use of minimum force in imposing penalties while pointing to the virtue of diverting offenders to the least coercive level of response compatible with their offence,[5] neither of these two principles has a firm or uncontested place in either sentencing practice or theory. Further, many influential theorists have accepted the proposition that the right to respect as autonomous persons is one of the things that is forfeited by offenders when they break the law.

We are left, then, with an unclear answer to our question: does the account we have been developing describe the function of sentencing and corrections as they are currently practised in modern democratic countries? There are aspects of sentencing theory and practice that fit the suggestion that the function of sentencing is to build or maintain public confidence in the capacity of the law to fulfil its various functions. However, the fit is not perfect by any means. This is, at least in part, because there is little if any consensus at the level of theory or practice about what the goals of sentencing should be. It is also because, as we shall see, contemporary approaches to sentencing and reform continue to need substantial reform.

It would seem to follow that whether we choose to adopt the view being presented will depend in large measure on what it implies for sentencing and sentencing reform, and whether the approach that it implies is both practical and morally justifiable.

Sentencing: the reparative option

If the goal of enforcement is reassuring the public that, contrary to any impressions a particular offence or sequence of offences might have created, they have good grounds for continuing confidence in the capacity of the law to fulfil its function, then reparative justice presents itself, on the surface at least, as an attractive sentencing orientation.

Central to the notion of reparations is the desire to overcome the alienation that is a normal consequence of a failure to live up to the legitimate expectations of others by making a gesture that acknowledges responsibility for harm inflicted and expresses regret. Apologies have this function. Where an apology is not adequate, we often accompany it with an offer of compensation. Where no effort is made to repair the damage caused by a failure to meet the legitimate expectations of others, the relationships involved are almost certain to be damaged.

Reparations undertaken in response to a formal offence have a similar function. They represent an attempt to correct the wrongs caused and rebuild the basis for cooperation. When they are offered as an expression of regret and an acknowledgement of responsibility for wrongs done, accepted as a sincere and adequate response to the harms caused, reparations fulfil what we have identified tentatively as the enforcement functions of sentencing. By offering to repair the damage caused by his offence, an offender acknowledges that an offence was committed contrary to law and that the picture of the victim projected by the offence is false. From the point of view of the authorities, reparations represent an acknowledgement on the part of the offender that he is not above the law. From the point of view of the public, reparations imply a desire and a willingness to live within the law by accepting responsibility for wrongdoing and undertaking to correct it. And from the point of view of the offender, reparations provide a basis for rebuilding trust that may have been undermined by the offence, thereby recreating the conditions for reassuming a normal place in society.

Reparative justice: obstacles and objections

Although reparations offer a clear and effective way of correcting the harms caused by criminal offences, the idea that the function of sentencing is to achieve reparative justice is open to significant criticism. We know from common experience that trust can be earned and that lost confidence can be regained. We also know from common experience that restoring confidence in the law, or in a particular offender, can be very difficult where distrust and fear have set in. Why is this so? There are many reasons, some of them very complex.

Offering compensation for harm caused is a basic reparative gesture, common in personal, business, professional, and employment relationships, to mention just a few examples. It is also available as a remedy in the case of criminal offences. The difficulty is that frequently there is no obvious direct form of compensation available. Where the only harm, beyond the loss of replaceable material goods, is inconvenience, an obvious remedy is to replace the loss. However, many crimes do not lend themselves so easily to this approach. Compensating for physical injury, emotional trauma, loss of life, permanent disability are examples. Where the harms sustained by a victim are intangible – fear, loss of confidence, or emotional distress resulting from the victimization of a spouse or child or friend – devising an appropriate form of compensation becomes more difficult and perhaps even offensive.

Where the victim is a group or community, similar problems emerge. Compensating for vandalism may be relatively straightforward. It is not at all clear, however, what might count as appropriate compensation for the harm that is caused when social relationships are damaged, or public confidence in institutions or professions or public standards is undermined.

It follows that finding an appropriate form of compensation for criminal offences will often be difficult and sometimes perhaps even impossible.

There is a second difficulty. The criminal law places the state between the offender, his victim, and the public. By acting as a buffer, the state can impose procedural safeguards designed to ensure that those accused of offences are fairly treated. The effect of the state's formal intervention, however, is to isolate offenders, making it more difficult for them to repair the harm their actions have caused and win back the confidence of those whose trust has been shaken.

For example, individuals and groups typically respond to conduct they regard as offensive by seeking to resolve their disagreements informally, or by creating social distance, where re-establishing or repairing relationships is not an option or is not successful. The reparative responses emerge from dialogue and mediation. However, where criminal offences are involved, the law formalizes the dialogue and stipulates the remedies.

By formalizing dispute settlement, the law shifts the primary responsibility for maintaining the background conditions of trust from individuals, interacting on an informal basis, to formal legal institutions. In a very real sense, this constitutes a loss of control by individuals over their own lives. By requiring that disputes be settled in accordance with law, the law defines the remedies available to individuals who have been victimized and requires that they rely on the law to ensure they are fairly treated. And when the conditions it lays down are met, it pronounces the matter resolved, whatever the attitudes of those who have been adversely affected by the offending behaviour. Thus, the law removes from individuals the right to decide for themselves the degree to which someone's actions have undermined his relationship with the community and what therefore constitutes an appropriate response. However, if sentences formally imposed fail to capture the expectations of victims and the community generally, they cannot fulfil a restorative function.

This gives rise to an additional problem. By interposing itself between offenders and those they have offended against, the state blocks direct dialogue. The trial is conducted by the state which assumes responsibility for gathering relevant information and assessing its significance. Victims are left to inform themselves. Lack of information, combined with the fear and distrust that crime can cause, can easily distort public perceptions of what counts as an adequate remedy for particular offences.[6]

Providing evidence that an offender can once again be trusted to live within the law is a serious difficulty. It is not, for example, a matter of formal proof or satisfying formal standards. The difficulty of reintegrating offenders into society, following the imposition of formal sanctions, is good evidence of this. The community is not necessarily persuaded that someone has earned the right to be treated normally just because he has served his sentence. This is illustrated by the serious difficulties offenders typically encounter when, having 'paid their debt to society', they attempt to find a productive place in society.

Finally, an inevitable imbalance of risks and burdens is imposed by any attempt to rebuild a place for an offender in the community. For the most part, when the law is broken, the burden of the offence is carried by the victim, who may have little to gain by cooperating with the person who has victimized him. Providing offenders with opportunities to rebuild a place for themselves also places uneven burdens on members of the community. An employer who is asked to take an offender or ex-offender onto the payroll may expose himself and his employees to substantial risks in return for relatively insubstantial personal gains.

Sharing the risks associated with providing offenders opportunities to rebuild their position in society in a fair manner poses real obstacles to accomplishing the goals of reparative sentencing. These obstacles seem to pale into insignificance, however, when faced with the objections that can be raised against this approach. Restoring confidence and rebuilding trust are by their nature voluntary, cooperative activities. Restorative justice cannot be imposed. It cannot achieve its objectives without the willing cooperation of offender and victim. In contrast, sentencing is by its nature coercive.

This problem is highlighted by the fact that those committing offences often feel no regret for their actions. Criminal activity may well be motivated by a simple rejection of the values reflected in the law. Or it may be motivated by serious grievances, either real or imagined. No approach to sentencing which does not acknowledge this fact can be adequate to its task.

Sentencing as social defence

It is the capacity of an action to undermine public confidence in the willingness of people generally and the offender in particular to obey the laws that gives offence and invites a coercive response. A sentence is one component of that response. It constitutes an intervention on the part of sentencing authorities in the life of an offender, motivated by the belief that the assumption that people can for the most part be trusted to obey the law does not apply to him.

What kind of response does such a loss of confidence justify? Is there a pattern in everyday life that provides guidance here?

Social life, we have suggested, occurs against a background of expectations. We expect those with whom we deal to respect general rules and values: to tell the truth, to resolve disagreements in acceptable ways, to fulfil their responsibilities as parents, or neighbours, or professionals and so on. Confidence that people can on the whole be trusted to meet legitimate expectations creates opportunities that would not otherwise exist. Plans can be made, activities can be engaged in, agreements arrived at that would not otherwise be possible.

Failure to meet those expectations can generate a wide variety of responses, from mild regret or disappointment to anger, resentment, fear, loss of respect, and so on. The disappointment may be simply shrugged off. Or it may result in changed relationships. Cooperation rests on trust. As trust is undermined, the possibilities for cooperation are affected. Relationships become strained, or perhaps are ended, as those involved seek to protect themselves from the exploitation or the hurt to which they feel they have become exposed.

What is an appropriate response to those who cannot be trusted to meet common expectations? What might one expect to happen when expectations collapse or are no longer warranted? Presumably, what is undermined and perhaps lost is the willingness, and perhaps even the capacity of those whose confidence has been undermined, to continue to relate as before to the person in whom trust has been weakened. In the first instance, those affected may simply watch more closely to see whether their suspicions are warranted. Or they may insist that the activities directly affected be supervised more carefully to ensure that the rules are observed. They may choose to end the activity. Or they may simply lose the capacity to continue it.

Invoking the law is one response available when expectations that are grounded on the law are not met. Crime surveys show that failure to obey the law generates the whole range of responses just outlined. Where little offence is given or those involved are committed to working through the problem informally, the law may not be invoked. However, the more serious or persistent the offence, the more difficult it will be simply to ignore it. This is particularly true of the law, whose basic function is to create a social framework for cooperation and to protect those working within that framework from the harms to which they would otherwise be exposed.

What can the law do to protect those willing to live within the law from those who are not? Presumably it can do what individuals do in the context of their own relationships, namely, reduce the exposure of those willing to live within the law to being harmed by those who are not. One obvious way of doing this is to offer protection by placing controls on those who might otherwise break the law. Control might be nothing more than supervision. However, it might also mean some form of isolation. The more severe the harm threatened, the more severe the control warranted.

This view of the function of sentencing fits the account we have been developing. Loss of confidence in the willingness of someone to meet legitimate informal expectations has the same effect on social relationships as is the case with expectations created through the establishment of formal rules or laws. And the responses to that loss of confidence follow similar patterns. The difference lies in the formal character of the law. If there is no formal response, the law loses its formal character. A sentence is a formal response. It is an essential component in maintaining confidence in the law.

Coercive intervention, with a view to protecting those who are prepared to respect the law from those who are not, can take many forms, from incarceration to supervision. Hence defensive measures can be shaped to meet the requirements of the minimum use of force principle. It is also consistent with respect for individual autonomy. The law creates a protective framework whose justification rests on its capacity to reduce the use of force in settling disputes and thus enhance the capacity of those falling under its authority to pursue goals in ways that would not otherwise be possible. Using force to enforce the law is therefore justified, if the law is to fulfil its function.

Social protection or protecting the public has become the dominant view of the purpose of sentencing in recent years.[7] Hence, to see the purpose of sentencing as social protection has the virtue of fitting widely shared perceptions of its proper function.

Sentencing as social defence: obstacles and objections

The view that the purpose of a sentence is to protect the public from harm at the hands of an offender, while attractive and popular, is not, however, an adequate foundation for a theory of sentencing. As the sole formal response to criminal activity, seeking to enforce the law by controlling offenders through supervision or incarceration cannot succeed. Neither is it consistent with the principles of enforcement we have articulated, or with common sense.

To begin with, seeking to protect the public from those in whom confidence has been undermined or lost through supervision or incarceration is an intrinsically negative response of limited short-term value. For example, isolating an offender from the public through incarceration may succeed in ensuring that he will not repeat his offence in the short term. But, unless the sentence imposes indefinite incarceration, it cannot provide long-term protection.[8] Supervision in the community is equally limited in value. Maintaining control over an offender in a community setting is extremely difficult in modern societies. Constant surveillance is virtually impossible, except in an incarceral setting.

The essence of the problem is that the law rests on voluntary compliance. Since not all members of a community can be trusted to comply voluntarily, the law must either seek to isolate permanently those who have shown they cannot be trusted, or create ways for those who have undermined confidence to regain the trust they have lost. Permanent or indefinite isolation is draconian and common fairness prohibits its frequent use. Furthermore, as we discovered earlier, its effect is to increase hostility and undermine the possibility of reintegration.

Finally, the purely negative objective of protection through supervision or isolation is one way of reaffirming commitment to the law and condemning criminal acts. It constitutes, therefore, one way of demonstrating commitment to the legal point of view. However, it ignores, except in the most simplistic way, the persuasive and enablement functions of enforcement. Persuading people that they should obey the law, as we have seen, is one effective way of building confidence in the assumption that most people are prepared to obey the law most of the time. So too is enablement. Both these elements of enforcement move beyond the coercive mechanisms of the law in an effort to win voluntary, i.e. non-supervised, compliance.

Subjecting an offender to supervision or incarceration is one way of communicating an unfavourable view of his behaviour. As such, and because it implies more or less extensive restraints on an offender's freedom to conduct his own affairs, the threat of supervision has the weight of a deterrent. Yet these are side-effects of an approach to sentencing whose goal is not change in attitudes but control based on mistrust.

Is there a third model available to us?

PART II: SENTENCING AS CONFLICT RESOLUTION

If the basic function of the law is to reduce recourse to violence in the resolution of disputes, then it would seem to follow that a basic task of law enforcement is to resolve conflicts with a minimum use of force. Is this a sound way of looking at sentencing?

It might be argued that the function of the criminal law is not to solve conflicts but to seek to avoid them by prohibiting harmful behaviour and stepping in to provide protection from those unwilling to obey the law. This description is not inaccurate, as we have seen. However, once the law is broken, conflict is the result. It is clear from our discussion that criminal activity brings offenders into conflict with victims, with the police and other enforcement authorities, and with the public at large. It is not uncommon, for example, to describe those who break the law as in conflict with the law.

What then sets criminal disputes apart from private law disputes? The answer, as we have seen, is their public character. Criminal activity requires a public response, because it challenges the authority of the law and has the potential to undermine public confidence in the law and therefore the sense of security that the law functions to create.

If sentencing is properly regarded as an activity whose goal is conflict resolution, what approach to sentencing is implied? The answer is not absolutely straight-forward. Since there are many views of the nature of human relationships, there are many different answers to this question. Indeed, each of the theories of punishment we have explored can be construed as a conflict resolution model. However, those approaches have already been examined at some length and criticized. Is there an alternative?

Conflict resolution is an area of human relationships that has been extensively studied. A surprising degree of consensus has developed. It is worth describing that consensus and then determining its applicability to an understanding of the role of sentencing and also of corrections.

Conflict is defined in Webster's Dictionary as 'a struggle between opposing principles and aims' or 'a clash of feelings or interests'. The language of conflict is the language of competition, opposition, hostility, anger, resentment, victory and defeat, and so on. Recourse to force is one way of resolving conflict by inflicting defeat. However, the use of force is itself morally problematic.

The essential problem with conflict is that it is self-perpetuating and has a tendency to escalate. It begins in a hostile act, one that is seen by its victim as unwarranted and unjustified, unfair, avoidably harmful, and so on. The problem faced by the victim is how to respond. He can ignore his victimization and hope it is not repeated. But this may be interpreted as weakness and does not correct the harm that might have been caused. Or he may seek to defend himself or to retaliate.

Any of these responses may escalate the conflict. A passive response may be interpreted as weakness and invite further abuse. A defensive response may stimulate an aggressive reaction. Retaliation may generate a further grievance to which there must now be a correcting response. The patterns in each case are familiar parts of everyday experience.

The primary goal of conflict resolution is to de-escalate the conflict. As Conrad Brunk points out:

> this means reversing the spiral of destructive or negative inter-actions – the expressions of anger, hostility, and alienation – which tend to build up in the conflict. It also means attempting to find a mutually satisfying outcome to the conflict – either by both parties obtaining most of what they want (ending the conflict) or by reaching an agreement on procedures for settling their on-going incompatibilities ('regulating the conflict').
>
> (Brunk 1988: 3)

Both research and common sense suggest that the preferred method of resolving disputes is using procedures in which the parties to the conflict produce a resolution directly through discussion. The problem is to overcome the obstacles in the way of the parties' ability to sit down with each other, make a rational assessment of the issues at stake in the conflict, and cooperate in the building of a solution. This, however, is the central dilemma. To work together, there must be a minimum level of trust. Unfortunately, this is the first casualty of escalating conflict. As Brunk puts it:

> The more severe the conflict becomes, the more trust is eroded, and the more difficult it becomes for the parties to deal constructively with their problem. A well-known dynamic in conflict is that the less trust there is between the parties, the more difficult it becomes for them to communicate, the more

179

they misperceive the nature of the conflict and the intentions of their opponent, and the more difficult it is for them to perceive a sincere, friendly gesture by the opponent as truly friendly. It is the classic 'positive feedback mechanism' where the conflict feeds on itself and expands.

(Brunk 1988: 4)

The pattern described here is a common one in corrections, as both experience and empirical research confirm.

How then can the obstacles be overcome? Much of the literature and research on the subject has focused on informal dispute resolution of the sort commonly encountered in community life – disputes between and among neighbours, family members, friends, colleagues, work mates and so on. The key is usually mediation, voluntarily agreed to, conducted by reference to a number of now relatively well-known and accepted principles. The mediator is neutral. His goal is to maximize communication so that the parties to the conflict can come to understand their opponents' point of view, identify common interests and goals, and find a solution which all can endorse, one that maximizes everyone's interests. The common parlance speaks of win/win solutions, rather than win/lose solutions.

There have been many attempts made to find a place for mediation within the sentencing and correctional process.[9] Most involve attempting to introduce mediation between the offender and victim and/or the offender and the authorities. The essential problem with the model is that it conflicts with basic features of the formal legal process. It is an attempt to divert disputes from a formal, i.e. legal, to an informal, i.e. non-legal, setting. In many cases, it is advanced as an alternative to the law and implies a lack of confidence in law as a way of resolving disputes.[10]

A criminal offence, however, brings an offender into conflict with the law itself. The law defines the dispute and stipulates appropriate responses. To introduce genuine mediation is to move the dispute from the jurisdiction of the law and make the applicability of the law a matter of negotiation, an approach which is an alternative to law, not a development of it.[11] It would seem therefore that the criminal law itself is an obstacle to the direct application of a mediation model. The court is not neutral. The judge is not a mediator in any true sense of the word. And the court cannot negotiate changes in the law.[12]

It does not follow, however, that a conflict resolution model of sentencing is inappropriate. It is the idea that the mediation might replace formal sentencing or that the role of the court could be changed to that of mediator between offender and victim that is inappropriate. The dispute is with the law. The court is a party to that dispute and is committed (if it is to retain the confidence of the public) to the legal point of view. The court as sentencing authority is not neutral; neither is it equal.

Conflict resolution and the idea of neutrality

The solution to our dilemma lies in recognizing that the principles of conflict resolution apply whether there is mediation or not. Mediation is a strategy for introducing principles of conflict resolution into a dispute. Its purpose is to provide a mechanism for guiding dialogue along specific channels. What is central to dispute resolution, however, are some basic principles.

The first is: *be friendly but firm*. This implies defending legitimate interests while avoiding the temptation to inflict defeat. There have been numerous studies that point to the importance of this principle. Francis Cullen and Paul Gendreau (1989), in a review of the effectiveness of correctional rehabilitation, argue persuasively that rehabilitation does work. However, effective programmes must adhere to specific rules. One of those is that the offender must be 'aware that he or she must abide by reasonable program contingencies spelled out, for example, by the probation order or the requirements of the therapeutic contract' (Cullen and Gendreau 1989). What is described as 'therapeutic integrity' is also essential. The basic rules and principles on which a rehabilitative programme is based have to be respected both by those offering the programme and by those taking it if it is to be successful (Cullen and Gendreau 1989).

Studies done in behavioural research and with Prisoner's Dilemma games confirm this view.[13]

A second principle is: *undertake to understand the opponents' position and to communicate one's own*. As Brunk points out, 'a major factor in all serious conflicts is the misperceptions the parties have of each other's intentions, character, and contribution to the conflict as well as the nature of the conflict itself' (Brunk 1988: 4). The significance of this point for criminal justice is apparent in many of the studies and experiments with victims and offenders over the past two decades. Martin Chupp, in a study 'Reconciliation Procedures and Rationale', puts the matter succinctly.

> Rarely have offenders had to face their victims and the human impact of their crimes. Offenders perceive their victims to be deserving of the crime and able quickly to recover losses. Victims have not only been overlooked by their offenders but many times by the entire criminal justice system.
>
> (Chupp 1989: 56)

Studies have shown that there is a good deal of misinformation about offenders among both victims and the public generally, as well as misinformation about what victims and the public generally both think and want from the criminal justice and sentencing process.[14]

The third principle is: *focus on common interests and propose solutions that an opponent is likely to have an interest in accepting.* Robert Fisher (1969) refers to this as giving yesable propositions. If a conflict is to be resolved, those involved have to see their way to a solution that both can accept as legitimate. Again, this observation is echoed in criminal justice experience. There is no evidence that sentencing oriented toward putting offenders down, or teaching harsh lessons, or deterring through harsh sentences is effective.

Principle four is: *be prepared to make unilateral gestures of cooperation.* Someone has to make the first move. This is simply common sense. And again, experience in corrections bears this out. Sentences whose impact on offenders is essentially negative do not reduce recidivism. On the other hand, experience with mediation and rehabilitation suggests that providing opportunities to participate in well-thought-out and well-administered programmes can assist offenders to reintegrate in the community.[15]

Conflict resolution and modern legal systems

At first glance, to approach sentencing in the manner suggested might seem incompatible with modern sentencing practice. Closer scrutiny undermines this appearance, however. The legal point of view requires that the law stand firm in the face of criminal behaviour. The law must be obeyed. The first principle, therefore, is not a hard one to integrate with current practices. Neither does respect for basic principles of criminal justice require that the court approach offenders in a hostile manner. To the contrary, placing the responsibility of responding to criminal behaviour in the hands of the state has, as one of its virtues, putting the task of sentencing in the hands of detached observers who are not emotionally involved in the conflict, and who can therefore respond to an offender in a detached manner.

Communicating the position of the law is also central to modern legal systems, no matter how ineffective they may be in that regard. Anthony Duff, for example, has argued that the central purpose of a trial, and any sentence that is subsequently imposed, is to communicate the community's view that the offending behaviour is unacceptable and should be repudiated by the offender. Further, as Duff (1986) has pointed out, many of the features of modern trials can only be understood on the assumption that a central purpose of a trial is dialogue and communication.

It is equally true that modern criminal procedure requires that an accused should be able to defend himself in court. Furthermore, pre-sentence reports, when they are available, invariably set out the offender's background. And one of the functions of defence counsel is to put the offender's view of an appropriate disposition of his case before the court before sentencing occurs.

Providing yesable solutions is perhaps more difficult to reconcile with modern practice. Some commentators reject the idea that the views or attitudes of offenders are relevant to determining an appropriate sentence. However, there is a good deal of evidence that this outlook does not dominate sentencing practice. If attempting to find solutions designed to win the cooperation of offenders were not a high priority in modern systems, many popular sentencing options currently in use would be difficult to explain, including probation, parole, victim/offender reconciliation programmes, community service orders, intermittent sentencing whose goal is to allow offenders to hold jobs and maintain community roles, and even rehabilitation.

Finally, it is clear from judicial commentary that our courts do on occasion initiate 'unilateral gestures of cooperation'. What is not clear is how modern courts understand their role in this regard.

Enforcement and conflict resolution

Earlier, we saw that law enforcement has three purposes: to demonstrate that widespread confidence in the capacity of the law to fulfil its function is justified; to persuade those who might not otherwise do so to live within the law; and to enable those who might not otherwise do so to obey the law.

Social defence, we suggested earlier, is one essential element of law enforcement. Intervening to protect the public from those whose behaviour has undermined confidence in their willingness to obey the law is also consistent with conflict resolution. Conflict cannot be stabilized, de-escalated, or resolved if the offending behaviour is not brought under control. Resolving conflict, we have seen, also requires communication. Active conflict blocks communication and prevents the rebuilding of trust. A first step in conflict resolution, therefore, is halting the conflict.

Bringing conflict to a halt by protecting the parties from each other is an effective demonstration of commitment to the legal process. A sentencing procedure with this as one of its objectives is consistent, therefore, with both a commitment to law enforcement and a commitment to conflict resolution.

A second component of enforcement is persuasion. This too is consistent with conflict resolution principles. One central task of law enforcement is to persuade those subject to the law to obey it. We have seen that persuasion has a place in policing and adjudication. It also has a place in sentencing. Persuading offenders to change their attitudes to the law is an effective way of protecting the public and building public confidence in the law. Equally important for conflict resolution is persuading the public to allow offenders a chance to re-establish trust. Here, too, the principles of conflict resolution and law enforcement are compatible.[16]

Finally, law enforcement should function to enable people to live within the law. This is also a principle of conflict resolution. Conflict resolution strategies require facilitating communication and understanding, providing support for participants, and assisting those involved to develop those skills needed if a mutually agreeable conclusion to the conflict is to be reached. Community conflict resolution projects typically involve teaching communication skills, finding jobs that allow reparations, and so on. There is an obvious place in sentencing and corrections for similar activities. Rehabilitation is not incompatible with enforcement, as the history of modern corrections shows. Indeed, providing offenders with the skills and the assistance they are likely to require if they are to live within the law has been a primary objective of correctional policy and penal reform for at least the past century.

The centrality of persuasion

If the purpose of sentencing and corrections is conflict resolution, then a central purpose of sentencing and corrections is persuasion. This, as we have seen, does not rule out the use of force for the purposes of restraint, where restraining an offender is a necessary first step in protecting the public. However, it places emphasis not on the negative goal of preventing harm but on the positive goal of winning voluntary compliance.

If the account we have set out is correct, there are good reasons, at least in principle, for living within the law. But many people choose not to. What are their reasons? Answering this question is now of real importance. For, if a central function of sentencing and corrections is to persuade individual offenders to live voluntarily within the law, they must be persuaded to change their attitudes toward the law. To do this will require an understanding of why they have the attitudes they do.

In fact there are many reasons that people might have to disobey the law. David Hume has some interesting observations in this regard. We learn the value of cooperation and the need for rules in the first instance, he suggests, in family-like settings. Children need adult support of very basic kinds. Parents need the cooperation of their children if their lives are to be ordered and rewarding. At this level, the point of cooperation will be clear to all but the most obtuse or insensitive.[17]

The environment in which children are raised, however, is very variable. Some families are supportive; some are hostile and alienating. A large percentage of offenders come from abusive backgrounds, broken homes, conditions of neglect and poverty, and so on. It is hardly surprising that people from such backgrounds might fail to grasp the point of living within the law.

Understanding the need and the point of cooperation at basic levels of social organization is not enough, however, to give someone a convincing set of reasons for obeying the law. That is because the point of living within the law is not learned simply by extrapolating from the benefits of cooperation in primary groups like the family to cooperation with strangers. Modern societies are complex and impersonal. The benefits to be derived from cooperating with those with whom we are in immediate contact are relatively obvious and direct. However, the benefits of laws are often indirect and unevenly experienced. This means that any harm resulting from an offence may be distant or even imperceptible. Or the distance between the offender and the victim, however that is measured, may be so great that the harm can be dismissed as of no great significance. Many offenders, for example, believe that those they harm either deserve their treatment or are not much affected by it. What is more, some crimes are directed toward impersonal targets, institutions, or companies where there are no direct victims at all in the normal sense.

We might expect, therefore, that the value of formal mechanisms for coordinating and guiding social behaviour might well remain obscure for many people. Where this is so, other factors might well override any sense that living within the law in particular situations was a priority.

What might those factors be? People are often influenced by the setting in which they find themselves. Friends, financial circumstances, disabilities, poor education, personal poverty may all have an influence. For those who are impoverished or chronically unemployed, obeying the law might seem to bring with it few benefits and substantial short-term disadvantages. Those who cannot read or write might feel they have no choice but to make their way in any way possible, even where that brought them into conflict with the law. Drug addicts or alcoholics or those with mental disabilities might simply have lost the capacity to live within the law.

It is also the case that people are often motivated by the perception of immediate advantage or immediate gratification. The law is constraining. If no one ever had a reason for breaking a law, there would be no need to impose it. Laws typically stop people from doing what from time to time they might otherwise be tempted to do. Short-term interests often clash with long-term interests. The immediate appeal of an article of clothing may seem to outweigh the risks of detection or any obvious harms that might be caused by stealing it. An entrepreneur may simply want to make a fast profit. Perceived self-interest, then, can provide reasons for disobedience.

Finally, the law itself may be an obstacle to obedience. No legal system is perfect. Neither are legal systems perfectly administered. Those who break the law may believe that the law itself is unsound. A sense of grievance or disagreement can provide motivation for disobedience.

Responding to disobedience

To win voluntary compliance, the law must respond to the reasons people have for committing offences. Those responses in turn will be morally acceptable only if the enforcement process respects the principles that justify the creation of legal mechanisms for resolving disputes. The minimum use of force principle is obviously key. If the function of the law is to reduce recourse to the use of force in settling disputes, then, in seeking to resolve conflicts with offenders, unnecessary use of force is unjustifiable. The principle of diversion is an application of the minimum use of force principle. It requires that conflicts be resolved with the minimum coercion consistent with protecting those the law is put in place to protect. Finally, to see sentencing as conflict resolution requires respect for the moral autonomy of the offender. Using force to resolve disputes is, by its nature, implicitly violent and has, therefore, the capacity to undermine the ability of those against whom it is directed to direct their own lives in accordance with values of their own choosing. It is the need to control the free use of force that justifies the use of force in enforcing the law. Hence, the goal of enforcement must be to achieve compliance through moral suasion, that is to say, by bringing those not otherwise disposed to obey the law to the view that compliance with the law is warranted.

Approaching sentencing from this perspective, what are the sentencing options?

PART III: PRACTICAL IMPLICATIONS

Conflict resolution and social defence

The criminal law is typically used to protect people from certain harms. It can fulfil this function, we have seen, only if people feel justified in assuming that those subject to the authority of the law are prepared to obey it for the most part. Until this assumption is undermined in some way, people will feel able to pursue those activities that the law facilitates.

By committing an offence, an offender provides others with grounds for thinking he cannot be trusted to conduct his affairs within the restraints of the law. If the law is to provide the protection it promises, it must therefore accomplish coercively what it has failed to accomplish in the offender's case through voluntary compliance. The coercive intervention is itself an expression of loss of trust.

What options are available? Placing restraints on the activities an offender can engage in is one. Confidence in the willingness of individuals to obey the law is not an all-or-nothing proposition. A person who has forfeited public confidence in his willingness to respect laws prohibiting drinking and driving may nevertheless in other respects be perfectly trustworthy. In such cases, protection of the public may require only the removal of a driver's licence.

Supervision in the community is another option. It expresses a loss of confidence in the offender but is flexible in its application. It can involve as little as periodic contacts. But it can also require daily checks and careful restrictions on what an offender can do. It can also be combined with some forms of incarceration.

Finally, there is the possibility of isolating an offender from the community.

Current sentencing practices make use of all these options, from community supervision in the form of probation and parole, the use of half-way houses or hostels, and electronic bracelets, to incarceration for varying periods under security conditions that range from open custody to high security and virtual isolation. A few states also use capital punishment.

How are these options to be integrated with a conflict resolution approach to sentencing? The response required of a sentencing authority is a function of three things: the harm that has been inflicted by the offender; the distrust that the offender has generated; and the threat of future harm that an offender represents. Using coercive measures to protect potential victims from an offender is a justified stage in conflict resolution. It is one aspect of 'standing firm'.

How should a sentencing authority determine what level of intervention is warranted? Two general observations are necessary. First, as we saw earlier, social defence cannot by itself resolve conflicts. It can only provide a buffer, a short-term protective intervention. Second, the goal of sentencing, as with enforcement generally, is to provide assurance that people are on the whole justified in assuming that those with whom they are likely to come into contact can be trusted to obey the law. With this in mind we can evaluate current practices.

Capital punishment

Capital punishment is the most severe intervention currently in favour in at least some quarters.[18] We cannot provide a detailed review of arguments for and against here. However, the basis for evaluation offered by the model here being developed is clear enough. Capital punishment is reserved in modern western societies for only the most serious and unsettling crimes, particularly the crime of murder. Those who defend its use do so either on retributivist grounds, which we have earlier suggested are not persuasive taken alone, or as an expression of a society's abhorrence of socially intolerable behaviour and its willingness to take the ultimate step in seeking to protect people from it. Studies that have been done, however, do not confirm that executions result in increased public confidence in the capacity or willingness of enforcement authorities to provide protection. Neither do they show that executions result in reduced incidents of murder. Indeed, public confidence in law enforcement seems lowest in those jurisdictions that still allow the execution of offenders.[19]

The failure of capital punishment to build or maintain confidence in the law is in fact quite consistent with the account of the function of law and of law enforcement here being developed. Capital punishment cannot build confidence that people can for the most part be trusted to obey the law because, by insisting that execution is the only appropriate way of dealing with them, it communicates fear and lack of confidence in the ability of the law to accomplish its goals in less severe ways. For a society to have to use this ultimate weapon, there must be real doubt that a significant number of people can be trusted to obey even the most fundamental of laws in the absence of this form of response. It is not surprising, therefore, that capital punishment is as likely to undermine public confidence in the capacity of the law to fulfil its function as it is to provide assurance.

In the absence of convincing evidence that capital punishment is a necessary step if public confidence in the law is to be sustained, the principle of minimum force requires turning to less coercive but equally effective measures. Incarceration is the obvious alternative.[20]

The use of incarceration

Is incarceration an effective and legitimate sentencing option? Certainly it has the value of separating an offender from the community, with all the protection this involves. However, as a solution its value is severely circumscribed. A recent British Government Green Paper explains why.

> Imprisonment restricts offenders' liberty but it also reduces their responsibility; they are not required to face up to what they have done and to the effect on their victim or to make any recompense to the victim or the public. If offenders are not imprisoned, they are more likely to be able to pay compensation to their victims and to make some reparation to the community through useful unpaid work. Their liberty can be restricted without putting them behind prison walls. Moreover, if they are removed in prison from the responsibilities, problems and temptations of everyday life, they are less likely to acquire the self-discipline and self-reliance which will prevent reoffending in the future.

The Green Paper goes on to say:

> Custody should be reserved as punishment for very serious offences, especially when the offender is violent and a continuing risk to the public.
>
> (Home Office 1988: 1 and 2)

The approach to the use of custody called for by the Green Paper reflects the approach implied by a conflict resolution model.[21]

Inconsistent with a conflict resolution model is any sentencing regime that imposes minimum sentences for specified offences, particularly minimum incarceral sentences, or prohibits the use of parole. The capacity of particular offences to undermine public confidence or create anxiety cannot be predicted in advance of their commission. It is true that the more serious an offence, the more likely it is to create anger and distrust. However, an appropriate response will seek to remedy the harm done. And what counts as a remedy will depend on the nature of the offence, what the offender had in mind in committing the crime, his response on reflection to the offence he committed, and the harm caused to the victims. What is more, the minimum force principle implies that, if custody is not required to provide adequate public protection, it is not warranted.

Probation, parole, gradual release, and electronic monitoring

Because, as the Green Paper points out, supervision in the community is more conducive to the goals of reparation and reconciliation than is incarceration, gradual release back into the community, probation, and parole have a clear place in sentencing practices built around conflict resolution. Can the same be said for electronic monitoring? Electronic monitoring is based on technology developed in the United States in the last decade. It was introduced ostensibly to provide a less expensive alternative to incarceration.

Current technology uses a bracelet attached to an arm or ankle that emits a signal that is monitored by a telephone receiver, and thus allows the authorities to impose house arrest on an offender without the need for direct supervision. The technology is attractive because it allows for more or less intensive or constant but relatively inexpensive supervision.

Electronic monitoring has been welcomed by correctional authorities in North America, confronted by prison overcrowding and the expense of building new prisons.[22] It has been roundly condemned, on the other hand, by a variety of advocacy groups for a variety of reasons. Electronic monitoring has the effect, some have argued, of turning an offender's home into a prison.[23] It impacts directly on those with whom an offender lives and constitutes an invasion of privacy. Most important, however, is its 'net widening' potential. Critics have argued that the introduction of electronic monitoring will not result in reduced prison population. Rather, it will be applied to offenders who might otherwise have received a suspended sentence, or a community service order, or probation, and so on.[24]

In a very real sense, the debate over electronic monitoring is not over sentencing principles, but rather over the difficulties of ensuring that innovations and reforms are used properly and not distorted in their applications by practical and political pressures. If physical supervision of those who have lost the trust of the community is in principle acceptable, then electronic supervision, which is in some respects less intrusive than custodial alternatives, can hardly be rejected as morally unacceptable.[25]

In fact, electronic monitoring creates a real dilemma for two reasons. First, where the goal of sentencing is seen as either control or social defence, sentencing authorities have a strong incentive to err on the side of public security where there is any doubt about the risk posed by an offender. And since risk prediction is notoriously unreliable, the possibility of erring on the side of severity in sentencing is substantial, as we saw in Chapter 2. Since electronic monitoring allows intensive surveillance at reduced cost, its use is therefore likely to lead to increased reliance on coercive intervention rather than less. Where the goal of sentencing is retribution, the use of community options like reparation and community service is likely to be seen as an alternative to punishment and therefore inconsistent with the goal of inflicting just punishments.

On the other hand, if the goal of sentencing is seen as conflict resolution, non-custodial sentences are clearly the preferred sentencing option. Were conflict resolution principles to be deeply embedded in sentencing practices, it is unlikely that electronic monitoring would have a net widening effect and therefore would not be seen as undermining penal reform aimed at reducing the use of incarceration for criminal offences.[26]

Conflict resolution and negotiated sentences

On some accounts of the matter, negotiation must involve compromise and therefore is incompatible with legally grounded sentencing. How can justice and negotiation with offenders coexist? Yet it is clear they do. Modern penal codes leave a great deal of room for judicial discretion. Indeed, discretion, as we have seen, is an unavoidable feature of law enforcement. Plea bargaining, pre-sentence reports, the right of Crown and defence to propose appropriate sentences all point to the fact that dialogue permeates every aspect of the sentencing process. Neither does negotiation require that those assigned responsibility for representing the legal point of view soften or compromise on their commitment to that point of view. Indeed, conflict resolution cannot occur unless those affected by the resolution see it as an adequate response to the harms caused by the offence.

Negotiation cannot successfully resolve a dispute, however, unless the point of view of the offender is also reflected in the sentence. Indeed, accomplishing this goal is essential, since the attitudes of the offender to the law are fundamental to the response of the law to the offence.

Resolving the conflict created by an offence requires that the offender be given an opportunity to rebuild the trust that has been undermined by his actions. Apologies, reparations for damage caused, public compensation, and even rehabilitation all have a role in this process.

Mediation does so as well. If we represent a sentence as the outcome of a process of dialogue between the law and its representatives on the one hand and an offender on the other, then clearly there is a role for mediators whose function is to assist the two sides to communicate their views clearly to each other and to reach a mutually acceptable solution to the conflict.

The explicit and acknowledged use of mediation models in sentencing is a relatively recent phenomenon.[27] They were introduced almost by accident in Kitchener, Ontario, by a parole officer looking for a creative way to deal with two young offenders who had vandalized the property of a number of private citizens, a church, and beer store.[28] After conviction but prior to sentencing, the two youths undertook to visit their victims under the supervision of a probation officer, with a view to discovering the effects of their offences on them. When they returned to court they were fined. They were also directed to make restitution to their victims. They were given three months to do both. Since that event, the use of mediation aimed at victim/offender reconciliation has been widely endorsed and used as a sentencing alternative.

Victim/offender reconciliation programmes (VORPs) have four goals: to encourage victim participation and facilitate acknowledgement and understanding of the victim's point of view on the part of the community and also the offender; to allow the offender to explain his actions and then to make amends, with a view to rebuilding trust and allowing for the resumption of a normal role in the community; to increase respect for the law and law enforcement; and to calm public anxiety or fear.[29] That is to say, formal mediation schemes seek to address all the harms that are typically caused by criminal offences to which, we have argued, a response is needed.

This is not to argue that formal mediation is a panacea. In fact, studies of actual mediation programmes are still sketchy. If mediation is attractive, it is because of the principles and values that motivate its use and not clear empirical evidence that, for example, it reduces recidivism or increases public confidence in the law.[30]

There is a fundamental problem, however, that debates about mediation and its role in the criminal justice system have raised. The criminal justice process is in practice unavoidably coercive. Mediation takes place in that context. Thus, although mediation programmes seek the voluntary participation of offenders and victims, inevitably pressures enter into the process. For example, in their review of a number of VORP programmes in the United States, Robert Coates and John Gehm (1989) found that most offenders participated in the projects they reviewed because they were required to by the court. Even where mediation is not court ordered, the possibility that participation will result in a reduced sentence is hard to avoid.[31] Neither is the process itself neutral. The search for a negotiated solution is carried out in the context of a commitment to the legal point of view. The purpose of negotiated sentences is to find a solution consistent with the law. Mediation assumes this context.[32]

This raises an important question. Do rewards and penalties have a place in the conflict resolution process?

Conflict resolution, and the role of rewards and deterrents

Is offering rewards a legitimate negotiating device in the pursuit of a resolution of a dispute? For example, is convincing an offender to participate in mediation by agreeing that to do so will be viewed favourably by the court a legitimate way to secure participation? Is winning a guilty plea by promising a reduced sentence a legitimate negotiating tactic? Is deterring non-compliance through the imposition of penalties a legitimate form of persuasion?

It is clear that rewards and punishments do have an entrenched and (for most people) an unproblematic role in human affairs. We do in the normal course of events use both to win agreement and cooperation in virtually all areas of social life. We reward those who cooperate with us or act in ways that we approve and we seek to deter those who we think might otherwise act in ways of which we disapprove. Children are rewarded for good behaviour and penalized for misbehaving. Good employees are rewarded with promotions; those who fail to fulfil their responsibilities adequately are held back, criticized and sometimes fired. Loyal friends of politicians are rewarded with appointments. Disloyal friends are ignored and ostracized. We reward with smiles, compliments, and praise, and punish with anger and criticism. Our governments construct systems of taxation with a view to discouraging some activities and encouraging others.

None of this is in principle controversial. Calculating the effects of our actions on others with a view to avoiding unfavourable reaction and soliciting supportive responses is a part of living. We even occasionally reward ourselves for achievements and penalize ourselves when we make mistakes. We do not consider any of this to be in principle unacceptably manipulative or morally suspect. Indeed, we could not eliminate rewards and disincentives as influences on our behaviour or as elements in our interpretation of the behaviour of others if we wanted to.[33]

What then sets apart legitimate and illegitimate uses of incentives and disincentives as devices for influencing the behaviour of others? Let us focus, for the moment, specifically on the matter of disincentives. It would seem that seeking to deter behaviour is illegitimate when it is used to obtain compliance in the absence of common or shared interests or values. That is to say, using deterrents is legitimate where they are used to draw attention to the point of acting in a particular way, when the point of so acting stands apart from the deterrent as a sound reason for the behaviour being called for. A deterrent, on this account, would be illegitimate, that is, unacceptably manipulative, where, in the absence of the penalty, the person to whom the deterrent was directed would have no adequate reason for acting in the way desired.

Let us take the example of smoking. Seeking to deter someone from taking up the habit or persuading him to give it up through incentives and penalties would not be thought to be unacceptably manipulative by those who view smoking as bad for one's health. Such people would likely support measures designed to discourage smoking even if they happened to be smokers. Those who were unpersuaded about the alleged health risks associated with smoking, on the other hand, might well see such devices as manipulative and offensive.

We also accept the use of rewards and penalties in situations where those to whom they are applied do not perceive the value of what is being encouraged or discouraged. Again, what is central is the purpose of the incentives. Where we believe there are good reasons to act in the way being encouraged, and, if we believe that people would so act were they to address the matter and give it sufficient thought, using incentives or disincentives to encourage the desired behaviour would probably be accepted as legitimate. This is particularly true in contexts where paternalism is seen as justified – disciplining children, for example. The child may not appreciate what he is being asked to do. He may even resent the regime of rewards and penalties to which he is being subjected. Yet we might still see the rewards and penalties as a legitimate way of bringing him to see the point for himself.

How does this apply to sentencing and corrections? We might put the matter this way. A central task for conflict resolution is to make someone aware of the grievance he has caused by his actions.

Imposing a penalty is often an effective way of doing just that. It symbolizes resolve and commitment and puts pressure on those against whom it is directed to take seriously the objections of those with whom they have come into conflict. Seen from this perspective, penalties are a strategy for opening the lines of communication.[34]

It follows that, if the point of a penalty is to bring those involved to a shared understanding of a genuinely common interest, its deterrent effect is not manipulative in a way that conflicts with respect for moral autonomy.[35] On the other hand, where avoiding a penalty is the only reason someone has for doing what is wanted, then imposing a penalty with a view to coercing obedience is manipulative. What is being communicated in this latter case is simply the dominant party's objection to a particular form of behaviour or activity, his willingness to use coercion to secure compliance, and the imbalance of power which allows him to do so.

The difficulty with the use of deterrents to obtain compliance with the law, then, is twofold. First, in a modern pluralistic society, we cannot assume that a consensus on what values the law ought to reflect is possible. There are no grounds, therefore, for assuming that sanctions imposed as deterrents will be anything but manipulative, at least in some cases. Second, paternalism is also a weak justification for winning compliance through the threat or imposition of penalties. It may well be true that the moral justification of law rests in part on the need for a formal system, if individuals are to be able to meet their basic needs and pursue effectively their various interests. However, coercing compliance cannot avoid raising questions about the law's commitment to its basic function, which is resolving disputes non-violently. Non-violent dispute resolution enhances autonomy. Paternalism either ignores or misunderstands autonomy, since autonomy cannot be imposed.[36]

On the other hand, the law requires compliance. This fact, combined with a commitment on the part of authorities to enforcement, cannot avoid having a deterrent effect on those who would not otherwise comply with the law. And so we find ourselves caught in a familiar dilemma. Enforcement is entailed by the legal point of view. Enforcement cannot avoid having a deterrent, and therefore potentially manipulative, effect on the behaviour of those subjected to it. Must we therefore simply accept that in practice enforcement is unavoidably manipulative? And if the answer is 'yes', as it seems to be, does it follow that seeking explicitly to deter disobedience through sanctions is also justified in spite of its manipulative implications?

The answer to the latter question is both 'no' and 'yes'. We have seen that there is little if any evidence that deterrent punishments for serious offences do play the role of drawing the attention of offenders or others in an effective way to the point of obeying the law. Neither is it easy to see how they could, for reasons already set out.[37] It follows that heavy penalties for any sort of offence cannot be justified in principle or in practice, if their primary purpose is to deter. In practice, such penalties have no ascertainable deterrent impact. Indeed, given the account we have defended, they cannot help but undermine respect for the law on the part of those toward whom they are directed. It is not surprising in this regard that research on the effect of penalties like long-term incarceration suggests that they can be counter-productive.[38]

On the other hand, using deterrent punishments to draw attention to the point of specific laws would seem to be quite appropriate. The point of regulating parking or disposal of garbage or the speed of vehicles on the road is obvious. Complying with such regulations is not normally a serious inconvenience. When they are disregarded, it is not for reasons of principle, but rather because of short-term interests. Deterrent penalties here help to align short-term and long-term interests and thus draw public attention to why the law should be obeyed, reasons that would normally be persuasive quite independently of the penalties attached to the law.

Fines fit into this category. If our analysis is correct, their use for a wide variety of offences is justified. Even heavy fines for offences whose point is clear – environmental protection, for example – are justified on this account.[39] Fines have a symbolic function. They communicate condemnation where imposing intrusive controls is not justified. Imposing heavy fines is a way of marking the seriousness of an offence and compensating the community for the harm imposed. What is not justified is imposing fines without regard to the capacity of an offender to pay. Fines that ignore the economic circumstances of those on whom they are imposed are as likely to distract from the point of the law being enforced as to emphasize it. Oppressive fines illustrate the manipulative potential of law enforcement, emphasizing the capacity of the law to force compliance quite independently of the merits of the law being enforced. Calculating fines by reference to an offender's income or earning power is one way of addressing this problem.[40]

It follows from our account, therefore, that both deterrence-oriented sanctions and fines have a relatively clearly defined, though limited, place in sentencing and corrections.

Rehabilitation and the role of coercion

Rehabilitation, too, has an obvious place in our account of sentencing. An example illustrates the point. Drinking and driving is now recognized as one of the major causes of traffic accidents. It is not surprising, therefore, that it is prohibited by law. Studies have shown, however, that many of those who drink and drive are alcoholics who are unable to control their drinking. A solution to recidivism in those cases normally requires either that they stop driving, a prohibition that is very hard to enforce, or that their problem drinking be addressed.

Let us imagine that a person with this problem appears in court, is convicted of the offence of driving while under the influence of alcohol, and then remanded for sentencing. At the sentencing hearing, the offender acknowledges the seriousness of the offence and accepts responsibility for his actions by offering to participate in a substance abuse programme. It is clear that, assuming that no harm had been done in committing the offence, solving this offender's drinking problem would also resolve his conflict with the law. Failure to address the problem, on the other hand, would be clear evidence that the offender was unwilling to take the steps required to reassure the court that he was sincere about wanting to live within the law. In this case, rehabilitation is central to resolving the conflict and therefore central to the sentencing project.

Let us now assume that the offender is someone who has appeared several times for the same offence. The court has been told on other occasions that the offender was committed to taking his problem in hand only to have him reappear for the same offence time and again. Would the court be justified in imposing treatment? Would such an action be consistent with a respect for his autonomy, his right to conduct his life in accordance with values of his own choosing, even where that brought him into conflict with the law?

Let us add one final element to the example. Let us assume that the most recent incident resulted in a serious accident and the loss of life. It is clear that the offender is a confirmed alcoholic and cannot be stopped from driving in the usual way, that is by simply confiscating his driver's licence. A penalty of incarceration is imposed. Should the offender also be required to participate in substance abuse programmes as a condition of early release via parole, for example? Further, would it be legitimate to offer him a choice of imprisonment or treatment of a serious and sustained variety?

We have already argued that coercive intervention in the lives of people is justified where its goal is to protect the autonomy of some from unjustified interference by others. To intervene in this way implies simply a defensive response. To seek to change the values and attitudes of others, however, can be morally intrusive and therefore can constitute an infringement of their autonomy. Respect for autonomy requires freedom of choice, including the freedom to choose to break the law, so long as the consequences of so doing are known.

The problem with coercive rehabilitation or coerced reconciliation or coerced cooperation of any form is that it would appear to be incompatible with treating offenders as rational and autonomous agents. This has led some people to argue that coercion and rehabilitation are simply incompatible. It has led others to argue that any attempt at mediation or reconciliation should be carried out only after an offender's sentence has been served or as an alternative to those proceedings. Only in this way, it is argued, could voluntary participation be assured.

There is something unrealistically utopian, however, about insisting that voluntary cooperation can occur only in settings absolutely free of manipulative pressures. It is utopian in part because no aspect of life has this character. As we have already seen, social life is influenced by the need to get along with others. What we do is a function in part of what others want us to do. And how badly they want our cooperation is signalled by the rewards they are prepared to offer and the disincentives they seek to put in our way.

If the use of rewards and the imposition of sanctions for the purpose of winning compliance with the law is a problem, it is because of the kind of power that enforcement authorities have over those that are placed in their power. But what this shows is that it is not the fact of power, but how it is used, that marks it as a threat to the autonomy of those against whom it is directed. It is coercing changes in values and attitudes without concern for the interests and values of the person being coerced which is unacceptable.

We have already seen that intervening to protect legally guaranteed rights is legitimate. So are interventions designed to deter people from breaking the law, where the purpose of the intervention is to reinforce respect for laws that those toward whom the deterrent is directed have an obvious reason to respect.

It would seem that positive and negative incentives to engage in rehabilitation are equally legitimate. The fact that respect for the autonomy of individuals has a positive as well as a negative dimension helps to explain why this is so.

Coercive rehabilitation and the notion of autonomy

In contemporary discussion, respect for individual autonomy has typically been interpreted to require respect for the right of individuals to pursue a life of their own making free from the unjustified interference of others. However, freedom from interference is only a necessary but not a sufficient condition for the exercise of autonomy. To be autonomous, an individual must have a view of what is worth doing, and the ability to act in accordance with that view in a manner which is consistent with the rights of others to do the same with their own lives. Furthermore, as we have already seen, no individual can acquire the ability to direct his own life without the cooperation of others.

What are the implications of this for a person living in a modern society? To direct his own life in today's world, an individual must have: elementary skills in reading and writing; the ability to find and hold a job; access to basic social services and counselling, together with a knowledge of how to use them. He must also be free of debilitating addictions.

Rehabilitation, as it has come to be understood in this century, involves acquiring the skills and knowledge needed to live in a modern world. Programmes offered to offenders typically provide educational and work skills upgrading, counselling, group therapy, substance abuse therapy, work opportunities, and so on. The rationale for encouraging offenders to participate in these programmes is clear. Unless they acquire the capacity to make their way in a modern society, cooperation with others is bound to be impeded. It will be much harder for someone who is unemployable to see the benefit of laws prohibiting theft than for someone for whom accumulating material goods is a genuine option. Rehabilitation that is designed to allow the option of complying with the law, with some hope of personal benefit, serves to enrich the options of those who take advantage of it, and thus strengthens their capacity to direct their lives in accordance with values of their own choosing.

Autonomy-oriented rehabilitation must respond to the needs of offenders, needs that are no different from those of other members of society. In the context of rehabilitation having this characteristic, incentives and disincentives are not unacceptably manipulative. They are manipulative to be sure. But since their goal is to widen the options available to offenders and to facilitate their participation in normal social life, they need not be morally objectionable. They will have this unobjectionable character where they are used to draw or entice participation in autonomy-enhancing activities. This conclusion is strengthened if we recall that the function of law is to enhance autonomy by reducing recourse to the use of violence in resolving disputes, where the objection to violence is its capacity to undermine the moral status of those against whom it is directed.

Let us return now to our example to see what this view justifies. In that example we were dealing with someone addicted to the use of alcohol whose actions demonstrated either an incapacity or an unwillingness to stop driving, even when prohibited from doing so. It is clearly in the interests of the public and the authorities that the addiction be cured. It is also in the interests of the offender, since having the right to drive in our society is an autonomy-enhancing right. Using the threat of penalties and the promise of rewards to convince such an offender to participate in a substance abuse programme would therefore not in principle be an unacceptable invasion of his autonomy. On the other hand, requiring such a person to undergo treatment in violation of explicitly stated objections on an offender's part would be unacceptable. So too would be incentives or penalties that bore little relation to the nature or the seriousness of the offence – the choice of treatment or solitary confinement, for example.

Coercive rehabilitation, then, is justified if it is imposed in a way that allows a positive answer to three questions. First, is the programme one that the offender would have good reason to participate in independently of the rewards offered to entice participation, rewards that bear no direct or intrinsic relation to the programme itself? Examples of such enticements might be a suspended sentence, a reduced period of incarceration, a favourable parole report, a reduced prison term, probation rather than incarceration, and so on.

Second, does involvement in the programme allow for disengagement by the offender from the programme without the infliction of penalties in addition to those that would otherwise have been appropriate, given the nature and seriousness of the offence? For example, in the matter of an addiction, is the approach taken to treatment compatible with the possibility that an offender might choose to withdraw from a programme earlier agreed to and live with his addiction, with all the consequences attached to so doing?

Third, are the incentives for participation or penalties for refusing to participate such that an offender would have little option but to respond to them, whether there were other reasons for so doing or not?

These questions not only provide a context for evaluating the merits of particular rehabilitative programmes, they also provide a guide for assessing the acceptability of any programme of incentives or penalties designed to entice cooperation with the directives or wishes of authorities. For example, it would not be acceptable, given these questions, to offer an offender early release or a lighter sentence in return for participation in a medical experiment (testing drugs, for example) or an experiment whose purpose was to test chemical weapons or protective clothing. In all these cases, the objectionable feature lies in the fact that the power of the state is being used to manipulate an offender's decisions for the benefit of others without regard to the intrinsic merits for the offender himself of what is being demanded.[41]

These questions also apply to alternatives to incarceration, for example community service orders, or restitution, or even mediation. For example, since taking responsibility for his actions could have a variety of beneficial consequences for the offender, requiring him to experience the reactions of others to what he has done could well enhance an offender's capacity to live within the law. To impose this solution on an offender, using the threat of punitive sanctions for non-compliance, could hardly accomplish its goal. In this case, the lesson for the offender would be the power of the law to coerce compliance, quite independently of the merits seen, from the offender's perspective, of what was being imposed. Here the coercive intervention is destructive of autonomy; it is not autonomy-enhancing.

It follows, then, that rehabilitation has a clear place in the account of sentencing being suggested here. It also follows, however, that the more coercive an option, the more likely that the point of cooperation will be lost in the resentment that coercion can engender.

In conclusion

We have argued that resolving conflicts in a manner that reduces recourse to the justified use of force is the fundamental justificatory function of legal systems. Approaching the law this way is compatible with the enforcement functions of both policing and adjudication. It is compatible with the practice of restricting the appropriate use of sanctions to those who could have avoided breaking the law had they so wished. It is also compatible with the way in which people informally assess the seriousness of misdeeds, and courts and legislatures gauge the seriousness of offences.

Discussion in this chapter suggests that sentencing and corrections can also be interpreted and described in this light. To view the function of sentencing and sentence administration as conflict resolution, whose goals are as we have described them, does without question depart from traditional understandings of its purpose. In particular, it departs from traditional understandings of the purpose of punishment. At the same time, it fits modern sentencing practice more comfortably than the traditional theories. It helps to explain the interaction of formal with informal elements in the sentencing process. And it opens the door to a defence of significant sentencing reforms that have found vocal support among reformers, but are not easily accommodated by traditional theories.

It remains, therefore, to show that the approach we have developed is compatible with, or provides an adequate option to, traditional and common sense views of the need for punishment. It is to this last task that we now turn.

8

TOWARDS A PHILOSOPHY
OF PUNISHMENT

Conflict resolution and traditional notions of justice

Throughout our discussion, our goal has been to construct an approach to punishment that was consistent with common sense and reflected basic moral sensibilities. Have we succeeded in that regard? Common sense suggests that punishment is an unavoidable feature of social life and a necessary component of law enforcement. Our discussion of retributivism led to the conclusion that fairness requires that we treat like cases alike, that people should be held responsible only for what they could have avoided doing, and that any harm or hard treatment inflicted for wrongdoing should be in proportion to the wrong committed. Our discussion of utilitarian or forward-looking views of punishment suggested that punishment should be imposed only where it could be shown to have beneficial consequences.

Does the account we have developed meet these conditions? First, it is clearly forward-looking. The function of law is to reduce recourse to the justified use of force in settling disputes. The function of enforcement is to hold or build public confidence in the capacity of the law to fulfil its function. Seen in this context, sentencing is an enforcement activity whose specific function is to seek to resolve the kinds of conflicts that are generated when the law is broken.

Our account also requires that like cases be treated alike. What makes an offence a criminal offence is its potential for undermining public confidence in the capacity of the law to fulfil its function. The goal of enforcement, we have argued, is to sustain that confidence or rebuild it when it has been undermined. To impose penalties for any other purpose is therefore unjustified. It follows that all offences must be treated alike. That is to say, the proper task of a sentencing authority is to formulate remedies appropriate to the harm caused by offences, with a view to assuring the public that continued confidence in the capacity of the law to fulfil its function is justified. The greater the harm caused, the more difficult it will be under normal conditions to correct it and, consequently, the more severe the remedy that will be required. Hence, sentences will be proportionate to the wrong committed.

But is all of this not perhaps just a gloss? To begin with, it is clear that if the appropriate role of sentencing is conflict resolution, then both the use of discretion in sentencing and the individualization of sentences are unavoidable. This problem is accentuated by the fact that conflict resolution requires that the attitudes of victims and the fears and anxieties of the public generally must be taken into consideration by sentencing authorities. Is this fair? And is it compatible with treating like cases alike, in something more than a purely formal sense?

The problem of fairness suggests a second objection. If the purpose of a sentence is to hold or restore public confidence, does this not expose offenders to the vagaries of public opinion? And did our discussions of retributivism not suggest that shielding offenders from the desire for vengeance is one important reason for creating formal systems of justice?

Finally, if common sense tells us that punishment is an unavoidable feature of social life and the enforcement of law, how can a model of sentencing whose function is not to impose punishments but to resolve disputes be satisfactory? Let us look at each of these difficulties in turn.

Conflict resolution and the exercise of discretion

The exercise of discretion in determining sentences has aroused strong opposition in recent years for a variety of reasons, connected in many instances to a rejection of utilitarian or purely forward-looking sentencing practices. A generalized objection to discretion assumes, however, that discretion always plays the same role regardless of the principles that guide its use. This assumption is not justified.

Guided by purely forward-looking principles, the function of discretion is to allow a sentencing authority to fit the sentence to the offender. If the goal is deterrence, then the sentencing authority must calculate what will suffice to deter the offender herself or others who might be contemplating a similar act. If the goal is reform, then an indeterminate sentence has the merit of allowing the authorities to maintain control over offenders until they have been reformed. Since what it will take to reform an offender will vary from person to person, it cannot be predicted in advance of the offence. Hence, to approach sentencing from this perspective requires the exercise of discretion.

It is clear from what we have said, however, that a conflict resolution approach to sentencing does not require this kind of discretion. Rather, the discretion it requires is needed: to ensure that the sentence arrived at reflects properly the nature of the offence committed, the values and attitudes that offence reflects, and its impact on all those affected by it; to communicate repudiation of the offence and the attitudes toward the law and its victims that the offence projects; and to provide an opportunity for repairing the damage caused. Correcting the harm done will require that sentences be moulded to fit the unique facts of each case. Discretion which has this as its objective is not incompatible with widely shared notions of fairness or justice. Indeed, it is exactly this kind of discretion that is required by models of retributive justice.

There is a good deal of evidence that there is wide public opposition to judicial discretion in sentencing. Studies show that this is in part based on a widely shared view that our courts should hand out similar penalties for similar offences. They also show that public opposition to the exercise of discretion is based in part on a belief that the judiciary cannot be trusted to impose sufficiently harsh sentences.[1]

As we have seen, unlike utilitarian models, a conflict resolution model of sentencing is not incompatible with the principle that the severity of a sentence should be proportionate to the seriousness of the offence committed. It also requires that sentencing authorities address explicitly the impact of offences on their victims in arriving at an appropriate sentence. Hence, as a model, it deals directly with a basic reason for public discontent with the exercise of discretion.

The fundamental objection to discretion in sentencing then is that it relieves sentencing authorities of an obligation to treat like cases alike in formulating sentences. What this analysis shows is that the culprit here is not discretion but a sentencing model whose focus is offenders and not their offences.

Conflict resolution and the individualization of sentences

This response, however, is not entirely convincing. A conflict resolution model does require that sentences reflect the offence committed. However, it also requires individualized sentences. Traditionally, the notion of individualized sentences has implied an abandonment of the principle that similar offences should be treated similarly.

A conflict resolution sentencing model calls for individualized sentences for a number of reasons. The first has already been discussed. There is a second reason. There can be no preset remedy for every offence because an adequate sentence must also reflect the needs of those affected, the victims, the wider public, and the offender herself.

For example, in some cases, restitution might present itself as an effective solution to a criminal offence. However, restitution will not always be possible or appropriate. In some cases, seeking victim/offender reconciliation might be unacceptable to the victim. To force mediation and dialogue in such cases would itself be unfair to the victim, in which case community service orders might be an alternative. Some offences might so undermine the willingness of members of the public to trust an offender that incarceration might be justified. However, even in these cases, if offenders are to be given an opportunity to rebuild the trust they have lost, the sentence of each offender will have to be individualized either by the sentencing authority or by correctional administrators. It is unlikely that the public would feel secure knowing that a paedophile had been released following even an extensive period of incarceration if, over his period of incarceration, he received no treatment.

Thirdly, the capacities and resources of offenders will vary. Some will have no difficulty compensating their victims financially or in some other way. Others will be unable to do so because they are poor or because they do not have the needed skills. The health, education, work skills, disabilities, and so on of an offender will all affect how best to bring a conflict toward an effective resolution. Thus, a conflict resolution model will require that sentences be tailored to the circumstances and characteristics of offenders themselves.

However, none of this is incompatible with the goal of ensuring that similar offences are treated similarly. What is required is that offenders make amends. How they do so or what is justified by way of helping them to see that they should do so will vary from offender to offender. However, variation in this case does not imply varying degrees of severity or leniency for similar offences. To the contrary, moulding sentences to the unique facts of each case and varying sentences with the severity of offences committed will be required if effective solutions to conflicts created by criminal offences are to be achieved.

Conflict resolution and the problem of public expectations

This discussion of discretion and individualization of sentences leads to a related objection. The function of enforcement and also sentencing, we have argued, is to retain or build public confidence in the law. Does this not open the sentencing process to the direct influence of public opinion?

Earlier we argued that one of the central virtues of state-imposed punishment was that it allowed sentences to be imposed by judges who were neutral or impartial and not emotionally involved in the outcome. To allow public expectations and desires to have a direct bearing on sentencing would seem to open the door to allowing emotions stirred up by disturbing or unsettling offences to influence directly sentences imposed.

There is another and related problem, that of fairness. Public attitudes are a function of a variety of factors that will often bear little relation to either an offender or her offence. Anger stirred up by one offence may colour public attitudes to the treatment of other unrelated offences. We know that this can happen. Much of the public unhappiness with parole, for example, is a result of anger and anxiety aroused by particularly spectacular but also relatively rare crimes.[2] Further, much of the resistance to involving victims in sentencing relates to the fear that this may well prejudice the process in unfair ways.

These objections to the model being presented are not convincing for two important reasons. First, there is a good deal of evidence that public attitudes are not nearly as harsh as many think. It is undeniably true that the public has been clamouring for increasingly harsh sentences for at least the past decade.[3] However, public attitudes are not as unambiguous as this general impression suggests. For example, research undertaken by the Canadian Sentencing Commission showed that members of the public seriously under-estimated the severity of sentences for a variety of crimes and seriously over-estimated the rate of crime in Canada. Other studies have explored public reactions to sentencing based on information gained through newspaper accounts compared with information based directly on court proceedings. When shown newspaper accounts of sentences handed down by the courts for a variety of offences, those being interviewed concluded for the most part that the sentences were too lenient. On the other hand, when given more detailed information of the kind available to the court, attitudes changed often quite dramatically. This suggests that public demand for harsher sentences is frequently based on inadequate knowledge of sentencing patterns and practices and is not a function of deeply held antagonism or an assessment of the intrinsic merits of harsh sentences (Archambault 1987: 87ff).

Research on attitudes toward rehabilitation tends to lead to the same conclusion. The study by Doble (1987) showed that there is strong support for a rehabilitation orientation toward sentencing. Paul Gendreau (Cullen and Gendreau 1989) reports that, while support for rehabilitation has dropped in the United States, it has nevertheless continued to elicit more public support than any other of the sentencing goals canvassed. Further, punishment as a goal of sentencing attracts the least support.[4]

A variety of empirical surveys has also indicated that people are not necessarily harsh or punitive in their attitudes. What they appear to want is serious attention addressed to their concerns and effective sentencing where necessary. Many studies have shown as well that the public demand for effective sentencing is as likely to mean adequate reparations or community service or rehabilitation as it is to imply a demand for punitive measures.[5]

Secondly, the proposal that sentencing and corrections be under-stood as a dispute resolution process whose goal is to instil public confidence in the law does not imply the direct involvement of the public in the process itself. What it does require is that those responsible for the process should understand that its purpose is to satisfy a public need for reassurance in the face of evidence that the basic assumption, that people they deal with are prepared for the most part to obey the law, might not be justifiable. What this implies in turn is that an effective sentencing process must lead to solutions that meet the expectations of victims in particular and the public in general, if it is to fulfil its function well.

Is there evidence that there is wide agreement about what people expect by way of solutions to conflicts caused by criminal offences? If there is not, conflict resolution will be difficult to achieve.

The discussion of the last four chapters suggests that on many of the points raised there is in fact consensus at a general level. There is wide agreement about the relative seriousness of various types of crime. Most people would rank murder as more serious than intentionally or carelessly inflicting serious physical injury, which is, in turn, more serious than property crimes, and so on. There are, of course, specific areas of conflict. But it is also clear that, where there is no consensus on the seriousness of particular offences, the sentencing process is unlikely to generate results that are widely perceived as satisfactory. Recent controversies over environmental issues and such things as abortion bear this out.

There is also a good deal of consensus on what should count as aggravating and mitigating factors.[6] This is not surprising, if the account of the role of expectations in social relations set out earlier is sound. Human relationships revolve around expectations that, if not shared, inhibit cooperation. Our general expectations, those related to the law among others, set standards for social interaction. There is and must be a fair degree of consensus about the implications of failing to meet those expectations for effective enforcement.

In addition, as we have just seen, there is more agreement than is commonly thought that restorative sanctions are preferable to those whose goal is primarily punitive and that the role of victims should be given a high priority.

Finally, there seems to be wide agreement that the sentencing process itself should be guided by authorities assigned that function on grounds of competence.[7]

This leaves us with a final objection. Is it not the case that the public expects and wants offenders to be punished for their offences? And is this not incompatible with viewing sentencing and corrections as a process of conflict resolution? To answer this question we must return to an explicit consideration of the theme of punishment.

Toward a theory of punishment

Let us begin this final assessment of the notion of punishment by distinguishing two questions. First, is punishment an unavoidable component of law enforcement? Second, does just law enforcement require that sentencing authorities deliberately or intentionally inflict punishment on offenders for their offences? The first question is straight-forward and requires a positive answer, as we shall see. The second question is ambiguous. On one of its interpretations, it too requires a positive answer. On a second interpretation, however, it is not a requirement of law enforcement that sentencing authorities deliberately inflict punishment on offenders for their offences.

Be that as it may, it is clear that the standard response, by philosophers at any rate, to the second questions is 'yes'. Received opinion is that the function of a sentence is to impose punishment with a view to deterrence, reform, denunciation, or on the grounds that justice requires it. This view is reflected in standard definitions by lawyers and philosophers. For example, Fitzgerald (1962: 199) defines punishment as 'the authoritative infliction of suffering for an offence'. Ted Honderich (1969: 1) asserts that 'punishment must involve some such thing as deprivation or distress, *which, indeed, is its aim*' (my emphasis). This view of punishment is explicitly captured by retributivism, as we saw in Chapter 1, where punishment is seen as the return of an evil for an evil.[8]

Not all definitions are so categorical, however. C.L. Ten (1987: 2) describes punishment as involving 'the infliction of some unpleasantness on the offender', or as depriving 'the offender of something valued'. H.L.A. Hart (1968: 4) includes in his definition of punishment the requirement that 'it must involve pain or other consequences normally considered unpleasant'.[9] It is clear that these two approaches to a definition of punishment are not identical. The second, as we shall see, is much closer to common usage. The first is, in essence, a stipulative definition that has emerged in the context of philosophical discussion. I shall therefore refer to it in what follows as the philosophical definition.

There are several reasons for rejecting the first definition, even though it normally sets the context for debate. First, it has the result of setting criminal punishment off from conventional or everyday uses of the word. The broadest definition of punishment is 'rough treatment' or 'suffering given or received'.[10] The philosophical definition requires, on the other hand, that punishment involve the deliberate or intentional infliction of pain, or suffering, or harm on someone for a misdeed she has committed, as something worthwhile in its own right or as a means to some end. Understood as a definition, this would seem to entail that a person cannot be punished for something she has not done.[11] It provides utilitarians with a way of dealing with the apparent implication of their theory that punishment of the innocent may sometimes be justified. Finally, it implies that ordinary language uses of the term are substandard[12] or in some other way deficient, and therefore misleading or inadequately precise.

The effect of adopting the philosophical view is to separate punishment in criminal law contexts from punishment as it is normally conceived. Yet the demand for punishment comes not from those trained in legal or philosophical terminology but rather from ordinary people, who have to live with the law and who see criminal offences and punishment in the context of other activities, where actions also give offence and merit punishment. We have a choice, then. We can see criminal punishment as finding a natural place within a broad range of punitive responses to unwanted behaviour. Or we can see it as a distinct phenomenon only tenuously related to its non-legal cousins. There is very little evidence, it must be said, that punishment for criminal acts, as it is discussed in the course of normal life, is understood in this second way.

There is more to be said on this issue, however. Most of the attacks on punishment are attacks on punishment defined as philosophers have defined it. For this concept of punishment assumes, among other things, that good can come from evil. It also sets punishment in conflict with rehabilitation. Imposing punishment with the aim of causing pain or suffering sets the offender off from others. It is an essentially negative act that classifies and stigmatizes the person it is directed against. Its classical expression is incarceration, execution, or banishment. Rehabilitation, on the other hand, has reintegration as its goal. Its object is to help an offender rebuild links with society. Many have concluded, therefore, that punishment and rehabilitation are incompatible.

Finally, this view of punishment sets sentencing against modern accounts of the evolution of cooperation, which imply that, as conflict resolution strategies, traditional theories of punishment are ineffective and likely to be counter-productive, something that experience with corrections confirms.

The second account does not have the implications of the first. Hard treatment need not be deliberately inflicted to be punishment. Rather, the second account views punishment as anything that causes pain or suffering, whether inflicted for that purpose or not. Thus we can speak of a punishing hike, a punishing game of hockey, a punishing attitude, or punishing demands.

To view the function of sentencing as conflict resolution is compatible with this second definition but not the first. Law creates and shapes human interaction and human expectations. It can function, furthermore, only if the expectations it creates are widely shared. To fail to meet those expectations is to create distance and tension and invite a re-evaluation of one's relationship with others. Offences alienate offenders from those against whom they have offended. If confidence in the law is to be maintained, criminal offences must be denounced and the right of victims to be protected and compensated affirmed. Law enforcement requires as a consequence that the law seek to identify offenders and require that they participate in a process designed to persuade them to acknowledge wrongdoing and to compensate for it in some way. The sentencing process, therefore, requires that offenders participate in an unpleasant process of evaluation and criticism, whose goal is to convince or require them to do painful or unpleasant things: acknowledge wrongdoing by paying a fine, admit guilt, apologize for misdeeds, make amends through compensation or community service, submit to surveillance because trust has been undermined, and so on.

It follows that the sentencing and correctional process will have the character of punishment for almost all offenders subjected to it. It will involve, that is to say, the imposition of penalties in the knowledge that they will be experienced as painful and perhaps even harmful, where that is unavoidable. But if the goal is conflict resolution, the penalties will be imposed or agreed to not with the aim of causing suffering, but with the aim of resolving conflict. It is true that the process will be engaged in with the knowledge that the outcome will probably be experienced as painful by those subjected to it. But it will not be engaged in *for the purpose of causing suffering*. And the solutions arrived at will not be advanced because of their pain-causing character.

Punishment as penance

The sentencing process seen as conflict resolution involves inflicting hard treatment on offenders in two ways. For an offender who is not prepared to seek a solution to his conflict with the law, the sentencing process will require imposing controls, whose purpose is to protect others from her. These controls, if effective in preventing the offender from breaking a law she would otherwise disregard, will be experienced as hard treatment, an unwanted imposition. Equally, for an offender who wishes to resolve the conflict in which she has become enmeshed, restoring the trust that has been undermined will require that she accept criticism for her actions and undertake to rebuild trust by making amends for the harm caused. An offender who is genuinely interested in repairing the damage she has done must face the task of rebuilding trust, a task that cannot help but be burdensome and unpleasant in some respects. She will be involved in a process that she would not likely choose to be involved in if she could avoid it.

But is this enough? Particularly, is this enough by way of compensation for the harm done? After all, the burdensome character of the process will not be experienced exclusively by the offender. Making amends cannot eradicate the burdens imposed on others by an offence. And those members of the community who cooperate by helping the offender to make amends – and she will need the cooperation of more than just the court – will also assume a burden that otherwise they would not have to carry and that, in a straight-forward sense, they do not deserve.

Is it not important, therefore, that pain and suffering be imposed not as an unavoidable concomitant of the imposition of control or the rebuilding of human relationships, but as a deliberately inflicted extra? If we set aside a traditional retributivist response to this question, are there any other reasons for thinking that reconciliation requires inflicting pain and suffering intentionally, simply because that is needed for reconciliation to occur?

Anthony Duff, drawing on religious notions of penance, argues that punishment in the philosophical sense is necessary. He argues that it is the decision to inflict pain which communicates the community's censure. Offenders must be brought to suffer as a way of communicating the wrongness of their offences. An offender who recognizes the immoral quality of her offence will welcome punishment as a way of doing penance, thus allowing her to communicate genuine repentance for the harm caused others. On this view, it is the willingness to endure pain and suffering which is the expression of repentance (Duff 1986: 233ff).

Duff's account, however, is incomplete. If this were not so, there would be no need to shape penalties in ways that enhance the possibilities of reconciliation. It would be necessary only to impose suffering in proportion to the moral gravity of the offence, in the hope that the offender would accept the justice of her treatment and repent her actions.[13] This in turn suggests that one cannot repent unless one wishes suffering on oneself. But surely to repent is to regret what one has done, and to wish or desire to make it good. Why should the experience of pain by itself be thought to communicate repentance more effectively than a gesture designed to contribute positively at some personal cost to the welfare of others?

There are two central difficulties with Duff's view. It sees reconciliation as achieved by repentance whose sincerity is affirmed by the willingness of the offender to suffer for what she has done. Yet communicating sincerity in admitting guilt is only a first step. Admitting guilt does not repair the harm done. Further, it does not demonstrate an understanding of what living within the law requires.

An example might help to illustrate the point. Showing remorse and accepting a punishment imposed by a court is a first step by which an alcoholic might begin to rebuild trust in his willingness and his capacity to avoid drinking and driving. But if the punishment involved simply the infliction of pain, there would be only limited grounds for confidence that the offender had 'learned her lesson' even if the punishment was accepted as penance.

Following her apprehension for the offence of drinking and driving, an alcoholic might well exhibit genuine remorse and accept the punishment imposed as a form of penance. This would not necessarily involve any change of heart on her part. She may always have been firmly opposed to drinking and driving, regarding it as deeply immoral, even before she committed her offence. Hence, the fact of remorse and the willingness to do penance might be weak grounds for assuming that the offence would not be likely to be repeated. On the other hand, an expression of sincere regret linked to compensation for the harm done, in so far as that was possible, combined with a commitment to take all necessary steps to bring her drinking under control through treatment or by becoming an active member of Alcoholics Anonymous, might well provide the basis for restoring confidence in her desire to live within the law.

Reconciliation is not just a matter of admitting guilt. It is a matter of repudiating the values or attitudes that led to an offence, showing a willingness to compensate for the harm done, and seeking to acquire the knowledge, skills, and habits that might reasonably be thought necessary for someone who had committed herself to not repeating her offence. Suffering cannot repair harm or rebuild what has been destroyed. It can only communicate a sense of wrongdoing.

215

Imposing suffering may communicate repudiation of wrongdoing. It cannot repair the harm done. On the other hand, resolving conflicts cannot be accomplished without an element of pain. Were this not so, we would not need to resolve conflicts. They would resolve themselves.

Punishment is an unavoidable component of the sentencing process. But, conflicts are not resolved through either the imposition of suffering or the acceptance of suffering as justly imposed.

Punishment is a logical concomitant of sentencing. It is not its proper purpose.

Sentencing, corrections, justice, and the role of other virtues

It is characteristic of the 'philosophical' view of law, justice and punishment that just enforcement of the law requires that considerations of mercy, compassion, and forgiveness be set aside until the demands of justice have been satisfied. It is this view that has led many to conclude that formal justice should be replaced with alternative informal approaches to regulating human behaviour. However, if the purpose of enforcement is first to help people avoid conflict and, on failing that, to help resolve conflict, then the philosophical view is unsound. Formal dispute settlement is a characteristic of formal legal systems. But resolving disputes formally is not incompatible with recourse to informal techniques of conflict resolution. In fact, adjourning formal proceedings so that informal discussion can occur is a characteristic feature of legal procedure.[14] Equally, giving offenders opportunities to demonstrate a willingness to accept responsibility for their offences is not incompatible with treating like cases alike and assuring that sentences arrived at reflect in appropriate ways the gravity of the offences committed.

Forgiveness, compassion, mercy, understanding, and related virtues facilitate reconciliation. They can, but need not, frustrate justice. We live the virtue of mercy when we give others another chance. We ignore justice if, in giving them another chance, we choose simply to ignore what they have done. In committing an offence, an offender inflicts harm on other individuals and on the public. To interpret mercy as requiring that the offence be overlooked or ignored sets mercy in conflict with justice, by shifting the burden created by the offence from offenders to their victims. But mercy need not work this way. The legal system shows mercy when it attempts to understand the needs of those who have come into conflict with the law, and seeks non-destructive solutions to the problems criminal activity creates. It shows compassion when it listens carefully to the stories of people who find themselves in conflict with the law, and seeks solutions that will enable them to resume a normal life. It finds a place for forgiveness when it allows offenders to deal with their offences in ways that open the door to understanding and, where possible, reconciliation.

Making room for these virtues might mean allowing an offender a chance to make good on his plea for a second chance by allowing the sentence to be worked out in the community. It might mean accepting a plea of guilty and allowing an offender to resolve her differences with those with whom she is in conflict through mediation, or even treatment. It might mean acknowledging the shattering impact of an offence and reconfirming a commitment to prevent offences in the future. It might mean accepting that the harm done by an offence was so deep and confidence so damaged that only a long period of incarceration could begin to restore the damage caused and the fear engendered.

None of these solutions requires assigning justice second place. All of them, with the exception, perhaps, of the most harsh options, require that punishment not be seen as the purpose of the response.

NOTES

AN INTRODUCTION

1 State punishment has been justified by some commentators, Walter Berns (1980) for example, as a way of rewarding law-abiding citizens for living within the law. See, for example, the same article reprinted in *Contemporary Moral Issues* (Cragg 1987: 167).

2 Readers familiar with the literature will recognize that in this regard, as in many others, the view I propose to develop deviates in significant ways from central features of recent philosophical discussions of the topic. Thus, for example, H.L.A. Hart (1968: 5), perhaps the most influential commentator on the topic of punishment in this half of the twentieth century, sets aside common informal examples of punishment as 'substandard' and moves to a definition of punishment that sets the understandings on which they are based to one side as not directly relevant to the task of understanding or justifying the phenomenon of punishment.

3 Support for the claims made in this introduction will be offered in later chapters. However, two references are particularly worth noting here. The first is a qualitative analysis of public opinion undertaken by the Edna McConnell Clark Foundation (Doble 1987), which revealed among other things a deep-seated distrust of the judiciary on the part of those interviewed and, by implication, the American public generally. The second is the report of the Canadian Sentencing Commission, which undertook a variety of careful studies of Canadian opinion on matters relating to sentencing reform (Archambault 1987).

4 For example, the recommendations of the Canadian Sentencing Commission are based on a justice model of sentencing. One of their recommendations is that parole be abolished, in as much as it is incompatible with the principles of fairness and proportionality. And although they propose that remission for good behaviour be retained, they recognize that their recommendations are, in this regard, inconsistent with the general principles of sentencing their report endorses, an inconsistency they justify on practical grounds (Archambault 1987: 247–8).

5 Contrasting positions on this subject are well illustrated by the writing of Walter Berns (1980), and of Hugo Bedau (1980).

6 The American report authored by Andrew von Hirsch (1976), entitled *Doing Justice*, contrasted with the Report of the Canadian Sentencing Commission is a good illustration of this phenomenon.

7 Two examples are found in the writing of Ezzat Fattah (1981), a distinguished Canadian criminologist who directed government research on the deterrence effect of capital punishment for the Canadian Department of Justice throughout the debates on that subject in Canada in the early 1970s, and of Terence Penelhum (1987: 560–1), a member of the Royal Society of Canada and a distinguished Canadian philosopher.

8 This claim will be defended at length over the next three chapters.

9 Ted Honderich in *Punishment: The Supposed Justifications* alludes to this fact in the initial stages of his examination of the traditional theories, when he discusses the assumption that 'punishment or some closely related practice is an indubitable social necessity' (1969: 9).

10 It is this kind of observation, of course, that has lent considerable weight to theoretical analyses designed to show that punishment should be replaced with alternative non-punitive responses to criminal behaviour.

1 PUNISHMENT AS RETRIBUTION

1 The idea that punishment might be replaced by some form of treatment is argued by Lady Barbara Wootton in a number of her publications. Her views will be evaluated at some length in Chapter 2. The idea that punishment might be replaced by a system of rewards for good behaviour is explored by B.F. Skinner (1971) in *Beyond Freedom and Dignity*. It, too, is referred to and briefly discussed in Chapter 2.

2 It is not uncommon to hear philosophers claim that the notion of restoring an imbalance created by injustice is incoherent, or so vague and metaphorical as to be of no value in an understanding of the nature and justification of punishment. Whether this is true is not material at this point in my argument. The point is that this kind of reasoning is very common and provides the underpinnings of a widespread understanding of the point of punishment. Even those philosophers who reject this justification as incoherent or inconsistent, because covertly utilitarian, e.g. Ted Honderich (1969) and Nicola Lacey (1988), confirm its social significance by according it the place they do in their own accounts.

3 For example, the Pocket Oxford Dictionary defines to punish as 'to subject (an offender) to retributive or disciplinary suffering'. Webster's Dictionary defines to punish as 'causing to suffer for some offence committed' or 'prescribing a form of suffering in penalty for (an offense)'.

4 I have in mind here Ted Honderich's attempt to capture the essence of what is commonly meant by the word in his definition: 'an authority's infliction of a penalty, something unwanted, on an offender, someone found to have broken a rule, for an offence, an act of the kind prohibited by the rule' (Honderich 1969: 1). As Nicola Lacey points out in *State Punishment* (1988: 7), this definition has a backward-looking quality

that implies a retributivist account of punishment. Once again, my goal is not to justify this outlook, but merely to establish its credentials as underlying popular understanding of the purpose of punishment.

5 The nature of revenge is discussed in more detail by Robert Nozick (1981: 363–97) in *Philosophical Explanations*. His account is summarized by C.L. Ten (1987: 43) in *Crime, Guilt and Punishment*.

6 This is essentially the position of James Fitzjames Stevens (1883) in *A History of the Criminal Law of England*. He is quoted by Jefferie Murphy (Murphy and Hampton 1988: 3). The merits of the position are discussed by Murphy at some length in *Forgiveness and Mercy*; see particularly Chapter 1.

7 In fact, Old Testament law required the death penalty for breaches of any of the Ten Commandments. In Deuteronomy, for example, the *lex talionis* is introduced in the context of a discussion of how those bearing false witness should be dealt with (Deuteronomy 19: 20). Elsewhere, Moses directs that those who fail to obey the first commandment to 'love the Lord your God with all your heart . . .' should be put to death by stoning (Deuteronomy 13). The same fate is commanded for murderers (Deuteronomy 19), adulterers (Deuteronomy 22: 13ff), and children who fail to honour their father and their mother (Deuteronomy 21: 18–21). For New Testament references, see the story of the woman caught in adultery (John 8: 1–11), the trial and execution of Jesus (e.g. Mark 14: 53–64), and the stoning of Stephen (Acts 7).

8 For a detailed discussion of this topic see Jefferie Murphy's account of 'Mercy and legal justice' (Murphy and Hampton 1988: 162ff).

9 I borrow this expression from Bernard Williams who introduces it in the context of a discussion of modern moral theories and their shortcomings in *Ethics and the Limits of Philosophy* (Williams 1985).

10 This idea will be explored in much greater detail below in Chapter 4 'The Function of Law and the Nature of Legal Obligation'.

11 This idea has been taken up by critics of conventional understandings of the nature of law and its relation to morality, and developed in many different directions. Marxist analyses of the nature of law are one example. The work of contemporary critical legal theorists, like Duncan Kennedy, is another.

12 This is made clear in Deuteronomy 5: 33 and in numerous other passages.

13 The Pentateuch contains graphic illustrations of how those who disobeyed the law would be punished. See, for example, Deuteronomy 28: 15–68.

14 The Book of Job in the Old Testament records Job's sense of deceit when these expectations fail to be met. His friends draw different conclusions, assuming, as they were entitled to do given the prevailing Hebrew understanding of the covenant, that, if someone was suffering, it was probably because he had broken the law. The end to the story illustrates the Hebrew belief that a just God would not allow the just to suffer and the evil to prosper.

15 John 8: 1–11.

16 This conclusion is reflected in the report of the Law Reform Commission of Canada entitled *Limits of Criminal Law – Obscenity: a Test Case* (1975b: 33).

2 THE POINT OF PUNISHMENT: FORWARD-LOOKING ACCOUNTS

1 Lady Barbara Wootton makes this connection in many of her writings, including *Crime and the Criminal Law* (Wootton 1963: 41, for example). So does H.L.A. Hart in *Punishment and Responsibility* (Hart 1968: 161, for example).
2 This is the view of the influential British judge Lord Denning who defends it in a number of places, including *The Changing Law* (Denning 1953). It is discussed at length by Hart in *Punishment and Responsibility* (Hart 1968: 36).
3 Much of the work of the Canadian Law Reform Commission is built on this form of reasoning. See, for example, *Limits of Criminal Law – Obscenity: a Test Case* (1975b).
4 Nowell-Smith seems here to be echoing arguments developed by Bentham (*Commentaries*, Book IV, Chapter II). Hart discusses Bentham's arguments at numerous points in *Punishment and Responsibility* (1968), particularly at pp. 18–20 and pp. 40ff.
5 Roger Beehler (1982) examines the ethics of aversive therapy in 'Containing violence', a discussion of *Clockwork Orange* (Burgess 1972). The belief that punishment can be used to condition those whom most would assume to be mentally disordered and who are seemingly not able to control their behaviour or to alter their behaviour patterns is well illustrated by the novel.
6 Another of Hart's reasons will be discussed in the next chapter, where Hart's own theory of punishment is examined at considerable length.
7 There are two different ways in which sentences can be indeterminate. A sentence is indeterminate if no specific penalty is set out for offences of that type, in which case sentencing authorities are left to choose an appropriate penalty. Offenders can also be sentenced to indeterminate sentences. Indeterminate sentences of the first variety need not lead to indeterminate sentences of the second. However, to have indeterminate sentences of the second type, the sanction for an offence must be indeterminate in the first sense.
8 This view of sentencing is common to many forward-looking theories. For example, Lady Barbara Wootton defends this approach in *Crime and the Criminal Law* (1963: 95).
9 This, of course, is exactly Hart's complaint. However, the inability to predict is a function not of strict liability but of a rehabilitation-oriented sentencing system. As we shall see, experience with indefinite sentences confirms the accuracy of this prediction.
10 This critique of reform-oriented theories is central to Hart's defence of a mixed or hybrid theory of punishment, which we review at some length in the next chapter.
11 This principle is persuasively advanced by Jeremy Bentham in his

influential defence of a deterrence-oriented utilitarian approach to punishment.

12 This suggestion is not as far-fetched as it might initially appear. In Ontario, for example, the owners of vehicles are responsible for paying any fines resulting from the operation of their vehicle, whether they were driving at the time the offence was committed or not. Although not intended as a form of vicarious punishment, imposing this rule has a similar effect.

13 Bentham offers the classical arguments in *The Principles of Morals and Legislation* (Bentham 1970). Complex and detailed discussions of these arguments and counter-arguments have been developed by a number of authors, for example C.L. Ten, who tracks very effectively, in *Crime, Guilt and Punishment* (Ten 1987), many of the arguments on this subject. Another thorough discussion is offered by Nicola Lacey in *State Punishment* (Lacey 1988: 37ff). Hart reviews Bentham's arguments in *Punishment and Responsibility* (Hart 1968), for example at pp. 18–20 and 40ff.

14 I have R.M. Hare in mind here, particularly the account he offers of two levels of moral thought in *Moral Thinking: Its Levels, Method and Point* (1981). For a detailed discussion of this point, see Ten's (1987) discussion of utilitarian accounts of punishment.

15 Nicola Lacey (1988: 38) cites the Dreyfus and the Yorkshire Ripper cases in this connection. Recent revelations about the treatment on the part of the British officials of a number of individuals found guilty of assisting in IRA terrorist activities provide further actual examples of the same phenomenon. The willingness of officials to break the law in defence of what they regard as important national interests is also well illustrated in recent American history, for example the Watergate and the Iran/Contra scandals. Other instances are not hard to find.

16 This was the year of the Gladstone Report, which brought about an immense change in the powers and responsibilities of judges in England (Hart 1968: 165). In particular, the report opened the door to individualized sentencing. Options available included probation, training schools, corrective training, preventive detention, and wide powers of absolute and conditional discharge.

17 David Garland (1985) supports this conclusion with detailed analysis, which he summarizes at p. 31. H.L.A. Hart (1968: 165) apparently also concurs with this judgement.

18 The impact of reform on sentencing over the last 100 years has been less consistent than its impact on thinking in the field of corrections. This is probably due to the fact that corrections is an administrative branch of government, while the judiciary has remained independent from administrative direction, leaving individual judges free to fashion their own individual approach to sentencing. Reform in sentencing has largely been accomplished by granting increasing discretion in sentencing to judges and by creating a variety of sentencing options. These changes implied a desire on the part of the government to see judges use a broader range of sentencing models. However, discretion is not direction. Judges have, as a result, been

free to use forward-looking sentencing principles or not, as they please.

A good description of the use of discretion by judges in sentencing is found in Hogarth's *Sentencing as a Human Process* (Hogarth 1971).

19 The evidence is carefully reviewed by von Hirsch (1976), particularly in the early sections of his report. The relevant evidence is also thoroughly discussed in *Justice as Fairness* (Fogel and Hudson 1981) and *The Effectiveness of Correctional Treatment* (Lipton et al. 1975).

20 The evidence here is massive. Von Hirsch reviews much of the data in his discussion of 'Predictive restraint' (1976: 19–27). 'Justice and parole: the Oregon experience' (Fogel and Hudson 1981: 101ff) is an interesting study on the same topic. Empirical research on the capacity of social scientists and psychiatrists to predict violent behaviour is carefully reviewed by Neil Boyd in 'Ontario's treatment of the "criminally insane" and the potentially dangerous: the questionable wisdom of procedural reform' (Cragg 1987: 198ff). On the other hand, there is also some evidence that, under carefully defined and controlled conditions, coercive treatment can have a reformative impact on the behaviour of offenders. That evidence, however, is not of the variety that would be required to resuscitate a rehabilitation- or welfare-oriented model of punishment. It is none the less important and should not be ignored. I explore its significance for a theory of sentencing with some care in Chapter 7 below.

21 Studies done in the last two or three decades provide substantial empirical support for this claim as the Law Reform Commission of Canada points out in *The Principles of Sentencing and Dispositions*, (1974b: 11). Hogarth's study (1971) of the sentencing patterns of Ontario judges and studies of indeterminate sentencing in California, where indeterminate sentences were widely used for a time, have uncovered the same patterns.

22 This fact has been confirmed both for the treatment of the mentally ill and for offenders. Boyd (in Cragg 1987) reviews the evidence in this regard. The 'logic' of this phenomenon is explored at some length in many places, including 'The indeterminate sentence and the right to treatment' by E. Barrett Prettyman, Jr (Fogel and Hudson 1981: 69ff).

23 Von Hirsch comments in his discussion of the individualization of punishment that 'many prisoners regard the indeterminate sentence as perhaps the worst feature of prison existence' (von Hirsch 1976: 31).

24 There have been innumerable studies of the deterrent effect of punishment. Recently, an extensive review of the literature was undertaken by the Canadian Sentencing Commission. The Commission concluded that, while punishment could be said to have a deterrent effect, the deterrent effect did not vary with the severity of punishment. Neither could specific types of offences be deterred through the application of special punishments, drinking and driving for example. What was true, they concluded, was that the deterrent effect of sanctions did vary directly with their certainty (Archambault 1987: 135ff). Two interesting reports commissioned by the Sentencing Commission are

Empirical Research on Sentencing (Roberts 1988) and *Legal Sanctions and Deterrence* (Cousineau 1988).

25 See, for example, 'The effectiveness of correctional rehabilitation: reconsidering the "nothing works" debate' (Cullen and Gendreau 1989).

26 C.S. Lewis (1953) is a good example here. His early criticism of 'humanitarian' theories involves a clear endorsement of retributivism. More important from a practical point of view, many social scientists with practical experience in the field of corrections have come to the same conclusion over the last two decades (see, for example, Fogel and Hudson 1981). Their views have become increasingly influential at the policy level during this period. That influence, combined with a collapse of confidence in the efficacy of rehabilitation-oriented sentencing, has resulted in a return to retributive punishment. This reversal of opinion is particularly well illustrated in *Doing Justice*, in which von Hirsch (1976) defends a retributive model for sentencing. In *Justice as Fairness* (Fogel and Hudson 1981), David Fogel and a number of other contributors to the volume, each of whom at one time was a faithful defender of a welfare model of sentencing, offer support based in part on first-hand experience for a return to a retributivism and discuss what that might involve. One very concrete manifestation of this reversal of opinion has been a systematic effort in a number of legal jurisdictions, particularly in the United States, drastically to curtail or eliminate judicial discretion in sentencing.

3 TWO HYBRID THEORIES

1 There are hints here and there in the text that point in this direction. For example, Hart says in the course of a discussion of capital punishment:

> Some punishments are ruled out as too barbarous or horrible to be used whatever their social utility; we also limit punishments in order to maintain a scale for different offences which reflects, albeit very roughly, the distinction felt between the moral gravity of these offences. Thus we make some approximation to the ideal of justice by treating morally like cases alike and morally different ones differently.
>
> (Hart 1968: 80)

This passage, however, is also consistent with the view that the amount of punishment inflicted should be determined by utilitarian considerations, with retributive principles operating as side constraints, as Mark Thornton has pointed out to me in discussion of this point.

2 Nicola Lacey makes this point in *State Punishment* in her discussion of the same topic (Lacey 1988: 46–52).

3 If there never was any conflict, the two approaches would be perfectly complementary and there would be no need to choose between them. The challenge for a hybrid theory is to propose modifications to each that bring them into substantial harmony in determining sentences for particular offences.

4 For example, Hart comments that 'fairness between different offenders

expressed in terms of different punishments is not an end in itself but a method of pursuing other aims which has a moral claim on our attention' (Hart 1968: 172). However, the appropriate interpretation of this passage would seem to be simply that Hart views fairness as a value which should be respected, except where it collides too vigorously with utilitarian considerations.

5 For example, in his discussion of Bentham's justification for retaining the notion of responsibility in determining guilt (Hart 1968: 20).

6 He makes these points in his discussion of Bentham's account, which is referred to in the previous note.

7 Jerome Bickenbach (1988) reaches this conclusion in his critical notice of Anthony Duff's book *Trials and Punishments*.

8 In a recent Nordic Conference of the International Association for Philosophy of Law and Social Philosophy hosted by the Canadian Section, Mark Thornton and Gene Dais argued at length that combining retributive and utilitarian principles into a coherent theory of sentencing was indeed possible. Their approach to this task is set out in their contributions to the proceedings of that conference, entitled *Retributivism and its Critics* (Cragg 1991). It is my view, however, that no defence of a hybrid theory of the sort that Hart defends can be evaluated in the absence of a relatively detailed description of how it would work in a sentencing context. Since neither undertakes this task, what they are actually advocating is fundamentally ambiguous, as indeed is Hart's own account, as this discussion shows.

9 This is implied by comments Hart makes in 'Prolegomenon to the principles of punishment' (Hart 1968: 22).

10 Hart implies, in his discussion of 'Punishment and the elimination of responsibility' (Hart 1968: 183), that to punish people for reasons of general deterrence is a form of manipulation.

11 This term is used by Hart in his discussion of 'Murder and the principles of punishment' (Hart 1968: 80–1).

12 Hart implies this view in a number of places. See particularly 'Prolegomenon to the principles of punishment' (Hart 1968: 22).

13 See Hart's discussion of 'Punishment and the elimination of responsibility' (Hart 1968: 172). It should be noted, what I think is in any case obvious, that these four propositions are a compilation taken from different discussions. The resulting interpretation is an attempt to construct a consistent answer to the question: 'How should the amount of punishment to be inflicted on offenders for their offences be determined?'

14 He makes this clear in *Punishment and Responsibility* (Hart 1968: 27). As previous discussion shows, there are good reasons for doubting that this view is in fact well grounded, a conclusion that will be strengthened as the argument progresses.

15 Though I do not propose to argue the point here, Hart rests his view of law and the nature of legal obligation on a modified form of legal positivism. His defence of that view is set out in *The Concept of Law* (1961).

16 I discuss this point at more length in 'Law, violence, and the limits of morality', *Law and Philosophy* (Cragg 1989).

17 For discussions of hybrid theories that support this point, see Nicola Lacey's *State Punishment* (1988) and C.L. Ten's *Crime, Guilt and Punishment* (1987), particularly Chapter 4.

18 See Jerome E. Bickenbach's critical notice of *Trials and Punishments* (1988: 765–87) and Duff's reply to that notice in the same issue (1988: 787–95).

19 Duff describes blaming as criticizing, rebuking, reproving, or condemning (1986: 40).

20 This conclusion is defended above. See pp. 65–6.

21 This is a conclusion that Duff himself implies does follow from his account. See, for example, his discussion of 'The ideal and the actual' (Duff 1986: 291). See also Bickenbach's (1988) analysis of Duff's views and what a critical evaluation of them implies for sentencing and corrections.

22 It is ironic, I think, that an account that is as uncompromisingly critical of utilitarian principles of sentencing should have this result. Yet this outcome seems unavoidable on Duff's analysis, as previous argument shows.

23 I have taken the notion of value sovereignty from Jerome Bickenbach's critical notice of *Trials and Punishments* (1988: 770).

24 I defend this claim at some length in the next chapter.

25 Nothing in Duff's analysis would seem to rule out the possibility that a system of personal values, grounded exclusively on self-interest, is a coherent option that an individual might rationally endorse. Certainly, it is a thesis that has been argued by contemporary theorists. See for example *Ethics and the Limits of Philosophy* (Williams 1985).

4 THE FUNCTION OF LAW AND THE NATURE OF LEGAL OBLIGATION

1 For example, the incarceration rate in the Netherlands is about one-tenth that of the United States. There are sharp differences also in attitudes toward capital punishment, which is still a common punishment for serious crimes in the United States but rejected as immoral in much of the rest of the western world.

2 This is certainly true of this century, as historical evidence to be reviewed below makes clear.

3 Recent Canadian experience with the treatment of young offenders offers a graphic example of this. It now seems fairly clear that what were regarded at the time (the 1970s) as significant reforms in the treatment of young offenders have resulted in significantly higher incarceration rates for this age group. The burden of the reform was a shift from a paternalistic to a responsibility-oriented model of treatment. In spite of the fact that penalties for young offenders have clearly increased in harshness over the intervening years, the Canadian government has promised to introduce measures that will result in even longer sentences for those young offenders perceived as a real threat to public

security, on the grounds that the Young Offenders Act does not treat sufficiently seriously the range of crimes young offenders are capable of committing.

4 Peter Stein (1984), in a book called *Legal Institutions*, provides a good review of the literature on this question. His Chapter 1 is particularly relevant in this regard. Dennis Lloyd (1964), in *The Idea of Law*, has equally useful things to say.

5 This is a crucial condition, as we shall see in what follows. There is not space here to discuss Hart's reasons for concluding that it is necessary for the existence of a legal system. For this, readers will have to turn to Hart's own account. However, Chapter 5 and subsequent chapters will provide substantial support for this view.

6 Recent discussion of this point suggests that it is necessary that only one official, namely the official having ultimate responsibility for administering the system, need approach the administration of law from an internal perspective, or from what I have described as the legal point of view. That is to say, only one person need regard herself as under an obligation to respect the law and respond to its demands, for a system of rules to qualify as a legal system. This is clearly an extreme case and would not be likely to occur in practice.

7 This characteristic has always played a central role in philosophical discussions of the nature of morality. Thus Socrates in *The Crito* sets out to convince his friends that, in deciding whether he should escape the death sentence imposed on him by the Athenian court, he should set aside self-interest as well as popular opinion and seek to be guided by a sound understanding of his moral duty. It is also a central insight in the Hebraic prophetic tradition. For example, when Micah, the prophet, asks what the Lord requires, he is told to do justice and love mercy, thus implying that the most basic values in deciding what to do are moral values (Micah 6: 8).

8 Hart seems not to recognize this in his own discussion of the subject (Hart 1961: 90). However, societies that rely on non-formal mechanisms for settling disputes do as a rule have moral authorities who are looked to for guidance. Amerindian cultures, with their system of elders, are a good example of this.

9 In the *Euthyphro* at 10c, for example.

10 It is important to note that this account of the moral point of view neither implies nor assumes moral relativism. It implies only that, in the last analysis, moral judgement rests with individuals.

11 Thomas Scanlon (1972: 215) seems to defend this approach to resolving the tension between the moral and legal points of view. It is a solution that Gerald Dworkin (1988) subjects to careful critical evaluation in the opening chapter of *The Theory and Practice of Autonomy*.

12 Nicola Lacey (1988: 81) criticizes Hart's account for what appear to be similar reasons. Peter Stein (1984) reviews some interesting research on the use of coercion in pre-law societies in the first chapter of *Legal Institutions: The Development of Dispute Settlement*. His observations support with empirical data the position being defended here.

13 It is significant in this regard that Hart (1961) asserts in his discussion

of 'Law as the union of primary and secondary rules' that a rule of recognition is a minimum condition that must be satisfied, if a legal system is to be said to exist. The basic function of a rule of recognition is 'to establish the proper way of disposing of doubts as to the existence of [a] rule' which people have a legal obligation to respect. His example of a primitive rule of recognition, namely the simple listing of written rules, is not convincing, however. The mere existence of such a list cannot establish that a rule has been broken, if there is a dispute over how the rule is to be interpreted. The Ten Commandments did not become a part of a legal system, as opposed to a moral system, until they were placed in the context of a system of adjudication. Hart implies as much in his discussion of rules of adjudication (Hart 1961: 94).

14 This theme is explored in considerable detail later in this chapter and in the chapters that follow.

15 Jan Narveson (1970) articulates the view here being discussed in an exploration of the coherence of pacifism.

16 Rousseau, in *The Social Contract*, is quite explicit about this. See, for example, Chapter 8 entitled 'Civil society'.

17 This aspect of morality has been frequently noted in the history of ideas. Plato's observation in the *Euthyphro* is a good example. Socrates is discussing the matter of good and evil with Euthyphro and says: 'But, as you say, people regard the same things, some as just and others as unjust – about these they dispute; and so there arise wars and fighting among them' (*Euthyphro*: 8).

18 It is this apparent independence of morality that has led some commentators to embrace legal positivism, the view that there is no logically necessary connection between law and morality. Legal positivism implies that the existence of a legal system can be established without reference to moral criteria.

19 Contempt of court is discussed in much greater length below under the heading 'Morality and the enforcement of law'.

20 This point is discussed again in the next chapter.

21 This point is reinforced by the discussion in Chapter 1, which outlines the merits of shifting the punishment prerogative from victims to the state.

22 See Hart's commentary on this aspect of informal enforcement in *The Concept of Law* (Hart 1961: 90).

23 Hart defends this position in his discussion of the minimum content of natural law in *The Concept of Law* (Hart 1961: 198). The argument in support of this view is echoed by Nicola Lacey (1988: 89–90) in her discussion of 'Legal obligation and the law's claim to obedience'.

24 These are the only conditions, Hart argues, that are required for the existence of a legal system, a view that implies legal positivism (Hart 1961: 113).

25 This test does not require that the obligation in question be explicit or clearly focused. However, if the officials of a particular system did not accord the minimum use of force requirement any legitimacy and

refused to acknowledge criticism in any form of enforcement activity based on it, that system would fail the test.

26 These principles are contained in Resolution 690 (1979) of the Parliamentary Assembly of the Council of Europe and are examined with commentary by J. Alderson (1984), former Chief Constable of Devon and Cornwall, United Kingdom.

27 The relevant articles are three in number.

> Article 2: 'In the performance of their duty, law enforcement officials shall respect and protect human dignity and maintain and uphold the human rights of all persons.'
> Article 3: 'Law enforcement officials may use force only when strictly necessary and to the extent required for the performance of their duty.'
> Article 5: 'No law enforcement official may inflict, instigate or tolerate any act of torture or other cruel, inhuman or degrading treatment or punishment . . .'
>
> (Alderson 1984: 184)

28 The Canadian Criminal Code provides many examples beyond just this one. Section 25(3) prohibits force 'that is intended or is likely to cause death or grievous bodily harm', except where someone believes 'there are reasonable and probable grounds that it is necessary for the purpose of preserving himself or any one under his protection from death or grievous bodily harm'. Subsection (4) directs that escape should be prevented in the least violent manner possible. Section 26 specifies that 'every one who is authorized by law to use force is criminally responsible for any excess thereof . . . '. Finally, Section 30, which is entitled 'Breach of Peace', authorizes the use of 'no more force than is reasonably necessary to prevent the continuance or renewal of the breach of the peace or than is reasonably proportioned to the danger to be apprehended from the continuance or the renewal of the breach of peace.'

29 This is implied by my account of the relation of law and morality and is illustrated by the specific clauses of the code of ethics contained in the European Council's Declaration on the Police referred to above.

30 This discussion obviously raises questions about the moral status of civil disobedience. I take up some of those questions in 'Violence, Coercion and the Legitimacy of Punishment' (Cragg 1986).

31 It is perhaps worth pointing out that it has not been my purpose in this chapter to develop a complete and all-encompassing account of the notion of legal obligation. My discussion has been limited to discovering the foundations of a theory of enforcement. While I think the argument is satisfactory for this purpose, it is obvious that there are important dimensions to the topic which have not been broached. I explore some, but by no means all, of those dimensions in 'Violence, Law, and the Limits of Morality' (Cragg 1989), 'Injustice, Disobedience, and the Problem of Violence' (Cragg 1981) and 'Violence, Coercion and the Legitimacy of Punishment' (Cragg 1986).

5 THE ENFORCEMENT OF LAW

1 Some of these reasons will be explored at greater length below.

2 This strategy is defended in two recent books on the subject, the first by Antony Duff in *Trials and Punishments* (Duff 1986: 267) and the second by Nicola Lacey in *State Punishment* (Lacey 1988: 169).

3 I have in mind here as examples Roman law and English common law.

4 These claims will be discussed at greater length later in the chapter where the evidence for them will be cited.

5 Jean Hampton explores this idea in *Forgiveness and Mercy* (Murphy and Hampton 1988: 116).

6 Anyone familiar with the vagaries of life could provide good examples of this phenomenon. Let me simply cite land claims that have been raised in countries like Canada that aboriginal people have tried with little success to resolve in courts of law.

7 Carlos Nino discusses these ideas at some length in an article entitled 'Moral Discourse and Liberal Rights', where he argues that protecting and enlarging the sphere of personal autonomy is a fundamental feature of the moral point of view. As he puts it, 'a person who is killed, raped, cheated, etc. has less opportunity for choosing and materializing moral standards' (Nino 1989: 167).

8 The intimidation factor in crime is reported in several of the *Canadian Urban Victimization Survey Bulletins* (Solicitor General of Canada 1983–8).

9 This message is communicated in many ways. For example, when the law fails to enforce family support orders with any vigour, it implies that the people for whose benefit those orders are issued do not really have the rights the law says they have, or, alternatively, that the people responsible for enforcement are not committed to fulfilling their duties conscientiously. The report of a recent Crime Victims' Trauma Conference provides important insights in this regard. It points out that:

> What all victims have in common is that they are often subject to *secondary victimization* – the additional emotional distress of not having one's needs and rights recognized and dealt with by law enforcement agencies, emergency room personnel, courts, the media and mental health professionals.
>
> (Randle 1985: 10)

10 Reference has already been made to the Canadian urban victimization survey (Solicitor General 1983–8). Further references to this and other crime surveys will be made below. What is important for our purposes here is that victimization surveys have all reported this finding.

11 I am not unique in thinking that the implications of law enforcement for those who break the law are important. Hegel, as is well known, argued that offenders have a right to punishment. Quite a number of modern commentators have echoed his ideas. It is certainly arguable that Plato's views implied much the same thing, though for quite different reasons.

An early publication of the Law Reform Commission of Canada entitled *The Meaning of Guilt* is interesting in this regard as well. The commissioners argue that imposing sanctions is justified in part because it benefits those being punished (Law Reform Commission of Canada 1974a: 5). In what follows, I attempt to understand the basis for these kinds of claim.

12 Information collected by the Canadian urban victimization survey allowed those doing the survey to prepare a profile of the typical victim of crime against the person. The survey found that a typical victim of crime against the person is 'a young unmarried male, living alone, probably looking for work, or a student, and with an active life outside the home – *not very different from the profile we might draw of the typical offender* [my emphasis] if we set aside the reference to students' (Solicitor General of Canada 1983, Bulletin 1: 4).

13 This is well illustrated by the B.C. court judgment quoted at length toward the end of the last chapter.

14 That failing to respond to the authority of police officers shows a kind of contempt is implied, for example, in the European Council's 'Declaration on the Police', which reads:

> A police officer who complies with the provisions of this declaration is entitled to the active moral and physical support of the community he is serving.
>
> (Alderson 1984: 173)

15 The Canadian urban victimization survey reported that 58 per cent of estimated instances of victimization never come to police attention. Similar findings have resulted from empirical research carried out in the United States and Great Britain.

16 This is the common law offence of 'contempt of court' discussed and illustrated toward the end of Chapter 4 above.

17 Recall that fewer than 50 per cent of criminal offences are actually reported and that of those that are reported only one case in ten results in a conviction.

18 As we have seen earlier, the more heavily the law leans on coercion to make this point, the more paradoxical its message will be, a feature of coercion which underlines its inherent inefficiency. The obvious and contrasting virtue of persuasion as a means of obtaining compliance will and does provide a continuing impetus for reform. Under normal conditions, persuading people to respect laws that are just and fair will be easier than persuading them to obey the law where it is evident that some important aspect of it is seriously deficient from a moral point of view.

19 The Canadian urban victimization survey showed that one reason that people have for not reporting crimes to the police is fear of retaliation. This factor is significant, for example, in cases involving physical abuse by family members. See Bulletin 2 (Solicitor General of Canada 1984a) for example.

20 This comment is subject to important provisos, of course. The mere fact of obedience cannot prove that public confidence is warranted, if the central reason for obeying the law is fear. Compliance

is a basis for confidence only where it is voluntary in the sense described earlier.

21 Sherman (1978: 25) comments on this aspect of police work and the conflict management role of the police.

22 *Habeas corpus* is actually an ancient common law writ that could be used to require judicial inquiry into the legality of a detention. The Habeas Corpus Act was enacted in 1679. *Habeas corpus* is now enshrined in the Canadian and American constitutions.

23 Anthony Duff's account (1986) in *Trials and Punishments* develops the view that a central function of a trial is persuasion. We explored his account at some length in Chapter 3. The central difference between his position and the one being defended here is that, on his account, the focus is individual laws. On my account, on the other hand, the task of the court is to persuade offenders that they have been treated fairly in accordance with law and that the court is justified in requiring that they obey the law, even if the law they have broken is a bad one in the view of the court or the offender. With this difference acknowledged, and it is a crucial difference, Duff's view of the persuasive function of a trial and my own are very similar. My view is supported by the cases cited in the last chapter. It is also supported by judgments of the Ontario Court of Appeal and the Supreme Court of Canada in the case of Morgentaler, who opened abortion clinics across Canada in apparent contravention of the Canadian Criminal Code and argued as part of his defence that the jury trying him should not enforce the law because it was immoral. The relevant citations are (1985) 52 O.R. 353 (Ont. C.A.) and (1988) 63 Ontario Report 281 (S.C.C.).

24 It is perhaps worth pointing out again where I disagree with Duff (1986) on this point. He argues that the goal of a trial is to convince an offender that his actions merit moral censure. My position, on the other hand, is that one of the purposes of a trial is to persuade those found guilty of an offence that the verdict was reached in accordance with law and is therefore justified. It is also the duty of the court to explain to offenders why the court is bound by the law and must proceed in accordance with the law in imposing a sentence. The judge need not be of the view that the law being enforced is morally sound. He does have an obligation to explain to an accused why he accepts an obligation to enforce the law, independently of his own assessment of its moral quality. Establishing the obligation of the court to apply the law as it finds it will be more necessary in some cases than in others, as our discussion of contempt of court in Chapter 4 makes clear.

25 As many studies have shown, the single most pressing grievance that victims have with the criminal justice process is its failure to keep them informed as 'their' case wends its way through the judicial system.

26 However, the fact that it is not provided for in a particular legal jurisdiction cannot be taken by itself to be a reflection of the basic values of the society in question. Providing legal aid is not just a matter of legal values. It may also be a matter of economic capacity, though deciding which is the dominant factor in any particular case may not be an easy task.

27 All of the empirical data in this paragraph are set out in a discussion of police discretion in *Canadian Criminal Justice*, Chapter 4, 'The powers and decision making of the police' (Griffiths and Verdun-Jones 1989: 81–143).

28 This list is drawn from the Canadian Law Reform Commission Working Paper entitled *Diversion* (Law Reform Commission of Canada 1975a: 9). A more detailed description of the discretion exercised by prosecutorial authorities is offered in *Canadian Criminal Justice* (Griffiths and Verdun-Jones 1989: 251–83).

29 Griffiths and Verdun-Jones (1989: 91) explore this aspect of discretion in police work.

30 This is confirmed by virtually all commentators. See, for example, the discussions of police and prosecutorial discretion in *Canadian Criminal Justice* (Griffiths and Verdun-Jones 1989: 90–3 and 251–70), 'Discretion in the application of the criminal law' (Saxton 1981), and 'Police discretion and public attitudes' (Cooley 1981), and the numerous studies to which these accounts refer.

31 Quoted from the *Report of the Canadian Sentencing Commission* (Archambault 1987: 45). See also *Arrowsmith* v. *Jenkins*, [1963], 2 Q.B. 561, in which the English court confirmed that it was proper for the police to exercise a wise discretion in determining when to prosecute.

32 See also *Canadian Criminal Justice* (Griffiths and Verdun-Jones 1989: 92).

33 A good example is the findings of the Royal Commission in Canada into the actions of the police in a 1974 drug raid on a hotel in Fort Erie, a border town in Ontario. Some forty-five female patrons of the hotel were strip-searched in the ladies' washroom by female officers. Very few charges resulted. The commission found that, while the actions of the police were within the law literally construed, they were foolish and unnecessary. Public commentary was equally harsh. (See Saxton 1981: 176.)

6 TOWARDS A THEORY OF SENTENCING

1 The study of public attitudes toward punishment has become a matter of increasing interest to researchers. Studies undertaken by the Canadian Sentencing Commission (set out in a chapter entitled 'Public knowledge of sentencing' – Archambault 1987: 87–102) suggest that demands for harsh punishment are often significantly moderated when people are presented with the detailed information available to judges when they hand down their sentences. A United States study funded by the Public Agenda Foundation, *Crime and Punishment: The Public's View* (Doble 1987), showed that public attitudes toward incarceration are frequently modified when individuals acquire a detailed understanding of the costs involved. And Martin Wright (1989a) highlights public opinion surveys that suggest that 'most members of the public would often be satisfied with restorative sanctions'.

2 These findings were reported by both the British Crime Survey (1988) and the Canadian urban victimization survey (Solicitor General of Canada: 1983–8).

3 Walter Berns acknowledges the implications of these kinds of fact for retributivist justifications of punishment in his otherwise categorical defence of capital punishment (Berns 1980: 527).

4 This theme is discussed extensively in Chapter 2.

5 See Chapter 2.

6 The foremost proponent of this view is Nils Christie, who develops his ideas in a number of places including *Limits to Pain* (1981).

7 This theme is explored in depth by Andrew Scull (1981) in 'Community Corrections: Panacea, Progress, or Pretence?'.

8 As we saw in Chapter 1 above.

9 It is not possible to 'prove' an assertion of this nature within the context of a general discussion of punishment, although much of what I have argued in previous chapters suggests reasons for thinking that it is true. The position on which my argument turns is therefore an assumption which not everyone will be prepared to accept. However, though it is only an assumption, exploring its implications for an understanding of punishment is surely justified, if only because it is so widely shared.

10 See, for example, the Canadian Sentencing Commission's comment: 'Even if punishment cannot ultimately be justified, it apparently satisfies a strong desire, seated both in moral thinking and human emotions, and it cannot be renounced' (Archambault 1987: 145), and their subsequent discussion of the need for restraint in sentencing at p. 164.

11 In a study entitled *Empirical Research on Sentencing* carried out for the Canadian Sentencing Commission, Julian Roberts comments: 'Research in social psychology upon the formation of attitudes has shown the ease with which people generalize from a single case to the larger population from which the case is drawn' (1988: 55). This is an important factor in the formation of attitudes that professional groups have to consider carefully in undertaking disciplinary proceedings against their members. It is also an important factor in law enforcement and in understanding how public attitudes about law enforcement are shaped.

12 Many of the findings of crime surveys referred to in this and following chapters provide empirical support for this claim. See, for example, *Justice for Victims* (Sinclair 1983: 57ff) or the Canadian Urban Victimization Survey Bulletins.

13 That it is widely accepted that public attitudes are revealed in this way is evident from both political debate and media reactions to sentencing decisions by the courts. Changing public response to instances of family violence, or sexual assault, or drinking and driving all provide good examples of this. Penalties for these offences have been under constant review for several years because of widely held views that the penalties attached to them were inadequate, and because sentences imposed and judicial commentary on those offences have suggested attitudes to which some people took serious exception.

14 The expression 'ought implies can' derives from Kantian moral philosophy. Kant understood it as a formal statement of a fundamental feature of moral judgement for reasons that are echoed in what follows.

15 In 1977, the Canadian Law Reform Commission reported that 77 per cent of all convictions in Canadian courts were for strict liability offences. Writing in 1963, Lady Barbara Wootton pointed out that, at that time in England, a majority of cases dealt with in criminal courts were for strict liability offences (Wootton 1963: 47).

16 The Canadian Criminal Code makes it an offence to drive a car with a blood alcohol count of more than 80 milligrams per litre.

17 Mewett and Manning (1978: 122) put it in the following way: 'the object of strict liability is to throw the responsibility of determining whether an Act was breached on the person whose activities [are] regulated by the Act.'

18 The view that this is how strict liability ought to be interpreted is defended by Mewett and Manning (1978: 131ff).

19 Hart argues in a number of places, for example 'Legal responsibility and excuses' (Hart 1968: 31), that the idea of a voluntary action is best understood in terms of excuses. The analysis that follows provides reasons in addition to those he adduces for accepting this view.

20 This has an important analogue in dealing with adult offenders, as we shall see below. Equally, understanding how to deal with adult offenders has significant implications for understanding our obligations to juvenile offenders, though exploring those implications is a task that, for the most part, will have to be set aside for another time.

21 What this implies for their treatment is perhaps one of the most difficult practical questions faced by a modern society. The behaviour of juveniles cannot be ignored, since their behaviour is capable of undermining confidence in the law. Yet we are not justified in treating them as though they were adults when they are not. Unfortunately, limitations of space and time prevent a thorough exploration of the implications of the treatment of young offenders in what follows. Suffice it to say that much of what we will say about the sentencing of adults will in fact have obvious implications for the sentencing of young offenders. It remains, however, that to respond to juveniles as though they were adults is simply to ignore the fact that youth is a legitimate excusing condition.

For further discussion on the distinction between children and adults and the expectations legitimately addressed to both, see the discussion of the handicapped, the third of the three categories of hard cases being discussed in this section.

22 Hart explores this question briefly in 'Punishment and the elimination of responsibility' (1968: 184–5), as does Nicola Lacey in *State Punishment* (1988: 73ff).

23 For example, the recent study of one hundred inmates in federal prisons in the Ontario region by Zamble and Porporino (1988). The findings of this study are summarized in *Liaison* (Amyot 1988).

24 See, for example, *An Empirical Study of the Use of Mitigating and Aggravating Factors in Sentence Appeals in Alberta and Quebec from*

1980 to 1985 by Shereen Benzvy-Miller (1988), prepared for the Canadian Sentencing Commission, as well as *Consumerist Criminology* by Leslie Wilkins (1984), particularly Chapter 9, 'An example of consensus: an empirical study'.

25 The Sentencing Commission study examined court records in two quite different provinces in Canada. Alberta is a prairie province with an English-speaking population and a broad ethnic mix, while Quebec is a French-speaking province with distinct legal and cultural traditions. Wilkins' study surveyed quite different groups of people drawn from widely separated geographical areas: members of a judicial council located in Canada; police attending a course in an eastern American state; professional research staff of one national crime research organization in the United States; students in a western Canadian university; students in an eastern American university; and participants from many countries at an international seminar at a United Nations Institute in Tokyo, made up mainly of judges and prosecutors.

26 See for example the Canadian Sentencing Commission study of deterrence (Archambault 1987: 135ff).

27 For example, a quick perusal of the lists of mitigating and aggravating factors compiled by both Wilkins and the Sentencing Commission study suggests criteria that have been used over time, but which might well be criticized in light of today's values. Nothing I have argued would suggest that critical appraisal of the components of such lists is inappropriate. To the contrary, assessment of the moral validity of tests the law uses to evaluate attitudes and values has an obvious place in law reform in light of the law's primary function as I have described it.

7 SENTENCING AND THE IDEA OF RESTORATIVE JUSTICE

1 See, for example, Feinberg's 'The Expressive Function of Punishment' (1965), Walter Berns' defence of capital punishment in his article 'Defending the Death Penalty' (1980), and Jean Hampton's recent article on 'The Expressive Function of Retribution' (Hampton 1991), as examples.

2 Berns is a good example of a retributivist who justifies punishment in part because of its capacity to 'teach law-abidingness' (1980: 167). Those theories which see education or moral education as their function are of course by their nature forward-looking, or, in a broad sense, utilitarian.

3 This in spite of the claim of the Ouimet Report (1969: 16) that 'it is being increasingly recognized that the law enforcement, judicial and correctional processes all share a common over-riding aim'.

4 The Canadian Sentencing Commission, to which reference has been made in earlier chapters, reaches this as one of their explicitly articulated conclusions. See Chapter 2, 'An historical overview', and Chapter 3, 'Current situation and problem' (Archambault: 1987).

5 See, for example, the Law Reform Commission of Canada's Working Paper on *Diversion* (1975a).
6 This constitutes one of the most serious obstacles to sentence reform today, as the studies of public attitudes to current sentencing patterns undertaken by the Canadian Sentencing Commission clearly show. This problem will be explored in more detail below.
7 See for example the Canadian Committee on Corrections report entitled *Toward Unity: Criminal Justice and Corrections* (Ouimet 1969). The Report of the Canadian Sentencing Commission points out that protection of the public is the most frequently invoked purpose of sentencing (Archambault 1987: 145).
8 The reason lies partly in the fact that the behavioural sciences are not able to predict with any degree of reliability whether an offender is likely to reoffend, a topic we explored in some depth in Chapter 2 above.
9 Perhaps the best and most comprehensive recent account is offered in *Mediation and Criminal Justice – Victims, Offenders and Community* (Wright and Gallaway 1989).
10 Chapter 4 explores many of the fundamental motivations behind these attitudes, but concludes that recourse to the creation of a legal system is justified as a way of reducing the level of violence that might otherwise occur as a result of the failure of informal systems.
11 It is not insignificant that the first serious efforts at victim/offender reconciliation (VORP) developed around an experiment in Kitchener, Ontario, undertaken under the jurisdiction of a court of law. What resulted was in essence an experiment with negotiated sentences. The experiment was quickly emulated elsewhere. It was widely viewed as a success, and as a genuine development of sentencing practice. However, not surprisingly in light of what has just been argued, it was struck down by the Canadian Supreme Court as an unlawful delegation of the court's sentencing authority. See Dean E. Peachy's description of the 'Kitchener Experiment' (1989).
12 All of this we have already explored in our discussion of *Trials and Punishments* (Duff 1986) in Chapter 3. Note that, as the Supreme Court judgment referred to in the previous note suggests, the law itself is not unaware of the apparent incompatibility of the mediation model and formal criminal justice.
13 This is, of course, a principle of law. It is implied by the legal point of view. However, it is also a central principle of conflict resolution, a fact that is emphasized both by social science research and by mathematical studies carried out by Robert Axelrod among others and reported in *The Evolution of Cooperation* (1984). Axelrod's studies consisted in inviting a group of mathematicians to play in an iterated 'N-person' Prisoner's Dilemma computer tournament, with a view to discovering the best strategy for winning. What he discovered was that tit for tat strategies, in which the first move was a trusting or cooperation-oriented move, were the most successful. Brunk calls these strategies 'nice' or 'firm but friendly', and then goes on to point

out that the essential weakness of tit for tat is that it is not sufficiently forgiving (Brunk 1989: 162).

14 Interesting and informative studies in this regard were undertaken by the Edna McConnell Clark Foundation (Doble 1987) and the Canadian Sentencing Commission (Archambault 1987). The Foundation study focused on in-depth interviews with small groups of Americans selected from a broad range of occupations and income levels. Those interviewed indicated that they believed crime to be produced by remediable circumstances – bad family environment, poverty, etc. They supported the reduced use of incarceration and more reliance on rehabilitation, and distrusted the judiciary (Doble 1987: 8). The Canadian Sentencing Commission discovered that most Canadians thought current sentencing patterns to be too lenient. However, individuals who thought sentences described in newspaper accounts were too lenient tended to change their minds when presented with more complete information. Indeed, in many cases, the final conclusion was that the sentences being reviewed were too harsh (Archambault 1987: 87–98).

15 The contributors to *Mediation and Criminal Justice: Victims, Offenders and Community* (Wright and Gallaway 1989) provide many examples of this phenomenon, as do many other authors.

16 It is perhaps worth pointing out here that one of the essential but difficult tasks of correctional administrators is convincing an often sceptical public that they should cooperate with proposals for community correctional facilities, like half-way houses, residences for young offenders, drop-in centres and so on, all of which are designed to assist those in trouble with the law to re-establish satisfactory relationships with the community.

17 See, for example, Hume's discussion of justice in *The Treatise* (Hume 1896: 534ff). For a more detailed discussion of Hume's views on this subject, see 'Hume on Punishment' (Cragg 1990: 67–9).

18 Capital punishment has in fact been abolished in most western countries. It is, however, still practised in some parts of the United States where the frequency of executions has been growing for more than a decade. There have also been calls for its reinstatement in most of those countries that have abolished it in recent years. However, even where public pressure has resulted in parliamentary debate and vote, proponents of capital punishment have not succeeded in having it reintroduced.

19 There are now so many studies of the effects of capital punishment that it seems redundant to list them here. Indeed, the inability to show that capital punishment has a deterrent effect is now widely accepted, even by those who continue to demand its reinstatement, for example the organization representing Canadian Chiefs of Police. It is also a well-known fact that those states in the United States that continue the practice have higher rates of crime than those that do not.

20 Alan Brudner (1980) offers an interesting analysis of capital punishment from this perspective. Ezzat Fattah's discussion (1981) of whether capital punishment is a unique deterrent is also interesting in this regard.

21 In other respects, however, the rhetoric and the approach of the Green Paper are quite incompatible with the approach to sentencing and corrections that a conflict resolution model implies. This is because the proposals in the Green Paper rest to a considerable degree on retributivism.

22 See, for example, 'Electronic Surveillance: Turning Homes into Jails', in *Liaison* (Amyot 1987). The article in question reports that by 1987, the date of the publication, 20 American states were using electronic devices to monitor more than 900 people. The Toronto *Globe and Mail* reports that, by May 1989, 33 American states were taking part in various programmes covering about 2,300 offenders. Up to the time of writing, only one Canadian province, British Columbia, had experimented with the technology. For a description and evaluation of the British Columbia pilot project, see Linda Neville's account (1989).

23 For example, the use of electronic monitoring has been condemned unequivocally by the Howard League (Great Britain), the National Association for the Care and Resettlement of Offenders (NACRO), and more cautiously by the John Howard Society of Canada. On the other hand, following a review of the British Columbia experience, it has been conditionally endorsed by the Canadian Bar Association and the American Civil Liberties Union. For a more complete account see the *Globe and Mail*, May 8, 1989. See also the *Liaison* article referred to in the previous note.

24 For an interesting discussion of 'net widening' see Anthony Bottoms' discussion of 'The dispersal of discipline thesis' in 'Neglected Features of Modern Penal Systems' (Bottoms 1983: 173ff). It should be noted that the potential for net widening is not just hypothetical. Studies have shown that only 12 per cent of those who have participated in electronic monitoring programmes in the United States had committed offences involving violence. On the other hand, the British Columbia experiment was restricted to offenders who had been found guilty of drink driving offences and who would otherwise have served time in a prison (Neville 1989).

25 A study by Steve Mainprize, a doctoral candidate in anthropology and sociology at the University of British Columbia, indicated that offenders in the experimental programme found electronic monitoring to be more just and humane than the alternative of incarceration. The study concluded that electronic monitoring 'constitutes a community correctional alternative to imprisonment that reduces or minimizes negative consequences of incarceration ... [and] has rehabilitative potential in that a greater level of alcohol abstinence support is offered to relevant offenders' (Neville 1989: 22–4).

26 Anthony Bottoms' study (1983), referred to above, develops a similar argument but with a focus on fine options. He argues that use of community options in sentencing does not necessarily imply net widening and may in fact signal quite a different understanding of the function of sentencing. His argument points to a return to classical notions of justice. My account calls, rather, for the development of quite a different model. However, the argument remains valid as

a critique of the net widening thesis. For a critique of Bottom's thesis, see 'From the Panopticon to Disney World: the Development of Discipline' (Shearing and Stenning 1984).

27 This comment has to be carefully interpreted. In fact, the use of legal counsel often gives rise to a form of mediation which is fundamental to the judicial process. The function of defence counsel is to ensure that the defendant's point of view is properly represented in the trial and sentencing components of the judicial process, and to represent the accused in both the formal and the informal aspects of the legal process.

28 Ontario is a Canadian province. In Canada, the administration of justice is a provincial responsibility.

29 See Dean Peachy's description of the Kitchener experiment (1989: 14) and John Harding's 'Reconciling Mediation with Criminal Justice' (1989: 32–3).

30 See the empirical assessment of VORP programmes by Robert Coates and John Gehm (1989).

31 Again, see the reviews of the Kitchener experiment by Dean Peachy (1989) and of the British experience with victim/offender reconciliation by John Harding (1989), which document this point.

32 For a useful initial exploration of some of the implications of this fact, see Sally Engle Merry's discussion of 'Myth and Practice in the Mediation Process' (1989).

33 This must surely be one of the basic reasons for the perennial appeal of utilitarian theories, as Kant seems to have recognized. However, interpreting the behaviour of others by reference to what Kant would call heteronomous factors does not imply that heteronomy provides a sound basis for evaluating human behaviour. It is simply to accept it as one element among others that have to be considered in seeking to understand and evaluate responses to human behaviour in general and criminal behaviour in particular. See Kant's discussion of hypothetical imperatives in *The Groundwork of the Metaphysic of Morals* (Paton 1956: 84ff).

34 Anthony Duff (1989: 140) explores this point in an interesting discussion of *Punishment, Custody and the Community* (Home Office 1988), to which we have already referred.

35 I am assuming here that the means are appropriate. Using excessively coercive means could never be justified on these grounds, for reasons set out in Chapter 4.

36 All of which is argued at length in Chapter Four.

37 In Chapter 4, for example.

38 Virtually all the research on the deterrence effect of punishment is relevant here. Some of those studies have pointed to the potentially counter-productive effect of severe forms of punishment, for example the study reported in *Crime and Delinquency* that points to the potentially brutalizing effect of capital punishment (Bowers and Pierce 1980). Much of the work of Paul Gendreau (Cullen and Gendreau 1989 and Gendreau and Ross 1987) is also of interest in this regard.

39 For a discussion of the conditions under which fines are justified, see

Anthony Bottoms' review of the subject of punishment and post-liberal society. Bottoms locates the discussion in a setting somewhat different from my own. However, his explanation dovetails with the one being set out here. One striking similarity between the two accounts is his account of the persuasive function of fines.

40 For a brief discussion of this point, see *Consumerist Criminology* (Wilkins 1984: 116).

41 By 'intrinsic' I mean the value of something, assessed independently of the rewards or punishments which are offered as special inducements to do as requested or required. For a sustained analysis of the distinction between intrinsic and extrinsic motivation, see Duff's account of 'Consequentialist Punishments' (Duff 1986: 151ff).

8 TOWARDS A PHILOSOPHY OF PUNISHMENT

1 The Edna McConnell Clark Foundation Report (Doble 1987) supports the first of these claims, as does the empirical research carried out by the Canadian Sentencing Commission and set out in Chapter 4 of their report, entitled 'Public Knowledge of Sentencing' (Archambault 1987). Public attitudes reflecting a desire for harsher penalties will be discussed below.

2 An example of this phenomenon has been the impact of a small number of very spectacular crimes on the use of parole in Canada over the last decade . Public pressure has also led governments to require those who have earned early release from prison for good behaviour to be placed on mandatory supervision on release. It has also led to the introduction of gating, a procedural device involving the release and immediate rearrest of an inmate at the prison gates. In all of these cases, correctional practices have been shaped by public attitudes in significant but almost certainly unjust ways.

3 In the United States, for example, support for capital punishment has grown from 40 per cent in the 1960s to over 70 per cent of the population in the 1980s. A 1987 survey showed that 84 per cent of those sampled thought that the courts do not deal harshly enough with criminals. The study sponsored by the Edna McConnell Foundation also discovered wide agreement among the people who were interviewed that the judiciary were too lenient in their approach to sentencing. Studies undertaken by the Canadian Sentencing Commission found that a high percentage of Canadians interviewed (80 per cent in 1983) thought that sentences were too lenient, though the percentage had dropped to 64 per cent by 1986.

4 This conclusion is based on a Harris poll conducted in the United States in 1983.

5 Martin Wright, in an article entitled 'What the Public Wants', surveys recent studies of public attitudes (Wright 1989b: 264). He concludes that many members of the public seem ready to shift the debate from the issue of lenient as opposed to harsh sentences to adequate forms of reparation and community service. A much more extensive evaluation of public attitudes is contained in a recent book, *Public Attitudes to*

Sentencing: Surveys from Five Countries, edited by Nigel Walker and Mike Hough (1988). The conclusion that emerges from the various studies is that the general public in western countries is not especially punitive. The studies also suggest that experience of victimization does not seem to be strongly related to punitiveness.

6 See, for example, the research of Leslie Wilkins, which is set out in Chapter 9 of *Consumerist Criminology* (Wilkins 1984). Also relevant is the research on mitigating and aggravating factors in sentencing appeals (Benzvy-Miller 1988).

7 This is one of the conclusions arrived at by Doble (1987).

8 The Oxford English Dictionary defines retribution as 'recompense for, or requital of, evil done; return of evil'.

9 It is clear from the other four elements in his definition, however, that Hart is in fact committed to what I shall describe as the philosophical definition of punishment, namely, that the aim or purpose of punishment is to cause pain or suffering.

10 This is taken from *Webster's Dictionary of the English Language*.

11 Quinton (1954) builds his well-known analysis on this definition in an attempt to marry retributivist and utilitarian accounts of punishment.

12 See Hart's comments (1968: 5), for an explicit statement of this view.

13 Wilkins (1984: 116) discusses a proposal for using electrical shocks as the only form of punishment. The virtue of electric shocks, it would seem, is that the pain they cause is subject to objective measurement. Using electrical shocks, therefore, would allow the punishment required for a particular offence to be precisely measured and accurately delivered. This would allow punishment to be administered in the knowledge that it was fair. Assuming this form of punishment were available, would submission to it as a penance further the cause of reconciliation? Would it lead to an enhanced sense of security on the part of a victim or the public? It is not at all obvious that it would. It might; but it also might not.

14 The reader might recall that this was the mechanism used by the Kitchener judge that allowed the idea of victim/offender reconciliation to be born.

BIBLIOGRAPHY

Alderson, J. (1984) *Human Rights and the Police*, Strasbourg: Council of Europe.

Amyot, D. (1987) 'Electronic Surveillance: Turning Homes into Jails', *Liaison* 13(10) (a publication of the Solicitor General of Canada).

Amyot, D. (1988) 'Prison, A Behavior Deep Freeze', *Liaison* 14(8): 4–9 (a publication of the Solicitor General of Canada).

Angeles, P.A. (1981) *The Dictionary of Philosophy*, New York: Barnes and Noble.

Archambault, J.R. (1987) *Sentencing Reform: A Canadian Approach* (Report of the Canadian Sentencing Commission), Ottawa: Ministry of Supply and Services.

Axelrod, R. (1984) *The Evolution of Cooperation*, New York: Basic Books.

Beccaria, C. (1963) *On Crimes and Punishments*, Indianapolis: Bobbs-Merrill Co.

Bedau, H.A. (1980) 'Capital Punishment and Retributive Justice', in Tom Regan (ed.) *Matters of Life and Death*, New York: Random House.

Beehler, R. (1982) 'Containing Violence', *Ethics* 92: 647–60.

Bentham, J. (1838–43) *The Works of Jeremy Bentham* (11 volumes), J. Bowring (ed.), Edinburgh: W. Tait.

Bentham J. (1970) *An Introduction to the Principles of Morals and Legislation*, J.H. Burns and H.L.A. Hart (eds), London: Hafner.

Bentham J. (1977) *Comment on the Commentaries*, J.H. Burns and H.L.A. Hart (eds), London: Athlone Press.

Benzvy-Miller, S. (1988) *An Empirical Study of the Use of Mitigating and Aggravating Factors in Sentence Appeals in Alberta and Quebec from 1980 to 1985*, Ottawa: Department of Justice, Canada.

Berns, W. (1980) 'Defending the Death Penalty', *Crime and Delinquency* 26(4): 503–27.

Bickenbach, J. E. (1988) 'Critical Notice of R.A. Duff: *Trials and Punishments*', *Canadian Journal of Philosophy* 18(4): 765–87.

Blake, J.A. (1981) 'The Role of Police in Society', in W.T. McGrath and M.P. Mitchell (eds) *The Police Function in Canada*, Toronto: Methuen.

Bottoms, A. (1983) 'Neglected Features of Modern Penal Systems', in D. Garland and P. Young (eds) *The Power to Punish*, London: Heinemann.

Bowers, W.J. and Pierce, G.L. (1980) 'Deterrence or Brutalization: What is the Effect of Executions?', *Crime and Delinquency* 26(4): 453–84.

Boyd, N. (1980) 'Ontario's Treatment of the "Criminally Insane" and the Potentially Dangerous: The Questionable Wisdom of Procedural Reform', *Canadian Journal of Criminology* 22(2): 151–67.

British Crime Survey (1988) *Home Office Research Study 111*, London: Her Majesty's Stationery Office.

Brudner, A. (1980) 'Retributivism and the Death Penalty', *University of Toronto Law Journal* 30(4): 337–55.

Brunk, C. (1988) *Hawks, Doves, and Two Models of Conflict Resolution*, Working Paper 88–4, Waterloo: Project Ploughshares.

Brunk, C. (1989) 'Nuclear Deterrence, Vulnerability and the Rationality of Unilateral Initiatives' in A.W. Cragg, L. Larouche, and G.J. Lewis (eds) *Challenging the Conventional*, Burlington, Ontario: Trinity Press.

Burgess, A. (1972) *A Clockwork Orange*, Harmondsworth: Penguin Books.

Christie, N. (1981) *Limits to Pain*, Oxford: Martin Robertson.

Chupp, M. (1989) 'Reconciliation Procedures and Rationale', in M. Wright and B. Gallaway (eds) *Mediation and Criminal Justice: Victims, Offenders and Community*, London: Sage.

Coates, R. and Gehm, J. (1989) 'Victim Offender Reconciliation Programmes', in M. Wright and B. Gallaway (eds) *Mediation and Criminal Justice: Victims, Offenders and Community*, London: Sage.

Cooley, J.W. (1981) 'Police Discretion and Public Attitudes', in W.T. McGrath and M.P. Mitchell (eds) *The Police Function in Canada*, Toronto: Methuen.

Cousineau, D. (1988) *Legal Sanctions and Deterrence*, Ottawa: Department of Justice, Canada.

Cragg, A.W. (1981) 'Injustice, Disobedience, and the Problem of Violence', *Laurentian University Review* 14(1): 5–13.

Cragg, A.W. (1986) 'Violence, Coercion and the Legitimacy of Punishment', *Studies on Aggression, Laurentian University Review* 19(1): 111–21.

Cragg, A.W. (1987) *Contemporary Moral Issues*, 2nd edn, Toronto: McGraw-Hill/Ryerson (1st edn, 1983).

Cragg, A.W. (1989) 'Violence, Law, and the Limits of Morality', *Law and Philosophy* 8: 301–18.

Cragg A.W. (1990) 'Hume on Punishment', in T.D. Campbell (ed.) *Law and Enlightenment in Britain*, Aberdeen: Aberdeen University Press.

Cragg A.W. (ed.) (1991) *Retributivism and its Critics* (Archives for Philosophy of Law and Social Philosophy – Supplementa) Stuttgart: Franz Steiner Verlag.

Cragg, A.W., Larouche L., and Lewis, G.J. (eds) (1989) *Challenging the Conventional*, Burlington, Ontario: Trinity Press.

Cullen, F. and Gendreau, P. (1989) 'The Effectiveness of Correctional Rehabilitation: Reconsidering the "Nothing Works" Debate', in L. Goodstein and D. MacKenzie (eds) *The American Prison: Issues in Research and Policy*, New York: Plenum.

Dais, E. (1991) 'Positive Retributivism and Despicable Justice', in W. Cragg (ed.) *Retributivism and its Critics* (Archives for Philosophy of Law and Social Philosophy – Supplementa), Stuttgart: Franz Steiner Verlag.

BIBLIOGRAPHY

Denning, Lord (1953) *The Changing Law*, London: Stevens.

Doble, J. (1987) *Crime and Punishment: The Public's View*, New York: The Public Agenda Foundation.

Duff, R.A. (1986) *Trials and Punishments*, Cambridge: Cambridge University Press.

Duff, R.A. (1988) 'A Reply to Bickenbach', *Canadian Journal of Philosophy* 18(4): 787–95.

Duff, R.A. (1989) 'Punishment in the Community – A Philosophical Perspective', in H. Rees and E.H. Williams (eds) *Punishment, Custody and the Community*, London: London School of Economics.

Dworkin, G. (1988) *The Theory and Practice of Autonomy*, Cambridge: Cambridge University Press.

Ekstedt, J. W. and Griffiths, C. (1988) *Corrections in Canada*, Toronto: Butterworth.

Ezorsky, G. (ed.) (1972) *Philosophical Perspectives on Punishment*, Albany: State University of New York Press.

Fattah, E.A. (1981) 'Is Capital Punishment a Unique Deterrent?' *Canadian Journal of Criminology* 23(3): 291–311.

Feinberg, J. (1965) 'The Expressive Function of Punishment', *Monist* 49(3): 397–408.

Finnis, J. (1980) *Natural Law and Natural Rights*, Oxford: Clarendon Press.

Fisher, R. (1969) *International Conflict for Beginners*, New York: Harper & Row.

Fitzgerald, P.J. (1962) *Criminal Law and Punishment*, Oxford: Clarendon Press.

Fogel, D. and Hudson, J. (eds) (1981) *Justice as Fairness: Perspectives on the Justice Model*, New York: Anderson.

Fuller, L.L. (1969) *The Morality of Law*, rev. edn, New Haven and London: Yale University Press.

Garland, D. (1985) *Punishment and Welfare: A History of Penal Strategies*, Aldershot, England: Gower.

Garland, D. and Young, P. (1983) *The Power to Punish*, London: Heinemann Educational Books.

Gendreau, P. and Ross, R. (1987) 'Revivification of Rehabilitation: Evidence from the 1980s', *Justice Quarterly* 4(3): 350–407.

Globe and Mail, Toronto: Canadian Newspapers Co. Ltd.

Griffiths, C.T. and Verdun-Jones, S.N. (1989) *Canadian Criminal Justice*, Toronto: Butterworth.

Hampton, J. (1991) 'The Expressive Function of Retribution', in A. W. Cragg (ed.) *Retributivism and its Critics*, Archives for Philosophy of Law and Social Philosophy – Supplementa, Stuttgart: Franz Steiner Verlag.

Harding, J. (1989) 'Reconciling Mediation with Criminal Justice', in M. Wright and B. Gallaway (eds) *Mediation and Criminal Justice: Victims, Offenders and Community*, London: Sage.

Hare, R.M. (1981) *Moral Thinking: Its Levels, Method and Point*, Oxford: Oxford University Press.

Hart, H.L.A. (1961) *The Concept of Law*, Oxford: Oxford University Press.

Hart, H.L.A. (1968) *Punishment and Responsibility*, Oxford: Clarendon Press.

Hobbes, T. (1952) *Leviathan*, Chicago: Encyclopedia Britannica (Great Books of the Western World).

Hogarth, J. (1971) *Sentencing as a Human Process*, Toronto: University of Toronto Press.

Home Office (1988) *Punishment, Custody and the Community*, London: Her Majesty's Stationery Office.

Honderich, T. (1969) *Punishment: The Supposed Justifications*, London: Hutchinson.

Hume, D. (1896) *A Treatise Of Human Nature*, 2nd edn, Oxford: Clarendon Press.

Lacey, N. (1988) *State Punishment: Political Principles and Community Values*, London: Routledge.

Law Reform Commission of Canada (1974a) *The Meaning of Guilt: Strict Liability* (Working Paper No. 2), Ottawa: Information Canada.

Law Reform Commission of Canada (1974b) *The Principles of Sentencing and Dispositions* (Working Paper No. 3), Ottawa: Information Canada.

Law Reform Commission of Canada (1975a) *Diversion* (Working Paper No. 7), Ottawa: Information Canada.

Law Reform Commission of Canada (1975b) *Limits of Criminal Law – Obscenity: a Test Case* (Working Paper No. 10), Ottawa: Information Canada.

Law Reform Commission of Canada (1975c) *Imprisonment and Release* (Working Paper No. 11), Ottawa: Information Canada.

Law Reform Commission of Canada (1977) *Contempt of Court: Offences against the Administration of Justice* (Working Paper No. 20), Ottawa: Information Canada.

Lewis, C.S. (1953) 'The Humanitarian Theory of Punishment', *Res Judicatae* 6: 224–30.

Lipton, D., Martinson, R., and Wilks, J. (eds) (1975) *The Effectiveness of Correctional Treatment*, New York: Praeger.

Lloyd, D. (1964) *The Idea of Law*, London: Penguin Books.

Marin, R.J. (1981) 'The Living Law', in W.T. McGrath and M.P. Mitchell (eds) *The Police Function in Canada*, Toronto: Methuen

McGrath, W.T. and Mitchell, M.P. (eds) (1981) *The Police Function in Canada*, Toronto: Methuen.

Merry, S.E. (1989) 'Myth and Practice in the Mediation Process', in M. Wright and B. Gallaway (eds) *Mediation and Criminal Justice: Victims, Offenders and Community*, London: Sage.

Mewett, A. and Manning, M. (1978) *Criminal Law*, Toronto: Butterworth.

Murphy, J.G. and Hampton, J. (1988) *Forgiveness and Mercy*, Cambridge: Cambridge University Press.

Narveson, J. (1970) 'Pacifism: A Philosophical Analysis', in Richard Wasserstrom (ed.) *War and Morality*, Belmont, California: Wadsworth.

Neville, L. (1989) *Electronic Monitoring System for Offender Supervision: Pilot Project Evaluation*, Victoria, British Columbia: Solicitor General, Corrections Branch.

Nino, C. (1989) 'Moral Discourse and Liberal Rights', in N. MacCormick and Z. Bankowski (eds) *Enlightenment, Rights and Revolution*, Aberdeen: Aberdeen University Press.

Nowell-Smith, P. (1948) 'Free Will and Responsibility', *Mind* 57: 45–61.

Nozick, R. (1981) *Philosophical Explanations*, Oxford: Oxford University Press.

Ouimet, R. (1969) *Toward Unity: Criminal Justice and Corrections* (Report of the Canadian Committee on Corrections), Ottawa: Information Canada.

Paton, H.J. (1956) *The Moral Law or Kant's Groundwork of the Metaphysic of Morals*, London: Hutchinson.

Peachy, D. (1989) 'The Kitchener Experiment', in M. Wright and B. Gallaway (eds) *Mediation and Criminal Justice: Victims, Offenders and Community*, London: Sage.

Penelhum, T. (1987) 'Our Technology and Our Moral Resources', in A.W. Cragg (ed.) *Contemporary Moral Issues*, 2nd edn, Toronto: McGraw-Hill/Ryerson.

Plato, *Protagoras*.

Plato, *Euthyphro*.

Quinton, A. (1954) 'On Punishment', *Analysis* 14: 512–17.

Randle, K.J. (1985) *Mental Health Assistance to Victims of Crime and Their Families*, Ottawa: The Canadian Council on Social Development.

Raz, J. (1979) *The Authority of Law: Essays on Law and Morality*, Oxford: Clarendon Press.

Rees, H. and Williams, E.H. (1989) *Punishment, Custody and the Community*, London: London School of Economics.

Roberts, J. (1988) *Empirical Research on Sentencing*, Ottawa: Department of Justice, Canada.

Rousseau, J.J. (1947) *The Social Contract*, New York: Hafner.

Saxton, B.J. (1981) 'Discretion in the Application of the Criminal Law', in W.T. McGrath and M.P Mitchell (eds) *The Police Function in Canada*, Toronto: Methuen.

Scanlon, T. (1972) 'A Theory of Freedom of Expression', *Philosophy and Public Affairs* 1: 215.

Scull, A. (1981) 'Community Corrections: Panacea, Progress or Pretence?' in D. Garland and P. Young (eds) *The Power to Punish*, London: Heinemann.

Shearing, C.D. and Stenning, P.C. (1984) 'From the Panopticon to Disney World: The Development of Discipline' in A.N. Doob and E.L. Greenspan (eds) *Prospectives in Criminal Law*, Aurora: Canada Law Book Co.

Sherman, L.W. (1978) *The Quality of Police Education*, San Francisco: Jossey-Bass.

Sinclair, D. (1983) *Justice for Victims*, Ottawa: Ministry of Supply and Services, Canada.

Skinner, B.F. (1971) *Beyond Freedom and Dignity*, New York: Bantam Books.

Solicitor General of Canada (1983) *Canadian Urban Victimization Survey Bulletin 1: Victims of Crime*, Ottawa: Communications Group, Programmes Branch, Ministry of the Solicitor General, Canada.

Solicitor General of Canada (1984a) *Canadian Urban Victimization Survey Bulletin 2: Reported and Unreported Crimes*, Ottawa: Communications Group, Programmes Branch, Ministry of the Solicitor General, Canada.

Solicitor General of Canada (1984b) *Canadian Urban Victimization Survey Bulletin 3: Crime Prevention, Awareness and Practice*, Ottawa: Communications Group, Programmes Branch, Ministry of the Solicitor General, Canada.

Solicitor General of Canada (1985a) *Canadian Urban Victimization Survey Bulletin 4: Female Victims of Crime*, Ottawa: Communications Group, Programmes Branch, Ministry of the Solicitor General, Canada.

Solicitor General of Canada (1985b) *Canadian Urban Victimization Survey Bulletin 5: Cost of Crime to Victims*, Ottawa: Communications Group, Programmes Branch, Ministry of the Solicitor General, Canada.

Solicitor General of Canada (1985c) *Canadian Urban Victimization Survey Bulletin 6: Criminal Victimization of Elderly Canadians*, Ottawa: Communications Group, Programmes Branch, Ministry of the Solicitor General, Canada.

Solicitor General of Canada (1986) *Canadian Urban Victimization Survey Bulletin 7: Household Property Crimes*, Ottawa: Communications Group, Programmes Branch, Ministry of the Solicitor General, Canada.

Solicitor General of Canada (1987) *Canadian Urban Victimization Survey Bulletin 8: Patterns in Violent Crime*, Ottawa: Communications Group, Programmes Branch, Ministry of the Solicitor General, Canada.

Solicitor General of Canada (1988a) *Canadian Urban Victimization Survey Bulletin 9: Patterns in Property Crime*, Ottawa: Communications Group, Programmes Branch, Ministry of the Solicitor General, Canada.

Solicitor General of Canada (1988b) *Canadian Urban Victimization Survey Bulletin 10: Multiple Victimization*, Ottawa: Communications Group, Programmes Branch, Ministry of the Solicitor General, Canada.

Stein, P. (1984) *Legal Institutions: The Development of Dispute Settlement*, London: Butterworth.

Stevens, J.F. (1883) *A History of the Criminal Law of England*, London: Macmillan.

Stevens, J.F. (1974) *Liberty, Equality and Fraternity*, London: Smith, Elder & Co.

Ten, C.L. (1987) *Crime, Guilt and Punishment*, Oxford: Clarendon Press.

Thornton, M. (1991) 'Against Retributivism', in A. W. Cragg (ed.) *Retributivism and its Critics*, Archives for Philosophy of Law and Social Philosophy – Supplementa, Stuttgart: Franz Steiner Verlag.

US President's Task Force on Law Enforcement and Administration of Justice (1967a) *The Challenge of Crime in a Free Society*, Washington DC: USGPO.

US President's Task Force on Law Enforcement and Administration of Justice (1967b) *Task Force Report: Crime and Its Impact*, Washington DC: USGPO.

von Hirsch, A. (1976) *Doing Justice: The Choice of Punishments*, New York: Hill & Wang.

Walker, N. and Hough, M. (1988) *Public Attitudes to Sentencing: Surveys from Five Countries*, Aldershot, England: Gower.

Wilkins, L.T. (1984) *Consumerist Criminology*, London: Heinemann.

Williams, B. (1985) *Ethics and the Limits of Philosophy*, Cambridge: Cambridge University Press.

Wootton, B. (1963) *Crime and the Criminal Law*, London: Stevens & Sons.

Working Group of the Canadian Correctional Law Review (1986) *Correctional Philosophy* (Working Paper No. 1), Ottawa: Solicitor General.

Working Group of the Canadian Correctional Law Review (1987) *Conditional Release* (Working Paper No. 3), Ottawa: Solicitor General.

Working Group of the Canadian Correctional Law Review (1987) *Victims and Corrections* (Working Paper No. 4), Ottawa: Solicitor General.

Wright, M. (1989a) 'Restorative Justice and Victim/Offender Mediation', unpublished PhD thesis, London School of Economics and Political Science.

Wright, M. (1989b) 'What the Public Wants', in M. Wright and B. Gallaway (eds) *Mediation and Criminal Justice: Victims, Offenders and Community*, London: Sage.

Wright, M. and Gallaway, B. (eds) (1989) *Mediation and Criminal Justice: Victims, Offenders and Community*, London: Sage.

Zamble, E. and Porporino, F. (1988) *Coping, Behavior and Adaptation in Prison Inmates*, New York: Springer-Verlag.

INDEX

251

10–29, 30–4; capital 3, 7, 12, 16, 18, 32, 60, 138, 168, 188, 189, 212; corporal 1, 10, 23, 80, 103; forward-looking theories of and their evaluation 30–57; hybrid theories of and their evaluation 58–78; the practice of 1–9, 142

rationality: and conflict resolution 179; and moral agency 68, 75, 76; and moral values 76, 77; and punishment 31, 51, 77
Raz, J. 84
recidivism 44, 53, 54, 77, 139, 182, 193, 198
reconciliation 137, 140, 182, 183, 190, 199, 214, 215; victim/offender 20, 193
reform: law *see* law reform; models of punishment 52, 55, 69–70; as moral education 42–3; or offender 211; penal 3, 7, 80, 103, 140, 147; as rehabilitation 43–6, 69, 70, 80, 206, 211
rehabilitation: and coercion 45, 198–203; concept of 43–4, 45; declining emphasis on 5, 81, 140; effectiveness of 3, 4, 181, 183; and enablement 170, 183, 184, 192; as a mitigating factor in sentencing 163; the progressive character of 44–5, 80; public attitudes toward 209; and punishment 46, 80, 212; and reparative 140; worries associated with 4, 44–6, 52–7
reliance: on force 141, 192; on incarceration 81; on law 99, 100; self- 190; and trust 113, 142–7
religion: and compliance with rules 84; discrimination on grounds of 168; and punishment 10
reparation(s): and conflict resolution 171, 184, 192; and law enforcement 171; and reconciliation 190; and sentencing 140, 171, 190, 192; and trust 171; *see also* justice, reparative

repentance and suffering 214, 215
responsibility: acknowledging 171, 198, 202, 216; age of 36; collective 27; and deterability 38–9, 47; difficulty in assessing the extent of 24, 25, 32; the impact of imprisonment on 190; and the notion of *mens rea* 24, 36, 40, 150–4; and the notion of voluntary action 39–42, 52, 190; the place of in assessing criminal liability 25, 35, 36, 53, 65, 138–68; taking 85, 86, 173
restitution: as an alternative to punishment 140; and mitigation 164; and reconciliation 193; as a sentencing option 202, 207
retaliation: the effects of 179; fear of 108, 117, 126; and vengeance 16
retribution: distinguished from vengeance 17; in the distribution of punishment 60; as the goal of punishment 4, 10–29, 60, 80; language of 61; -oriented sentencing 54, 192
retributivism: criticisms of and objections to 5, 20–9, 30–4, 80; and capital punishment 189; chief rivals to 5; and the justification of punishment 8, 10–29, 59, 170; and penal reform 80–1; practical and philosophical concerns with 16–20; rendered compatible with utilitarianism 59–67; and restorative justice 158–9, 204, 205, 206, 211, 214; teleological 67–78
rewards: a feature of social life 1; merited 20; and punishments 38, 47; the proper use of 1, 194–8
Rothman, D. 5
Royal Canadian Mounted Police 120, 121

self-interest: and punishment 69; as a reason for disobedience 102, 186; and violence 89

256

For Product Safety Concerns and Information please contact our EU
representative GPSR@taylorandfrancis.com
Taylor & Francis Verlag GmbH, Kaufingerstraße 24, 80331 München, Germany

* 9 7 8 1 1 3 8 9 9 5 2 0 8 *